KRISHNAMURTI
THE YEARS OF FULFILMENT

KRISHNAMURTI
The Years of Fulfilment

MARY LUTYENS

FARRAR STRAUS GIROUX
New York

Published simultaneously in Canada by
McGraw-Hill Ryerson Ltd., Toronto
First published by John Murray (Publishers) Ltd, London, 1983
First American printing, 1983
Printed in the United States of America
Library of Congress Cataloging in Publication Data
Lutyens, Mary.
Krishnamurti: the years of fulfilment.
Includes index.
1. Krishnamurti, J. (Jiddu), 1895–
2. Philosophers—India—Biography. I. Title.
B5134.K754L87   1983   ~~181'.4~~ [B]   83–1620

Krishna-
murti

I wish to express my thanks to the following for their kind help: Mary
Cadogan, George Wingfield Digby, Pupul Jayakar, Anneke Korndorffer,
Erna Lilliefelt, Marcelle de Manziarly, Doris Pratt, Vanda Scaravelli,
Susunaga Weeraperuma (for information supplied from the Supplement
to his Bibliography of Krishnamurti before publication), and, above all,
to Mary Zimbalist.

I am most grateful to Victor Gollancz Ltd, to Harper & Row and to the
Krishnamurti Foundation, England, for permission to quote from Krishnamurti's writings. I am also grateful to Chatto & Windus, to Alfred A.
Knopf and to Sybille Bedford for permission to quote from her biography
of Aldous Huxley; and to Eyre Methuen, to Farrar, Straus & Giroux and
to Christopher Isherwood for permission to quote from *My Guru and His
Disciple*.

Contents

Illustrations

Foreword

This second volume of Krishnamurti's biography, which brings the story of his life up to 1980, has, like the first, been written at his suggestion and with his full co-operation. But, as before, he has not asked, nor been asked, to approve the text which is entirely my responsibility.

Krishnamurti is regarded by thousands as one of the great religious teachers of all times. His message is simple to those who give it close attention, though extremely hard to implement. From 1930, when he emancipated himself from Theosophy, he has been travelling the world trying to find words to convey as clearly as possible to his ever-increasing audiences the solution he has found to the violence and sorrow of mankind. He maintains that there can be an ending of sorrow. If his own words are not understood, no amount of interpretation will elucidate them, so I have not attempted to interpret him; nor do I make any apology for my presence in the book, for I have found it necessary to tell part of the story through my own experience.

One of the most fascinating aspects of Krishnamurti is the dichotomy between the man and his teaching. Having known him virtually all my life (indeed I have now known him longer than anyone else alive), I find it hard to reconcile the shy gentleness and almost vacant mind of the sixteen-year-old boy, who first came to England in 1911, with the powerful teacher who has evolved a philosophy that cannot be shaken by the most prominent thinkers of the day—particularly hard since there is still so much of that boy remaining in the man. In this book I have tried to explore his mystery. Who or what is Krishnamurti?

Mary Lutyens

I

The Years of Awakening

The first volume of my biography of Krishnamurti—*Krishnamurti: The Years of Awakening*—took the story of his life up to the age of thirty-five. This chapter is a recapitulation of the events of those years with the addition of two letters from Mrs Besant not then available to me.

Jiddu Krishnamurti was born on May 11, 1895, at Madanapalle, 150 miles north of Madras, the eighth child of Telegu-speaking Brahmin parents. His father, Jiddu Narianiah, was a rent collector employed by the British, so the family, though obscure, were not poor by Indian standards. Krishna's mother died when he was ten, and nearly four years later, Narianiah, who had now retired and who had been a Theosophist for many years, moved with his four surviving sons to the International Headquarters of the Theosophical Society at Adyar, Madras, to work as an assistant secretary. The eldest son, Sivaram, who was to become a doctor, was fifteen; then came Krishna, not yet fourteen, then Nityananda (Nitya), three years younger, and finally Sadanand, aged five, who was mentally deficient.

Soon after the move to Adyar, Krishna was picked out on the beach one evening from a crowd of other Indian boys by Charles Webster Leadbeater to be the vehicle for the World Teacher (the Lord Maitreya, the Christ). Most Theosophists at that time believed that the Lord Maitreya was soon to manifest in human form, as two thousand years ago he had manifested in the body of Jesus and before that in the body of Sri Krishna. Leadbeater, a leading figure in the Theosophical Society, who claimed to be clairvoyant, chose this particular boy because of the beauty of his aura which, he declared, had not one trace of selfishness in it. Leadbeater could hardly have chosen him for his outward appearance, for the boy was scraggy, dirty, ill-nourished, with crooked

I

teeth, his hair shaved in front as was then the Brahmin custom, and with a vacant, almost moronic expression. Moreover, he had a persistent cough and a weak, sickly look resulting from the many bouts of malaria he had suffered throughout his childhood.

Mrs Annie Besant, the President of the Theosophical Society, who was in Europe at the time Krishna was 'discovered', was soon notified by Leadbeater that a 'vehicle' had been found. Mrs Besant, who had had psychic powers herself at one time, had relinquished them in order to release more energy for the struggle for Home Rule for India in which she was engaged. She now relied entirely on Leadbeater in all occult matters.

Leadbeater removed Krishna and his brother Nitya from the school where Krishna was being beaten every day for stupidity and began to teach them himself with the help of two of his young secretaries. He also built them up physically with nourishing food, long bicycle rides, tennis and swimming, with the result that Krishna's appearance changed within a few months. With his teeth straightened, his hair grown and a new look of health, giving life to his huge dark eyes, he had become beautiful. The boys' spiritual training was undertaken by Leadbeater's own occult master, Kuthumi, who, with other masters, was said to live in an ever-young human body in a ravine in Tibet and who could be visited nightly on the astral plane during sleep. Kuthumi accepted the boys as his pupils, and not long after Mrs Besant's return to Adyar, Krishna took his first occult Initiation on January 11, 1910.

In March, Mrs Besant, with their father's consent, became the legal guardian of the two boys. A few weeks later she took them with her to Benares where she had a house in another Theosophical compound and where Krishna started teaching a group of adults the truths which the Master Kuthumi had taught him on the astral plane. Among this group was George Arundale, a man of thirty-two, Principal of the Central Hindu College founded by Mrs Besant at Benares in 1898, and E. A. Wodehouse, elder brother of P. G. Wodehouse, Professor of English at the College. Krishna's teaching to this group was published the following year in a little book called *At the Feet of the Master* which was translated into forty languages and is still in print. Since Krishna's English was very poor at that time it has always been a matter of dispute whether the book was written by him or by Leadbeater. Krishna himself never claimed to have written it; he stated in a foreword, 'These are not my own words but the words of the Master who taught me.'

In January 1911 an organisation was started by Mrs Besant and Arundale called the Order of the Star in the East with the object of preparing the way for the Coming of the World Teacher. Krishna was made the Head of this Order. Two months later Mrs Besant took the two boys to England where many converts were made to the O.S.E. and where they met for the first time Lady Emily Lutyens (my mother), wife of the architect, Edwin Lutyens, and a recent convert to Theosophy, who was to become Krishna's closest friend in the years ahead.

Mrs Besant and the two boys returned to India in the autumn. On December 28, at the T.S. Convention at Benares, while Krishna was handing out certificates to about 400 new members of the O.S.E., those who came up to receive them started prostrating at his feet. According to Leadbeater the hall had all at once filled with a tremendous power which was evidently flowing through Krishna. This was said to be the first manifestation of the Lord Maitreya, the World Teacher.

In February 1912 Mrs Besant again took the boys to England where they remained until 1920. Their father was now trying to regain custody of them. He brought an action against Mrs Besant in the High Court of Madras which he won. She appealed and lost, but, undaunted, took the case to the Privy Council in London who quashed the ruling of the Madras Court in May 1914. By that time Krishna had reached his majority according to Indian law and needed no guardian.

The boys meanwhile had been studying in England with two Theosophical tutors—George Arundale and C. Jinarajadasa, a prominent lecturer for the T.S., who were both Initiates. It had been ruled by the Master Kuthumi, through Leadbeater, that Krishna must always be accompanied by two Initiates. It was hoped that both boys would pass into Oxford or Cambridge or, failing that, into London University. A very rich American Theosophist, Miss Mary Dodge, who lived in England with her friend, also a Theosophist, Muriel, Countess De La Warr, had in

1913 settled £500 a year on Krishna for life and £300 on Nitya. This gave them a certain sense of independence.

I remember Krishna well in the war years 1914–18. I was two when he first came to England so I have known him since the dawn of my memory. His nature was then, I believe, what it has been from the beginning—affectionate, generous, shy, diffident, dreamy, docile, self-effacing. At times he appeared quite vacant and oblivious of his surroundings. He was completely unspoilt— I might say untouched—by all the adulation he had received since he was first 'discovered'. He liked poetry—Keats, Shelley, Shakespeare—and some parts of the Old Testament which Lady Emily read aloud to him. He also enjoyed P. G. Wodehouse and Stephen Leacock, light comedies at the theatre and exciting films, but his favourite occupations were playing golf (he became a scratch player) and tinkering with his motor-bicycle. He has always loved mechanical things—watches, cameras, motor cars— an unexpected trait in his character.

Krishna was very dependent on his brother Nitya, a bright lovable boy. They shared everything and were as close as twins although anything but identical in appearance. Nitya was smaller, had great charm of face and personality but none of Krishna's beauty. Three years younger than Krishna, he seemed to be the older of the two.

Before the end of the war the Initiate-tutors had returned to India and the boys were living with Miss Dodge in the luxurious house on West Side Common, Wimbledon, which she shared with Lady De La Warr, coming daily to London to study at London University. It was at this time that they learnt to dress well and feel at ease in a rich aristocratic household. Nevertheless, Krishna was not happy. He had lost his belief in the Masters and the Lord Maitreya and shrank from the role he knew he would be called upon to play in return for all that had been done for him. 'Why did they have to pick on me?' he often asked Lady Emily.

Eventually in January 1920 Mrs Besant, despairing of Krishna ever passing an examination (he had failed his matriculation three times), sent him to Paris to learn French while Nitya remained in London studying for the Bar. It was a wrench for Krishna to leave Lady Emily whom he loved better than anyone at that time, but in Paris he was to meet a delightful French-Russian family—the de Manziarlys—an ardent Theosophical Russian mother with three daughters and a son who all became his devoted friends. By July Madame de Manziarly had reawakened in him some enthusiasm for Theosophy and the O.S.E. as well as stimulating him mentally by taking him to picture galleries and concerts. However, as he told Lady Emily, he far preferred natural scenery to any picture. At the end of the year he spoke voluntarily at a Theosophical meeting.

In May of the following year it was discovered that Nitya had tuberculosis. He went to Paris to be under a nature-cure doctor recommended by Madame de Manziarly, and then to Villars in Switzerland to be treated by a specialist. By November he was pronounced cured and that month he and Krishna returned to India after nine years' absence. Mrs Besant had sent for them. Krishna was now twenty-six and she believed that he was ready to play his part as Head of the O.S.E. In December, at the Theosophical Convention at Benares, he gave four of the Convention lectures on the subject of Theosophy and Internationalism. Public speaking was at first a torture to him. Lady Emily, who had followed him to India, recalled that he obviously had great difficulty in putting his thoughts into words although he had thoroughly prepared his lectures. He never considered rebelling against what he believed to be his duty in spite of the acute embarrassment he felt at the reverence with which he was now again treated.

Leadbeater had been living in Sydney since 1917 as head of a Theosophical community. An ex-curate in the Church of England he had now become a bishop in a new church—the Liberal Catholic Church, derived from the Old Catholic or Jansenist Church (called after Cornelius Jansen, a seventeenth-century reformer who had broken away from the Church of Rome), which claimed Apostolic Succession and which, according to Leadbeater, had the blessing of the Lord Maitreya. There was to be a T.S. Convention in Sydney in April 1922 and it was decided that Krishna and Nitya should attend it with Mrs Besant. They had not seen Leadbeater since 1912. They found him dressed as a bishop, wearing a large amethyst ring and a pectoral cross. Krishna was repelled by all the ceremonial of the church services he was expected to attend.

Nitya became very ill again in Sydney and was advised by the doctor to return immediately to Switzerland via San Francisco, the quickest route. Krishna, determined to go with him, told Mrs Besant that he did not feel his 'mental body' was developed enough and that he wanted to take eighteen months off from all Star and Theosophical work in order to study 'quietly and uninterruptedly economics, religion and education' in Switzerland. Mrs Besant and Leadbeater both approved of this plan.

Krishna and Nitya had not intended to stay in California more than a few days but they liked America so much that when an American member of the O.S.E. offered to lend them a cottage at the upper end of the Ojai valley, 360 miles south of San Francisco, 1500 feet above sea level and with a dry climate suitable for Nitya, they accepted the invitation. They both fell in love with this beautiful valley full of orange groves where Nitya at once began to feel better. In the event they were to stay there for nearly a year. During that time a trust was formed (the Brothers Trust) which bought for them the cottage and six acres of land with money raised in England.

This was the first time the brothers had been alone together, though Mr Warrington, the General Secretary of the T.S. in America, was staying in another cottage near by. Between August 17 and 20 Krishna underwent a three-day spiritual experience that transformed him. Mr Warrington was present at the time, and afterwards he, Nitya and Krishna all wrote accounts of what had taken place. Krishna was out of his body for much of the time during those three days, and in the evenings he would sit in meditation under the pepper tree outside the cottage.*

Krishna emerged from this experience in a state of ecstasy. He wrote to Lady Emily, 'I have changed and with that change in me I am going to change the lives of my friends . . . I am going to help the whole world to climb a few feet higher . . . You don't know how I have changed, my whole inner nature is alive with energy and thought.' And to Leadbeater he wrote: 'As you well know I have not been what is called "happy" for many years; everything I touched brought me discontent; my mental condition

---

* Krishna's and Nitya's accounts are given in full in *Krishnamurti: The Years of Awakening*.

has been as you know deplorable. I did not know what I wanted and everything bored me in a very short time and in fact I did not find myself.' He then recounted something of his experience and the ecstasy he had found.

Nitya too was deeply affected by what had taken place. He told Mrs Besant that 'the whole world has so changed for me since these things happened, I feel like a bubble which has suddenly become solid . . . I feel as if I have never really lived before, and now I could not live unless I served the Lord.'

Krishna concluded his own account of what had happened with the words: 'The fountain of Truth had been revealed to me and the darkness has been dispersed. Love in all its glory has intoxicated my heart; my heart can never be closed. I have drunk at the fountain of Joy and eternal Beauty. I am God-intoxicated.'

Leadbeater and Mrs Besant both affirmed that this experience had been Krishna's third Initiation (he had taken his second Initiation in 1912) but they could find no explanation for what occurred afterwards. From six o'clock every evening for about an hour, Krishna became semi-conscious, with the most excruciating pain in his head, neck and spine. He also became so sensitive that the slightest noise became a torture to him and he could not bear to be touched. The pain would gradually ease off but it left him exhausted. This 'process', as it came to be called, went on for years with greater or lesser intensity whenever he was quiet or alone with close friends. It would stop as soon as he had to travel or meet strangers. (It still goes on to some extent.) With the exception of one Theosophical woman doctor, who was baffled by his condition, no medical practitioner has ever been consulted about 'the process' and Krishna has never taken any kind of pain-killer for it. He has always been certain that it was something he had to go through—some kind of expansion of consciousness that could not be avoided. It was at its most intense and agonising for several months on end in 1924 when he and Nitya returned to Ojai after a summer in Europe. By that time the Brothers Trust had bought for them a larger house and more land at Ojai while still keeping on the cottage. They called the large house Arya Vihara, meaning Noble Monastery.

After the experience of August 1922, Krishna began to write poetry which he continued to do for several years. He also took on a new stature and authority. He had no more doubts as to what his mission in life was to be. He became less vague and more beautiful. From that time onwards most of his friends and followers started calling him Krishnaji—the suffix ji being a term of respect in India. In the first volume of his biography I referred to him as Krishna up to the time of his '22 experience and then as K which is how he refers to himself now, nearly always in the third person. I shall follow the same practice in this book and call him K hereafter.

*   *   *   *

In 1923 Baron van Pallandt made over to K his beautiful eighteenth-century ancestral home, Castle Eerde, near Zwolle in Holland, with 5,000 acres of woodland. Since K did not want to own any property personally another trust was formed to receive it, of which K was President, and Eerde became the international headquarters of the O.S.E. In the summer of 1924 the first Star Camp was held on part of the property at Ommen, a mile or so from the Castle. This camp was to become an annual event up till the war.

During another visit to India and Sydney in 1924-5 Nitya became very ill again. On the voyage back to San Francisco from Sydney in June '25 he nearly died and he remained dangerously ill throughout the summer at Ojai. K nursed him devotedly, slept in his room and did for him all those tasks that have to be done for a bedridden patient. K did not go to Europe that summer on account of Nitya, but the Star Camp was held at Ommen in August, presided over by Mrs Besant. George Arundale, now a bishop in the Liberal Catholic Church, and another Theosophical leader and Liberal Catholic bishop, James Ingall Wedgwood, were also there. Arundale and Wedgwood claimed clairvoyance and 'brought through' all kinds of messages from the Masters and announced various Initiations. Arundale's young Indian wife, Rukmini, was said to have taken three Initiations; Arundale and Wedgwood took their fourth (Arhathood) and Mrs Besant and Leadbeater their fifth and final one (Adepthood). None of these amazing happenings was confirmed by Leadbeater from Sydney; nevertheless, Mrs Besant trusted Arundale so completely that during the Camp she publicly announced the names of ten of the twelve people who were to be the Lord's apostles when he came, according to information 'brought through' by Arundale. Among these were Mrs Besant, Leadbeater, Nitya, Lady Emily, Jinarajadasa, Wedgwood, Rukmini and Arundale himself. Leadbeater was 'visibly distressed' when he heard of all these pronouncements, and K was not consulted about them; he was merely informed of them by cable and letter.

Lady Emily, who had been at the Camp and had been carried away by the hysterical excitement there, was one of those who wrote to K telling him about it all. She received letters from him in return, full of a most unhappy scepticism. He felt that something sacred had been defiled and she soon realised what a gullible fool she had been. At K's request she destroyed all the letters she received from him at that time; he feared that if they fell into anyone else's hands his criticisms of Mrs Besant, whom he dearly loved, would be misunderstood. He believed that she was growing senile—she was seventy-eight—and was being imposed upon by those she trusted. She had written to ask him to confirm what had taken place at Ommen to which he had replied, 'I am afraid I do not remember [on the astral plane] any of those happenings over there as I am much too tired as I have to sleep with Nitya and be constantly wakeful.'

Mrs Besant wanted K to attend the Jubilee Convention of the T.S. at Adyar, Madras, in December. He was assured that Nitya would not be allowed to die; the Masters had said so, for he was needed for the Lord's work. Mrs Besant asked K to travel with her to India in November. Since Nitya was a little better and Madame de Manziarly offered to go and look after him, K reluctantly agreed.

Lady Emily, the Arundales, Wedgwood and others travelled with K and Mrs Besant on a ship leaving from Naples on November 9. There was a distinct coolness between K and Bishops Arundale and Wedgwood in their spectacular regalia. As soon as they embarked K received a telegram to say that Nitya had influenza, and at Port Said on the 13th another telegram arrived: 'Flu rather worse. Pray for me.' Even then K was not unduly worried. As he said to Shiva Rao, one of his first tutors at Adyar with whom he was sharing a cabin, 'If Nitya was going to die I would not have been allowed to leave Ojai.' His faith in the

Masters' power to save Nitya's life seemed to Shiva Rao to be 'unqualified and unquestioning'. That same night came the announcement of Nitya's death. According to Shiva Rao the news

broke him [K] completely; it did more—his entire philosophy of life— the implicit faith in the future as outlined by Mrs Besant and Mr Leadbeater, Nitya's vital part in it, all appeared shattered at that moment. At night he would sob and moan and cry out for Nitya, sometimes in his native Telegu which in his waking consciousness he could not speak. Day after day we watched him, heartbroken, disillusioned. Day after day he seemed to change, gripping himself together in an effort to face life—but without Nitya. He was going through an inner revolution, finding new strength.

By the time K arrived in Bombay he had written a piece about Nitya which was published in the magazine of the O.S.E.—the *Herald of the Star*:

On the physical plane we could be separated and now we are inseparable . . . For my brother and I are one. As Krishnamurti I now have greater zeal, greater faith, greater sympathy and greater love, for there is also in me the body, the Being of Nityananda . . . I know how to weep still but that is human. I know now with greater certainty than ever before, that there is real beauty in life, real happiness that cannot be shattered by any physical happening, a great strength which cannot be weakened by passing events, and a great love which is permanent, imperishable and unconquerable.

These were not just words. A friend who was at Adyar to greet him recalled that his face was radiant; there was not a shadow on it to show what he had been through. I myself noticed that he had gained a new power of love and sympathy when he came to Colombo to meet Leadbeater and a party, of whom I was one, coming from Sydney for the Convention. Leadbeater greeted K with the words, 'At least *you* are an Arhat'.

Mrs Besant was greatly torn in her loyalties. Her personal love and reverence for K were unshaken as were his for her, and she still believed him to be the vehicle for the Lord Maitreya, but she also dearly loved George Arundale. She made one last effort to reconcile him and K. She gathered together in her drawing-room Leadbeater, Jinarajadasa, Arundale and Wedgwood, and taking K by the hand and-seating him beside her on the sofa, she asked him if he would accept them as his apostles. He replied that he would accept none of them except perhaps Mrs Besant herself. There never was a reconciliation. Arundale, however, stopped 'bringing through' messages, unlike Leadbeater who went on doling out Initiations to his own flock.

The T.S. Convention was followed by a Star Congress on December 28. At the first meeting at 8 o'clock in the morning under the great banyan tree in the compound a dramatic change took place while K was speaking about the World Teacher: 'He comes only to those who want, who desire, who long . . .' and then a new expression radiated his face, his voice changed and rang out—'I come for those who want sympathy, who are longing to be released, who are longing to find happiness in all things. I come to reform and not to tear down, I come not to destroy but to build.'

For those of us who noticed the change to the first person this was a spine-tingling moment. Among the few who noticed nothing were, not surprisingly, Arundale and Wedgwood. Mrs Besant certainly noticed the change, for at the last meeting of the Congress she declared: '. . . the event [of December 28] marked the definite consecration of the chosen vehicle . . . the final acceptance of the body chosen long before.'

K himself did not doubt what had happened. Speaking to the National Representatives of the O.S.E. he said, 'You have drunk at the fountain of wisdom and knowledge . . . When He comes again, and I am sure that He will come again very soon, it will be for us a nobler and far more beautiful occasion than even last time.' And at a meeting on January 5, 1926, he said: 'A new life, a new storm has swept the world . . . I personally feel quite different since that day . . . I feel like a crystal vase, a jar that has been cleaned and now anybody in the world can put a beautiful flower in it and that flower shall live in the vase and never die.'

*   *   *   *

In July of the same year, 1926, K held the first of what were to be many small gatherings at Castle Eerde before the Ommen Camp. This group came by invitation and K talked to them for an hour every morning. Mrs Besant, who was lecturing in Amsterdam, was not invited. She wrote pathetically to K on July 10:

My beloved son,

Thank you for your loving letter. I seem very far away. I hear of many delightful poems, which I, of course, do not see, and I am sure you are giving delightful talks. I am like the prophets and kings who desired to see and hear the things that the lucky people round you see and hear, but which the poor ps and ks did not see and hear.

Don't leave off loving me because you have many who are more demonstrative than your loving old Amma [Mother]

And on July 18 she was writing again, this time from Huizen, close to Ommen, the centre of the Liberal Catholic Church in Europe, presided over by Bishop Wedgwood:

My beloved,

Thank you very much for your dear little letter. It is sweet of you to love me, and I love you and wish to serve you.

I am sorry and glad that your spine and head are troublesome, for it means that He will come and use His body, His, my darling, for you have given it to Him, your great and splendid privilege.

We can only help by not hindering. I, too, would like to be with you, but I have to help all those gathered here from all parts of Holland.

May all the Devas guard you, dear one, the happy crowd that love Shri Krishna and listen to hear His flute call them to their joyous service.

Always your own loving Amma[1]

Mrs Besant attended the Camp at Ommen with Wedgwood. Several times it seemed that the Lord spoke through K at the meetings. At one evening talk round the Camp fire it was unmistakable: 'I belong to all people, to all who really love, to all who are suffering. And if you would walk you must walk with me.' One woman who heard him that evening described how 'His face had grown strongly powerful and stern and even his voice sounded deeper and fuller. The power went on increasing in every word he uttered.'

Mrs Besant and Wedgwood were in the audience and after the talk Wedgwood whispered to Mrs Besant that it was not the Lord Maitreya who had spoken through K but a powerful black magician whom he knew well. When Mrs Besant passed this on to K he was dumbfounded. He said that if she believed that he would never speak again. She made no more reference to it but thereafter whenever K said anything not approved of by Wedgwood he claimed that 'the Blacks had got him'.

At the beginning of 1927 K wrote to Leadbeater, 'I know my destiny and my work. I know with certainty and knowledge of my own, that I am blending into the consciousness of the one Teacher and that He will completely fill me.' In April that year at Ojai, where Mrs Besant was staying with K, she made a statement to the Associated Press of America which ended with the words, 'The World Teacher is here.' Because of this belief the name of the O.S.E. was changed to the Order of the Star, and the *Herald of the Star* to the *Star Review*.

But during the Ommen Camp in August that year K was disconcerting many of his followers by saying, 'No one can give you liberation, you have to find it within . . . He who has attained liberation has become the Teacher—like myself. It lies in the power of each one of us to enter the flame, to become the flame.' He was saying in effect that the Masters and all other gurus were unnecessary, that everyone must find truth for himself. He had written and spoken a great deal about 'union with the Beloved' and caused even greater consternation when in a later talk at the Camp he tried to explain what he meant by this:

When I was a small boy I used to see Sri Krishna, with the flute, as he is pictured by the Hindus . . . When I grew older and met with Bishop Leadbeater and the Theosophical Society, I began to see the Master K.H. [Kuthumi]—again in the form which was put before me . . . Later on, as I grew, I began to see the Lord Maitreya. That was two years ago and I saw him constantly in the form put before me . . . Now lately it has been the Buddha whom I have been seeing . . . I have been asked what I mean by 'the Beloved'. I will give a meaning, an explanation which you will interpret as you please. To me it is all—it is Sri Krishna, it is the Master K.H., it is the Lord Maitreya, it is the Buddha, and yet it is beyond all these forms. What does it matter what name you give? . . . What you are troubling about is whether there is such a person as the World Teacher who has manifested Himself in the body of a certain person, Krishnamurti; but in the world nobody will trouble about this question . . . My beloved is the open skies, the flower, every human being . . . Till I was able to say with certainty, without undue excitement, or exaggeration in order to convince others that I was one with my Beloved, I never spoke. I talked in vague generalities which everybody wanted. I never said: I am the World

Teacher; but now that I feel I am one with my Beloved, I say it, not in order to impress my authority on you, not to convince you of my greatness, nor of the greatness of the World Teacher, nor even of the beauty of life, but merely to awaken the desire in your hearts and in your own minds to seek the Truth . . . It is no good asking me who is the Beloved. Of what use is explanation? For you will not understand the Beloved until you are able to see him in every animal, in every blade of grass, in every person that is suffering, in every individual.

A year later at one of the Camp meetings K said he would abolish the Order at once if it 'claimed to be a vehicle which held the Truth and the only Truth'. At a subsequent meeting he told his audience, 'I hope you will not listen to anyone, but will listen only to your own intuition, your own understanding, and give a public refusal to those who would be your interpreters.' These 'interpreters' were, of course, the leaders of the T.S. He added that he did not want disciples:

> Every one of you is a disciple of the Truth if you understand the Truth and do not follow individuals . . . There is no understanding in the worship of personalities . . . I still maintain that all ceremonies are unnecessary for spiritual growth . . . Is it not much simpler to make Life itself the goal—Life itself the guide, the Master and the God— than to have mediators, *gurus*, who must inevitably step down the Truth, and hence betray it?

He had warned his listeners that they were to be shaken to their foundations. The great majority of them were. They wanted him as their guru, they wanted to be his disciples and for him to tell them what to do and how far advanced they were on the occult path.

From the time the O.S.E. had been founded in 1911, the leaders had been warning the members that when the Lord came his teaching might be so contrary to all they expected that they would be in danger of rejecting him. Now they had fallen themselves into the very trap they had warned others against. Leadbeater, Arundale and Wedgwood had rejected him because as well as denying that they were his apostles he would not accept the Liberal Catholic Church or Co-Masonry, the other ceremonial in which they had given themselves high degrees, while Mrs Besant, although she remained as infinitely loving to him as he was to her and even longed at moments to resign from the Presidency of the T.S. in order to follow him wherever he went, could not give up her occult Master. Jinarajadasa, the other important leader, though remaining quite friendly, was too entrenched in Theosophy to change. There was no place in K's teaching for any of them. They had been in positions of great power which they were not prepared to relinquish.

At the Star Camp at Ommen on August 3, 1929, in the presence of Mrs Besant and over 3,000 Star members, K formally dissolved the Order.

I maintain that Truth is a pathless land [he began], and you cannot approach it by any path whatsoever, by any religion, by any sect . . . I do not want to belong to any organisation of a spiritual kind . . . If an organisation be created for this purpose, it becomes a crutch, a weakness, a bondage, and must cripple the individual, and prevent him from growing, from establishing his uniqueness, which lies in his discovery for himself of that absolute, unconditioned Truth . . . Because I am free, unconditioned, whole . . . I desire those who seek to understand me, to be free, not to follow me, not to make out of me a cage . . . You are all depending for your spirituality on someone else . . . No man from outside can make you free . . . You have been accustomed to being told how far you have advanced, what your spiritual status is. How childish! Who but yourself can tell you if you are incorruptible? . . . For two years I have been thinking about this slowly, carefully, patiently, and I have now decided to disband the Order, as I happen to be its Head. You can form other organisations and expect someone else. With that I am not concerned, nor with creating new cages, new decorations for those cages. My only concern is to set men absolutely, unconditionally free.

At the end of the year K also resigned from the Theosophical Society.

2

The Completeness of Life

No one has ever taken the place of Nitya in K's life and heart, but after Nitya's death in November 1925 an Indian friend, D. Rajagopalacharya, became his most constant companion. Rajagopal, as he was called, was a South Indian Brahmin born in 1901. He had been a protégé of Leadbeater's and had been sent to England in 1920 to go to Cambridge. Rajagopal met K in the autumn of that year and asked whether he might work for him when he had taken his degree. K liked him and agreed. Rajagopal spent the summers with him and a party of friends in France, Austria and Italy in 1922, '23 and '24; he went twice to Ojai, once to help look after K when his 'process' was at its most intense in 1923-4, for which he took a year off Cambridge, and again in the summer of 1925, after taking his degree in History, to help in nursing Nitya in his last illness.

Rajagopal returned to England with K in the autumn of '25 and went with him and Mrs Besant to India. Travelling with them was a pretty American girl of twenty-two, Rosalind Williams, whom K and Nitya had met when they first went to Ojai and who had also helped to take care of Nitya at the end. Rosalind and Rajagopal were thrown much together after Nitya's death and in October 1927, with Mrs Besant's full approval, they were married in London. Thereafter, they made their home at Ojai, an arrangement that suited K very well. He continued to sleep at his cottage (now called Pine Cottage) but took his meals at Arya Vihara where the Rajagopals lived. Rosalind kept house for him.

Since Rajagopal was with K at the time of Nitya's death he stepped quite naturally into Nitya's shoes—shoes that never quite fitted him—and K appointed him Organising Secretary of the O.S.E. in Nitya's place and made him International Treasurer of the Order, a new appointment.

Rajagopal, though slim and tall with beautiful hands, was a very different physical type from K and Nitya, being curly-haired and rather snub-nosed. He was far more Western than Eastern in temperament—practical, highly efficient and tidy almost to the point of obsession. K's vagueness irritated him almost as much as his bossy pernicketyness irritated K. As well as affection and a good deal of laughter there were frequent clashes between them; nevertheless, K was content to leave all practical matters, which bored him, especially financial matters, in Rajagopal's undoubtedly capable hands.

After the dissolution of the Order there was no falling off in the audiences attending K's talks; new people took the place of those who abandoned him and donations towards his work continued to pour in. K's only personal source of income was the £500 a year settled on him by Miss Dodge; all other income came from donations and the sale of his books. From 1926, for nearly forty years, Rajagopal organised K's tours and talks, arranged for the publication of his books and acted as his secretary-courier. For several years K helped Rajagopal to correct the talks for publication. His early books, most of them consisting of poems, were published by the Star Publishing Trust which K had set up at Castle Eerde, its chief centre, Hollywood, London and Madras, though the books were printed in India. They were sold at meetings and through a mailing list.

The sole function of the Publishing Trust was the dissemination of K's teaching. Rajagopal was also chief editor of the monthly *Star Review* which had agencies and representatives in eighteen different countries and was translated into as many languages. There was an *International Star Bulletin* as well.

Rajagopal had no money of his own, yet there was no question of his being offered a salary. It would not have occurred to K that he might have wanted financial independence, especially after his marriage to a girl who had nothing of her own either. All his needs were provided for as Nitya's had been, and K treated him with the same generosity, the same sense of sharing everything (K's and Nitya's shirts, handkerchiefs and socks had been marked with their joint initials); besides, now that Rajagopal held the purse strings it was for him to decide what his and K's needs were. It was an arrangement that worked perfectly so long as there was complete mutual trust.

In physical appearance K had by the thirties reached a maturity of beauty; with his straight black glossy hair, smooth brown skin, great luminous black eyes with long, long lashes, flat ears, ideally proportioned nose and mouth, a supple athletic slim figure and slender hands and feet, he was as perfectly formed as a human being could be. Numberless women had been, and still were, in love with him, and he had been in love with two or three girls, a fact he has completely forgotten now and dismisses as of no importance. He was not of more than average height, yet an erect carriage gave him presence. A natural thoughtfulness for others, a self-effacingness, would have ensured good manners even if he had not been trained in the politenesses of good English society. Moreover, he was extremely elegant.

K has often been criticised for dressing so well. Many people are conditioned to think that 'a holy man' should not care for appearances; they expect to see a swami in a loin cloth with wild hair and beard. K, on the contrary, believes in caring for the body in every way—seeing that it has the right food, the right amount of exercise and rest, keeping it scrupulously groomed, and dressing it not only well but appropriately. Thus in Europe and America he wears European clothes—suits and ties in towns and informal clothes in the country—and changes into Indian dress as soon as he arrives in India. His good taste in clothes, as in all things, is natural to him. He has always been to the best tailors and shirt-makers and had his shoes made to measure—a necessity owing to the extreme narrowness of his feet. He looks after his clothes as he does his body, hanging up his suits as soon as he takes them off, never failing to put trees in his shoes (he always wears brown shoes) which he polishes himself so that they shine like horse-chestnuts. Taxi drivers in London invariably stop for him, taking him for a prince or a millionaire.

With all this, I have never known anyone so completely detached from his body as K is. He looks after it because it has to serve him for his work. He cares for it as he does a motor-car. It is unthinkable that he would go out in a car of his own that had not been washed and polished. On going to see him one always endeavours to look one's best, for he notices everything, not in a critical or disapproving spirit but from his habit .of keen observation.

This tidiness in appearance and excessive care of the body may seem incompatible with K's dreamy, vague nature as may his life-long interest in machinery. A Pathek-Philippe watch, left to him many years ago, is the only possession he really seems to cherish, yet even that he would be capable of giving away. He would give away all his clothes to someone in need. He once gave away his only overcoat. Emerson has said, 'A foolish consistency is the hobgoblin of little minds, adored by little statesmen and philosophers and divines. With consistency a great soul has simply nothing to do.' If in nothing else, the inconsistencies in K's character would make him a great soul.

*   *   *   *

From the time K was 'discovered' he had never yet travelled alone, and after Nitya's death it was Rajagopal who usually travelled with him. When they went to India Rosalind remained at Ojai, though she did sometimes go to Europe with them. After the dissolution of the Order, the annual camps were open to the public, thus attracting new people. These camps became expertly organised under Rajagopal's direction; attendance was limited to 3,000 people apart from those who came for the day. In 1931 Castle Eerde and most of the land was returned to Baron van Pallandt by a deed of transfer. Only 400 acres on which the camp was held were retained. Thereafter a moderate-sized house called Heenan, near Ommen village, became the headquarters from which Rajagopal and his Dutch helpers ran the Star Publishing Trust, edited the *Star Review*, organised the camps and transacted other business. Many people who regularly attended the camps had now built huts at their own expense on the Star land. The building of these huts, unobtrusively erected among the pine trees, was strictly controlled. K himself had his own quite luxurious hut and Rajagopal had another.

Since 1929 an annual camp had also been held in the spring at Ojai. This was on land some eight miles from Arya Vihara at the western, lower end of the valley bought for K's work with funds raised as a result of an appeal by Mrs Besant in 1927. When the weather permitted, K gave his talks there out of doors in a grove of holm oaks or ilexes, the so-called Oak Grove.

Despite their loyalty in attending the camps, several of K's old devotees were unable to follow him into what seemed to them mists of abstraction. One of these was Lady Emily Lutyens who had been his follower for some twenty years and to whom he had revealed as to no one else his innermost feelings in regular long letters. Old enough to be his mother, she had for love of him neglected her husband and five children (of whom I was the youngest)—had, indeed, been ready to forsake them altogether at a word from him—a word she longed for. She had given all her energy, first to preparing the way for the coming of the World Teacher and then to serving him when he came; now she could not accept the fact that he did not want followers. For several years after the dissolution of the Order she felt empty, listless, hopeless. K continued to write to her and she to him, though their letters became less and less frequent. Since 1913 he had always addressed her as 'Mother' or 'Mum', just as he called Mrs Besant the Indian equivalent, 'Amma'. He tried his hardest to carry her with him, to make her understand that she must not depend on him or anyone else for her happiness, that she must be a light unto herself. But she had always been a follower and seemed to have no inner resources. As she wrote in her autobiography:

> Krishna had managed to transcend personal love but I could not. It was not that he did not love, but no one person was necessary to him any longer. He had attained to universal love. As he said himself: 'Pure love is like the perfume of the rose, given to all. The sun does not care on whom it shines . . . The quality of true love, of pure love, knows no such distinctions as wife and husband, son, father, mother.[2]

*　　　*　　　*　　　*

After the Ommen Camp of 1930 K went with Rajagopal to France and then Switzerland where he became very ill with bronchitis, and afterwards to Taormina in Sicily for six weeks to recuperate. It was a happy, peaceful time. 'Those warm sunny days and quiet have opened up many ideas and I feel a great warmth in my heart. I have written and filled my note book while I was there.' Thus he wrote to Lady Emily on December 11 from the Grande Bretagne Hotel, Athens, where he had arrived with Rajagopal the day before and where talks had been arranged for him. It was his first visit to Greece. The meeting on the day of his arrival had been crowded: 'I believe 1,000 were turned away and there were more than 2,000 in the hall. Somebody said that if I stayed there for a fortnight I would become the Mayor of Athens!! I think I had better leave! They are very enthusiastic and I can't go out without a crowd, literally, coming after me.' He continued in this same letter:

I have never seen anything more beautiful, simple, forceful than the Parthenon. The whole of the Acropolis is amazing, breath taking and *everything* else in nature of the expression of man is vulgar, mediocre and confused. It's magnificent. I would come to see it a thousand miles. What people those wonderful few Greeks were. You must see it, and everything else that is not in the way of the eternal is so puny, ridiculous and stupid.

K had not been so enthusiastic about a work of art since he had seen a stone head of Buddha in the Boston Museum in 1924.* The only other man-made object that had so far thrilled him was the *Winged Victory* in the Louvre.

This visit to Athens was the start of K's first extensive tour of Europe which lasted five months. After four days in Athens he went with Rajagopal by sea to Constantinople; then, after another four days, on to Bucharest where he had been invited to give public talks. Because he spoke against organised religion and nationalism, some nationalistic Catholic students in Bucharest had threatened to kill him, a threat the authorities took so seriously that they insisted on a four-man, plain-clothes police guard following him wherever he went and staying outside his room during the four nights he spent at the Athenée Palace Hotel. K himself regarded the danger as a great joke.

Queen Marie of Roumania, a grand-daughter of Queen Victoria, asked to see him. He spent three hours with her in her palace. He found her 'an awfully nice woman . . . Possessions, power, authority—but suffering,' he told Lady Emily. 'Men are men whether Kings or Queens or beggars.'

* K wrote an article about this head of Buddha in the *Herald of the Star*, March 1924.

The Completeness of Life

In January and February 1931 K and Rajagopal were in Jugoslavia and Hungary; then back to Ommen at the end of February for a last gathering at Castle Eerde before it was returned to the Baron. This was followed by two public talks in London at the Friends Meeting House in the Euston Road. By now K was speaking with fluency and confidence. In all his talks at this time he was constantly using the word 'completeness'. For instance, in his second talk in London on March 9:

In everything, in all men, there is the totality, the completeness of life ... By completeness I mean freedom of consciousness, freedom from individuality. That completeness which exists in everything cannot progress: it is absolute. The effort to acquire is futile, but if you can realise that Truth, Happiness, exists in all things and that the realisation of that Truth lies only through elimination, then there is a timeless understanding. This is not a negation. Most people are afraid to be nothing. They call it being positive when they are making an effort, and call that effort virtue. When there is effort it is not virtue. Virtue is effortless. When you are as nothing, you are all things, not by aggrandisement, not by laying emphasis on the 'I', on the personality, but by the continual dissipation of that consciousness which creates power, greed, envy, possessive care, vanity, fear and passion. By continually being self-recollected you become fully conscious, and then you liberate the mind and heart and know harmony, which is completeness.

K has often been asked about physical healing. He undoubtedly possesses a power of healing but has always played it down. In answer to a question at this same meeting—'What is your attitude to spiritual healing?'—he replied:

I once had a friend whom I healed. Some months later he was taken to prison for some crime. Which would you rather have: a Teacher who will show you the way to keep permanently whole, or one who will momentarily heal your wounds?... Miracles are fascinating child's play. Miracles are happening every day. Doctors are performing miracles. Many friends of mine are spiritual healers. But although they may heal the body, unless they make the mind and heart also whole, the disease will return. I am concerned with the healing of the heart and the mind, not with the body. I hold that no great Teacher would perform a miracle, because that would be a betrayal of the Truth.[3]

From London the European tour extended to Edinburgh, Berlin, Hamburg, Frankfurt and Vienna, in all of which places K gave talks, attracted followers and made many new friends. Then back to Ommen for another camp in July–August. It was not until October that he returned to Ojai having been away for sixteen months. He was ecstatic at being back there. Rosalind and Rajagopal now had a baby daughter, Radha, born in July, who delighted him.

Lady Emily, out of her state of emptiness, and worried by family matters, wrote at this time to accuse him of escaping from the realities of life into his beautiful secluded valley. He replied on December 30:

The ecstasy I feel is the outcome of this world. I wanted to understand, I wanted to conquer sorrow, the pain of detachment and attachment, death, continuity of life, everything that man goes through, every day. I have. So, my ecstasy is real and infinite, not an escape. I know my way out of this incessant misery and I want to help people out of the bog of this sorrow. No, this is not an escape.[4]

And on February 4, 1932, still at Ojai, he was writing again:

It's not an escape when you see that certain things are unnecessary for you, not to plunge into them. I saw that family life with all its charms and entanglements were not needed for me so I kept out of it. Surely, mum, that is not an escape. The same way I could have earned money, quite a lot [he had received a serious offer to appear as Buddha in a film], but I didn't want, not out of laziness or lack of opportunity but because I wanted to do something very definitely and I don't care about money. I am quite happy to be a beggar, which I am. If Miss Dodge stopped I would still not be worried because I need very little and I can always be warm in India! And begging there is an honourable profession unlike here! As to these beautiful places I didn't deliberately choose them and I really don't care where I am, honestly, as long as it's quiet.[5]

Rajagopal was in Hollywood recovering from a tonsilectomy with Rosalind and the baby. K, alone at Ojai, wrote that he was spending his days in solitude, 'and it's tremendous, tremendous is the only word for it. I have revolutionised myself!! I can't tell you, mum, what a glorious thing it is to have realised the highest and the most sublime thing. I wish I could help you to it.'

On March 26 after the Rajagopals had returned, he was writing again:

I am trying to make it clear, trying to build a bridge for others to come over, not away from life, but to have more abundantly of life. I feel that, especially the last month, I have realised something that gives greater fullness to life. All this is so badly expressed and by constantly expressing and talking about it one hopes to make it clearer and clearer . . . I am trying to incite as many as I can to live rightly and by heaven, there are few alright!! It's all very strange. I can't lose my enthusiasm, on the contrary it's intense and I want to go and shout and urge people to change and live happily. The more I think of what I have 'realised', the clearer I can put it and help to build a bridge but that takes time and continual change of phrases, so as to give true meaning. You have no idea how difficult it is to express the inexpressible and what's expressed is not truth.[6]

K has never lost his enthusiasm, never ceased trying to 'build a bridge' or to find new words in which to express the inexpressible.

*   *   *   *

For many months Rajagopal had been suffering from rheumatism, especially in his hands, and it was feared that he might have arthritis. The tonsilectomy, from which he took a long time to recover, relieved him only temporarily.

During the early months of 1932 K spoke regularly in the Oak Grove at Ojai; then in June the camp was held there. This same month, K started on a four-month tour of the U.S. and Canada, and in December returned with Rajagopal to Europe en route to India, where he had not been since early in 1929.

In January 1933 K gave six public talks in Benares and afterwards toured northern India for a month, speaking in every place he visited. At the end of this programme he fell ill with a very bad attack of chicken-pox. In May he saw Mrs Besant at Adyar. It was the last time he stayed there and the last time he saw her. By now she had completely lost her memory and barely recognised him. 'Dear Amma, it is tragic to see her like this,' K wrote to Lady Emily. 'It's all so sad for them all.' She was to die in September in her eighty-sixth year.

K and Rajagopal sailed from Bombay on May 11. K wrote to Lady Emily from board-ship on the 17th that he was being constantly interrupted by people wanting to talk to him. One lady had said to him, 'You look so intelligent and nice that you must have some philosophy of life'. Still unable to shave owing to the chicken-pox spots, he had grown a full black beard. 'I look like the conventional Christ,' he reported, 'a merveille, and you can imagine the fun the passengers get out of it.'

They left the ship at Port Said and went to Cairo and Alexandria before going on to Athens again for another gathering. This time they stayed with friends a few miles outside the city and K was even more enthusiastic about the place than he had been in 1930, writing to Lady Emily on June 18:

It's like California but more beautiful, more mature, softness in the air and the people are extraordinarily friendly. It would be a pleasant land to live in. Violet hills, quantities of flowers, vineyards, cypresses, olive trees and wild thyme in purple bloom. What a country. The Acropolis is matchless and I am in love. Unfortunately the lady is in marble. It is just my luck!! She's the goddess of Justice, Themis. It's really superb and I've completely lost my heart and mind to her.

Rajagopal's rheumatism had returned very badly, so after Athens he and K went to Salsamaggiore in Italy for Rajagopal to take the mud baths, then on to Stresa at the end of June for another gathering. The Ommen camp followed in July. Rosalind and baby Radha joined them there, returning to Ojai when they went to Oslo where K gave some talks. On the way to India in October they stayed in Paris, and then in Rome with a new acquaintance, Lady Berkeley, an American, who had a luxurious house there and had arranged some meetings for K.*

K and Rajagopal arrived in Madras a month after Mrs Besant's death and stayed for the first time at Vasanta Vihar, 64 Greenways Road, a recently built house in six acres of newly-acquired land, put up by the Star Publishing Trust for its Indian headquarters. It was a much larger house than K had wanted or expected. It is on the north side of the Adyar River whereas the 260-acre

---

* Daughter of John Lowell of Boston, she had in 1924 married the Earl of Berkeley as his second wife. When he died in 1942 the title became extinct.

compound of the Theosophical Society is on the south side stretching east to the sea.

Leadbeater had been summoned from Sydney when it was known that Mrs Besant was dying. He had arrived just in time to see her alive and was staying on at Adyar for the T.S. Convention in December. K described to Lady Emily his reception by the Theosophists:

C.W.L. [Leadbeater] met me at the station with a garland and so did others but it was an empty show, and there was a largish crowd in the hall at Adyar, another farce. George [Arundale, the new President of the T.S.] was there and patted my hand. The atmosphere there was awful, no friendliness and falsification. Some of the old friends who used to come round keep a safe distance, if seen near me they mightn't get steps [on the occult Path]. Others come round and whisper I am the real stuff but they are old and they can't leave off their old habits, though their hearts aren't in it. Beneath the candle is the darkness; so it is at Adyar. I never felt so tired in my life as there and I was really glad to leave it. C.W.L. is distinctly old and garrulous. I went to see him twice and we talked about everything that was of no importance. He seemed to be friendly but—! All over India I have huge crowds, but quantities without any quality. There was in this morning's paper, an interview with me saying how spoilt I was etc.

K wrote this on January 21, 1934, from Colombo from where he and Rajagopal were to sail for Australia on the 27th. After the Adyar Convention, which he had attended, K had driven to the Rishi Valley School which he had founded in 1928 in Andhra Pradesh, ten miles from Madanapalle, his birth-place, and some 170 miles north of Madras. About 2,400 feet above sea level, the beautiful Rishi Valley is dominated by the Rishi Konda mountain. The co-educational, non-profit-making residential school has a campus of 300 acres, including a farm. The school also runs a rural centre where seventy children from adjacent villages are educated and given medical care. It was originally constituted as a charitable institution under the name of the Rishi Valley Trust of which K and Mrs Besant, among others, were trustees. G. V. Subba Rao was the first Principal of the school, a post he held for thirty years. Rishi Valley was the first of what are now eight Krishnamurti schools. While K was there that year he talked to the teachers for five hours a day for a week.

Education has been one of K's most passionate concerns since the start of his mission. He feels that the best hope for the world's sanity lies in the right education of children from the earliest age. If children can be brought up without national and racial prejudices, without competitiveness or any of the cultural traditions and ideologies that divide man from man, there might be peace. But how can children thus be educated unless there are enough unconditioned adults to teach them? It is obviously far harder for an adult to *un*condition himself than for a child to remain unconditioned. For the adult it means a complete transformation. All the prejudices he has been nurtured on have to be discarded, all his ideals, assumptions and aspirations. To give up one's prejudices is virtually to give up one's personality. 'Try it and see,' K says. It is immensely difficult, bearing in mind that ideals such as patriotism, loyalty and heroism are as much prejudices as a sense of national or racial superiority or inferiority.

*   *   *   *

On the way to Sydney K spoke at Fremantle, Adelaide and Melbourne to 'huge audiences'. The press, particularly in Sydney, was very friendly; not so the T.S. people. In Sydney he stayed with Mr and Mrs John Mackay in the suburb of Mosman, close to The Manor where Leadbeater had his community, with whom he had stayed when he first went to Sydney with Nitya in 1922.

Leadbeater, who had returned to Australia on another ship, died in Perth on March 1. His body was sent to Sydney for cremation. K happened still to be there and went to the funeral service, though he stayed outside the chapel. He reported to Lady Emily that 'The Manor people are bewildered by his death, and were asking who was going to tell them when they had taken steps [on the Path] now he had gone'. This dependence on others to tell them their state of spirituality was one of the things K had so deplored about Theosophists.

In Auckland, New Zealand, K's next destination, which he and Rajagopal reached at the end of March, he found the newspapers even more friendly than the Sydney ones. He was not allowed to talk over the air, however, because he was 'anti-religious'. 'Bernard Shaw, who is on a visit,' he wrote, 'told the people that it was scandalous as I am a great religious teacher. He wrote to me about it. Unfortunately I didn't meet him. I had tremendous meetings and a good deal of interest and I think the friends there will keep it up.'

Shaw, who had been an intimate friend of Mrs Besant's before she became a Theosophist, had met K once or twice when lunching with Lady Emily in London. Shaw described K as 'the most beautiful human being he ever saw'.[7]

3

The Stream of Suffering

Constant travelling for more than two years left K exhausted on his return to California at the end of April 1934. He stayed in Los Angeles with Dr John Ingleman, a Swedish friend of long standing, who gave him massage and generally looked after his health. The Rajagopals meanwhile stayed at 2123 North Beechwood Drive, Hollywood, the headquarters of the Star Publishing Trust in the U.S.A. where there was a flat above the office. Rajagopal, who was still suffering from rheumatism or arthritis in his hands, saw a round of doctors and was put on a strict diet. In May they all returned to Ojai. 'Radha is lovely,' K told Lady Emily, 'chatting away all the time. She treats me as another child, plays with me etc.' (She was nearly three.) K has always loved children and felt at ease with them. In one of his books he gives a memorable description of a little girl in India:

A little child, without the prompting of her mother, came and sat close by, wide-eyed and wondering what it was all about. She was freshly washed and clothed and had some flowers in her hair. She was keenly observing everything, as children do, without recording too much. Her eyes were sparkling, and she did not know what to do, whether to cry, to laugh or to jump; instead she took my hand and looked at it with absorbing interest. Presently she forgot all those people in the room, relaxed and went to sleep with her head in my lap.[8]

Rajagopal had now built an office at Ojai with living quarters above it close to Arya Vihara, and a young American, Byron Casselberry, a former pupil of Leadbeater's, who had edited the *Star Bulletin* at Eerde for a time, was living there, helping Rajagopal with his administrative work. K still slept in Pine Cottage and had his meals at Arya Vihara. Before the Ojai camp in June he went with the Rajagopals to the Big Bear Lake in the San

Bernadino mountains about 150 miles from Ojai and at an altitude of 7,000 feet. He had been there twice before.

A long tour of South America had been planned for December. In order to be ready for it Rajagopal took a complete rest in Hollywood with Rosalind and the baby for the whole of August. K, left alone at Ojai, was, as always, particularly happy when alone. 'I am having a good time by myself,' he wrote to Lady Emily on August 14, 'writing, reading, and going for walks late in the evening.' It was a very hot summer. The temperature reached 114° in the shade on some days. When the heat became too much for him he would motor with friends for an evening picnic to the beach at Ventura where there was such a difference in temperature that they had to build a fire.

Rajagopal had sent Lady Emily a typed newsletter reporting on the Ojai camp and K's talks, during the week it lasted. She was evidently critical of some of K's activities and the things he was saying and the closeness of his new house at Adyar to the T.S. headquarters, for he was writing to her on August 27:

You say, mum, in your letter à propos of Rajagopal's news letter—
1. That I have denied being the W.T. [World Teacher]. You know, mum, I have *never* denied it. I have only said that it does not matter who or what I am but that they should examine what I say which does not mean that I have denied being the W.T.—2. With regard to schemes, there are very few we deliberately started. They grew out of the past with all its confusions.—3. You say I destroy their [the Theosophists'] ideals and smash what they hold sacred. Their ideals and their beliefs and their sacred things are in no way different from that of the world. It's the whole of man's illusions that I am trying to tackle not that of the Theos. only. What I am saying is to me more true than ever and if no one understands or cares for it, I shall go on. I am saying this not out of the tragic heights of superiority but because I can't help it—to go on. I am in love with it more than ever, and it is more immense, profound and unforseeable than ever and I am bursting with it.

With regard to the land for the S.P.T. [Star Publishing Trust] Rajagopal and I felt Madras was the best place for various reasons, for printing, people, workers etc. We tried to get land away from the T.S. headquarters. After hunting around Madras, we finally settled on this place. We have nothing against the T.S. and its tenets. I am *not* fighting *them* but the world's ideas, ideals. I don't feel competitive or a rival to them. If I did and had bought land near them, it would have been very,

very bad taste. Mum, the world is like the average T.S. person and I am
really tackling the world problem and not particularly the T.S. people's
but if it applies to them what am I to do? I hope I am making myself
clear. I am bursting with ideas and I write every day.

He begged Lady Emily in this letter to criticise him as much as
possible: 'The more one is critical the more we can understand
each other.' He went on to tell her that Rajagopal had to go into
hospital in Hollywood at the end of the month for a serious sinus
operation which it was hoped would cure his rheumatism. His
hands had become numb. In the event, the operation was postponed and K and the Rajagopals went to Carmel, an attractive
little town on the coast some 265 miles north of Ojai, for the
months of September and October. They stayed there as guests of
friends who ran a small hotel called the Peter Pan Lodge on a hill
behind the town. K went for solitary walks of six or seven miles a
day while they were there. 'It's impossible to describe these walks,'
he told Lady Emily on October 16, 'they are lovely and I have a
great time in my solitude.' He had begun this letter by apologising
for not having written for so long 'but something is happening
inwardly which takes most of my leisure'. He and Rajagopal spent
every morning correcting talks and working on a book.

I can find no record of this book unless it was a book of talks.
K had published his last book of poems in 1931—*The Song of Life*
—for which he had written a foreword: 'The attainment of Truth
is an absolute, final experience. I have recreated myself after
Truth. I am not a poet; I have merely attempted to put into words
the manner of my realization.'[9]

K met one of America's greatest living poets at Carmel,
Robinson Jeffers, who had built himself a house there by the sea
with his own hands. He and his wife were Communists, though
they did not belong to the Party. K also met Lincoln Steffens, who
lived at Carmel, and his wife who was 'a blood red Communist'
according to K, though not a member of the Party either.* They
all had some 'very interesting talks together' in K's words. The
opening lines of a poem by Jeffers called *Credo*, published in 1935,

---

* Lincoln Steffens was a well known journalist and author. He had published his
autobiography in 1931. He died in 1936, aged 70. He had married his second wife,
Ella Winter, in 1924. Robinson Jeffers was born in 1887 and died in 1962.

probably refer to K: 'My friend from Asia has powers and magic, he plucks a / blue leaf from the young blue-gum / And gazing upon it, gathering and quieting / The God in his mind, creates an ocean more real than the / ocean, the salt, the actual / Appalling presence, the power of the waters.'

The author, Rom Landau, came to Carmel from Europe on purpose to talk to K and write about him in his book *God Is My Adventure*. He visited Robinson Jeffers while he was there and reported that Jeffers was so attracted by K's personality that they had soon become friends. Landau asked Jeffers if he thought K's message would ever become popular. 'Not at present,' Jeffers had answered. 'Most people won't find it intelligible enough.' 'What struck you most when you met him?' Landau then asked. 'His personality,' was the reply. 'Mrs Jeffers often makes the remark that light seems to come into the room when Krishnamurti comes in, and I agree with her, for he himself is the most convincing illustration of his honest message. To me it does not matter whether he speaks well or not. I can feel his influence even without words. . . . It is his very happy personality that seems to diffuse the truth and happiness of which he is always talking.' Jeffers went on to say that his message would be mature when its words were intelligible to everyone.

Landau talked to K alone on several consecutive days and quotes pages of what K said to him, mostly in response to questioning. The salient points were that truth, liberation or God, whatever you chose to call it, could not be found through the intellect or through experience. Truth was the release of the mind from all the burdens of memory. Truth was constant awareness of life within and without oneself. Life should be lived completely at every moment. There was no need to search for truth. It was always there, hidden behind a whole heap of old experiences. Eliminate all of them and truth would be there. Happiness, truth or God could not be found through the ego. The ego was nothing but the result of the environment. 'Do you really mean to say,' Landau asked at one point, 'that you have never read philosophy?' 'Do you seriously think you can learn from books?' K had replied. 'You can accumulate knowledge, you can learn facts and technicalities, but you cannot learn truth, happiness or any of the things that really matter. You can only learn from living

and acknowledging the life that is your very own. But not from
the lives of others.'

During one conversation K had said, 'You asked me just now
about personal love, and my answer is that I no longer know it.
Personal love does not exist for me. Love is for me a constant
inner state. People sometimes think that I am superficial and cold.
But it is not indifference, it is merely a feeling of love that is
constantly within me and that I simply cannot help giving to
everyone that I come into touch with.'

In their last conversation K spoke about free will in a startling
way: 'Only the unintelligent mind exercises choice in life. When
I talk of intelligence I mean it in its widest sense, I mean that deep
inner intelligence of mind, emotion and will. A truly intelligent
man can have no choice, because his mind can only be aware of
what is true, and can thus only choose the path of truth. It simply
cannot have any choice. Only the unintelligent mind has free will.'

'How did you come to that state of unity with everything?'
Landau asked on his last day at Carmel, to which K replied:

People have asked me about it before, and I always feel they expect to
hear the dramatic account of some sudden miracle through which I
suddenly became one with the universe. Of course nothing of the sort
happened. My inner awareness was always there; though it took me
time to feel it more and more clearly; and equally it took time to find
words that would at all describe it. It was not a sudden flash, but a
slow yet constant clarification of something that was always there.

Although Landau accurately reported K's ideas, one cannot
hear his authentic conversational voice in such articulate words.
Back at Ojai K's voice is heard again in a letter to Lady Emily
written in late November:

My own dearest Mother,
    I would love to see you just now, as I want to talk to you about so
many things. I am bursting with the immensity of love, anything one
likes to call it. I am intoxicated, intelligently, wisely. It's amazing and
it's so absurd to put it into words; it becomes so banal. Imagine the
state of the man who wrote Song of Songs, that of Buddha and Jesus,
and you will understand what mine is. It sounds rather bombastic but
it's not—so simple and consuming. I wish I could talk to you, mum.
Some day we will, dearest mum.

The Stream of Suffering

In his letters to Lady Emily, K often wished that they could spend a quiet time together as they had done at Ehrwald and Pergine (in the summers of 1923 and '24) when his 'process' had been going on so intensely; and when he heard that she was having a holiday in Cornwall he recalled their time together at Bude (in 1914–16), though he believed that he and she had been alone there except for Nitya, whereas in fact he had been there with his tutors and she had paid him only occasional visits. Right up to her death, nearly thirty years later, he never failed to remember her birthday.

There has always been some mystery as to how much K really remembers. When I was writing the first volume of his biography in 1972 he tried his utmost to bring back recollections for me. Of his childhood and youth he remembered nothing except what had been told to him. He had vague memories of his middle years but could not be relied upon for accurate dates. He remembered that he had had a brother called Nitya to whom he was devoted but was unable to recall his face, yet when I showed him some old group photographs he was able immediately to put a name to some of the people I could not identify. When I showed him the same photographs a few days later he failed to remember any of them. At times he can startle one with some recollection that seems to come with the same intuitive flash as his recognition of the faces in the old photographs, but for the most part his memory of the past is now a blank—he cannot even remember the times when his 'process' was at its most acute. This is in no way due to senility; far from it, for he is extraordinarily alert. But he has never dwelt on the past, never carried the burden of it over from one day to another, nor is he concerned with the future. How much the minds of the majority of us are occupied with past hurts, failures and triumphs, and future hopes and dreads. K's mind is focused sharply on the present.

*   *   *   *

Rajagopal had an operation on his right antrum at the beginning of November. K, who was with him during the operation in the hospital in Hollywood, described it as 'rather ghastly'. Rajagopal had a great deal of pain. A second operation on the left antrum had to be postponed because he was not in a condition to undergo

34

it. He was in bed for three weeks. During that time K was with him in Hollywood and spent a large part of each day correcting his own talks. 'I am going it alone,' he reported; 'I am learning. It's a long tedious affair.' He was also trying to learn Spanish from a linguaphone in preparation for the South American tour which had been postponed until March 1935. Apart from English, K could speak only French (he was later to learn Italian). He had entirely forgotten his native Telegu and knew no other Indian languages except enough Sanskrit to be able to chant in that tongue.

Lady Emily was recommending and sending him books to read. She also sent him the *New Statesman* in batches. He wrote on December 10: 'I haven't had time but shall get "The Lost Horizon" [by James Hilton]. I got the New Statesmen and have not read them as yet. Thank you for sending "God the Invisible King" [by H. G. Wells]. I read a review of H. G. Wells' Autobiography. I must get it and read it, it sounds interesting.'

It is doubtful whether he did more than dip into any of the books Lady Emily sent him. If he did read them he has certainly forgotten them. In October 1929 he had read Keyserling's *Creative Understanding* and had commented, 'Keyserling is very good, put in more philosophical language what I say.' It is hard to believe that he read the whole of this great tome of nearly 500 pages. As I have already said, he had read some Shakespeare, some Keats and Shelley, and certain parts of the Old Testament. At one time he knew the 'Song of Solomon' almost by heart. At Pergine in Italy in 1924, he had read aloud to us *The Gospel of Buddha* told by Paul Carus, and he had read *The Light of Asia*. He disclaims ever having read the *Bhagavad Gita* or the Gospels. One well-known English literary critic, now deceased, argued that Krishnamurti could not be a real religious teacher since he had never read the Gospels!

For years now K has read very little apart from thrillers—Rex Stout and Frederick Forsyth being among his favourite authors. During a flight he will look at the *Reader's Digest* and *Time*, and he immensely enjoys the jokes in the *New Yorker*. When in Europe and America he watches television in the evenings and is particularly interested in the news. Since he meets so many people all over the world in different walks of life, whom he is eager to question, he has a very good idea of what is going on in every country. One of his chief pleasures is, and has always been, a good exciting film. The last film I went to with him was the *Raid on Entebbe*. In the end he was shaking so much from excitement that he could hardly walk out of the cinema. He does not care for science fiction in films or books.

*　　*　　*　　*

Rajagopal's second operation at the end of January 1935 was much more serious than the first and he suffered 'appalling pain' afterwards, according to K. K set off for New York in late February where he stayed a fortnight and spoke three times to large audiences and gave a talk on the radio. He then went on to stay with Robert Logan and his wife, Sarah, who had a house and large estate, Sarobia (a combination of their Christian names) at Edington, Bucks County, near Philadelphia. He had known the Logans for several years. (It was Mr Logan who left him the Pathek-Philippe watch he is so fond of.) K gave three talks in Philadelphia while he was there.

Since Rajagopal was still convalescent it was Rosalind who accompanied K to New York and Sarobia, but when he returned to New York, where Rajagopal and Byron Casselberry met him, Rosalind went back to Ojai. The three men sailed for Rio de Janiero, Brazil, via Bermuda, on March 3. This tour of South America, a continent K had never visited before, was to last eight months. Altogether he was to give twenty-five talks while he was away—seven in Brazil (Rio, St Paulo and Nichteroy) in April and May, four in Uruguay (Montevideo) in June, six in Argentina (Buenos Aires, La Plata, Rosario and Mendoza) in July and August, four in Chile (Santiago and Valparaiso) in September, and, on his return, four in Mexico City in October and November. He spoke only in English. Hundreds of people attended his talks who could not understand a word, yet, apparently, sat 'spell-bound throughout'. K prefaced his first talk in each new place by a declaration that he did not belong to any religion, sect or political party, 'for organised belief is a great impediment, dividing man against man and destroying his intelligence; these societies and religions are fundamentally based on vested interests and exploitation. What I want to do is to help you, the individual, to cross the stream of suffering, confusion and conflict, through deep and complete fulfilment.'

K had been invited to Montevideo by the Minister of Education and his talks there were broadcast. The editor of one of the leading newspapers was a friend who gave him plenty of publicity. In Buenos Aires too there was so much publicity and so many photographs of him were published in the papers that he could not go out without collecting a crowd which he found 'rather unpleasant'. 'Here too,' he told Lady Emily, 'they broadcast all my talks and also at several points in the city there were loudspeakers, so the people really had to hear what I said, whether they liked it or not. Of course the Roman Catholic priests and priests generally have been secretly and publicly opposing very strongly.'

Buenos Aires was a Roman Catholic stronghold and many articles antagonistic to K's ideas were published in the Catholic newspapers. One Catholic priest issued a pamphlet, *Contra Krishnamurti*, which was distributed by boys all over the city. The Catholics even tried to get him deported. However, two papers took his side 'so whole-heartedly' that they printed all his talks in Spanish translations.

Rajagopal went back to California from Buenos Aires. He was still unwell and it was thought that Chile would be too cold for him. K continued the tour with Byron Casselberry. The high spot of those months was, for K, the crossing of the Andes in a Douglas twin-engine plane, a flight of one hour and twenty minutes which he had been told was the most dangerous in the world. Several people had begged him not to risk this flight but he was enjoying his independence and did not feel afterwards that there had been 'the slightest danger, though, of course, if anything did happen to the engine in the middle of the Andes, then good-bye'.

In Santiago his talks were translated into Spanish phrase by phrase as he spoke. 'I am really surprised there is so much interest and enthusiasm,' he wrote to Lady Emily. At one of the talks some men belonging to a Roman Catholic organisation came in with tear-gas bombs intending to break up the meeting. 'Some people asked them why they did not throw their bombs, and they said they did not know exactly. There have been a lot of curious incidents like this.'

The Stream of Suffering

An authentic report of K's talks in Latin America, revised by K himself, was published by the Star Publishing Trust in 1936. More than five years after the dissolution of the Order of the Star he was putting forward in essence the same ideas as he had propounded then, though he had found different words in which to express them. In his first talk in Rio de Janeiro he had said:

If you really think about it, you will see that your whole life is based on the pursuit of individual security, safety and comfort. In this search for security naturally there is born fear. When you are seeking comfort, when the mind is trying to evade struggle, conflict, sorrow, it must create various avenues of escape, and these avenues of escape become our illusions. This drives you from one religious sect to another, from one philosophy to another, from one teacher to another. This you call the search for truth, for happiness.

Now, there is no security, no comfort, but only clarity of thought which brings about understanding of the fundamental cause of suffering, which alone will liberate man. In this liberation lies the blessedness of the present. I say there is an eternal reality which can be discovered only when the mind is free from all illusion. So beware of the person who offers you comfort, for in this there must be exploitation; he creates a snare in which you are caught like a fish in a net.

In answer to a question about immortality he replied:

Now I can say there is immortality, to me it is a personal experience; but it can be realized only when the mind is not looking to a future in which it shall live more perfectly, more completely, more richly. Immortality is the infinite present. To understand the present with its full, rich significance, the mind must free itself from the habit of self-protecting acquisition; when it is utterly naked, then there is immortality.

The only real change in K's philosophy was his attitude to sex which no longer filled him with the horror it had done in the early twenties. In answer to a question at the end of another talk: 'What is your attitude to the problem of sex, which plays such a dominant part in our daily life?' he had answered:

It has become a problem because there is no love. When we really love there is no problem, there is an adjustment, an understanding. It is only when we have lost the sense of true affection, that profound love in which there is no sense of possessiveness, that there arises the

38

problem of sex. It is only when we have completely yielded ourselves to mere sensation, that there are many problems concerning sex. As the majority of people have lost the joy of creative thinking, naturally they turn to the sensation of sex which becomes a problem, eating their minds and hearts away.

On September 21 K and Casselberry embarked from Valparaiso for Mazatlan, the port of Mexico, where they arrived on October 11. It was a slow voyage, changing at Bilbao and Panama, and stopping almost every day at a different port. There was no rest for K because at every port reporters came on board wanting to hear what he had to say 'from the horse's mouth' as he put it.

Rajagopal met them at Mazatlan and went with them to Mexico City where K gave the last of four talks on November 23. He had been away from Ojai for nine months.

4

Pacifism and Aldous Huxley

K took a long time to recover from the effects of this tour. Early in 1936 he went with the Rajagopals to Carmel for a month where they stayed again at the Peter Pan Lodge. Back at Ojai he wrote to Lady Emily on April 21:

> I am just beginning to pick up my strength again. Somehow the South American tour rather exhausted me, and I have lost some weight, which I cannot afford to do [he weighed under eight stone]. All the same I am feeling much better, more energetic. I hardly go to Los Angeles except to Hollywood once in a while but spend most of my time here, seeing people, correcting my talks and thinking. I must say I have had a very good time lately thinking about things, and this seems to be so endless, so extraordinarily variable, and the more one penetrates the deeper it seems to lead.

This 'thinking', going deeply into himself, was K's form of meditation. He was later on to regard thinking, except for practical purposes, as an activity leading to sorrow and confusion. He gave eight talks in the Oak Grove at Ojai in May; then after visits to New York and the Robert Logans again at Sarobia, Philadelphia, in both of which places he gave public talks, he sailed on July 1 with the Rajagopals for Rotterdam from where they went straight to Ommen for the camp.

At the beginning of August K flew by himself to London, principally to see Lady Emily but also to buy clothes. He stayed with Lady Emily at her large house, 13 Mansfield Street, near Cavendish Square. They had not met for three years, the longest time they had been parted since he first came to England in 1911. There were not many old friends left for him to see in London. Lady De La Warr had died in 1930 and Miss Dodge in 1935 (K's income has continued since her death), but Mrs Jean Bindley,

whom he had known for many years and who had been National
Representative for the Order of the Star in Edinburgh, had now
moved to London where he was delighted to see her.

After a few days in London K returned to Ommen for a gathering of some sixty-five people of different nationalities. As in former
days at Castle Eerde these gatherings were by invitation only.
Lady Emily now felt too old to attend them or the camps.
Towards the end of September K went to Paris where he stayed
with Carlo Suarès and his wife Nadine at their eighth-floor
apartment at 15 avenue de la Bourdonnais. Carlo Suarès was
Spanish and his wife Egyptian. K had known them since 1927 and
had become increasingly friendly with them. Suarès had translated
several of his books into French.

Among friends in Paris was Marcelle de Manziarly whom K had
first met in 1920 when she was nineteen. A fine musician, pianist
and composer, a pupil of Nadia Boulanger, Marcelle is perhaps
the only person alive today who has been unswervingly devoted
to K and his teaching for sixty years. Marcelle's elder sister, Mima
Porter, a widow, who was also very friendly with K at this time,
had had a house at Ojai since 1930. K was also devoted to their
brother Sacha, a man of outstanding charm with a huge zest for
life in spite of having lost a leg in the first war.

In October K went with Rajagopal to the Hotel Montesano at
Villars near Montreux, where, as he then remembered, he had
been with Nitya in 1922. It was cold, the mountains were covered
in snow, but he loved the Swiss air and the views of Mont Blanc,
the Dent du Midi and the Lake of Geneva. He was thankful for
this month's holiday before the heat of India. He was to sail with
Rajagopal from Brindisi to Bombay on October 28 after spending
a few days again with Lady Berkeley in Rome.

On January 13, 1937, K was writing to Lady Emily from
Vasanta Vihar at Adyar to say that his public talks in Madras had
been well attended. Jinarajadasa had been two or three times to see
him from the T.S. Headquarters; he was friendly but K did not
know how genuinely.

We haven't been inside the T.S. [he continued]. Isn't it peculiar?
So easy to turn love into hatred or indifference. Now there's definite
antagonism. Curiously, but for obvious reasons, all the people we
used to know and be 'intimate' with have dropped off like leaves in a

storm. There are no new ones, as yet. This smashing of the old, the crystalised, is not a day's process; there needs to be constant, choiceless awareness. I am intoxicated and thrilled with it all. Smashing is coming in every direction but only the people who are awake will not again crystalise, making of themselves into vessels. That's the constant difficulty, to be open, to love without withholding. Yes, we are always wanting or differentiating the vessel but we hardly ever let go of the vessel and drink the water.

'Choiceless awareness' were words that K was to use thereafter over and over again, and still uses. It is doubtful whether Lady Emily quite understood them. Choice implied direction, the action of the will. What K was talking about was awareness from moment to moment of all that was taking place inside oneself without any effort to direct or change it—a matter of pure observation, perception, which would result in change without effort.

K was appalled by conditions in India. The Indians believed that the problems of starvation, disease and unemployment could be solved by nationalism.

It's the fault of everybody [he wrote], the English and the Indians themselves. It's something terrible each time to see it, poverty, misery, dirt and degradation. Human dignity is being destroyed, as it's so sedulously being done in Europe. There's so much hatred and I suppose it will end in a jolly war or revolution. There are so many unemployed students here, begging and losing all sense of dignity . . . We have to find new people [for his work] and that's difficult. We must begin here as if nothing had happened here for the last ten years.

In K's view, no kind of social reform could ever be the answer to the fundamental question of human misery. It was scratching the surface. His work was concerned with the nature of man. Until man himself changed radically all other change was useless and irrelevant.

*   *   *   *

On the way from India to Ommen in the spring of 1937 K and Rajagopal spent three weeks in Rome, staying with Lord and Lady Berkeley. All public talks in Italy had been banned by Mussolini, so a small gathering had been arranged for K at the house of Contessa Rafoni in the via Morgani. At this gathering he met Vanda Passigli, daughter of Alberto Passigli, an aristocratic landowner, very prominent in Florentine society. All the arts were important to the Passiglis, though music most of all; they were friends and patrons of most of the great musicians of their time—Toscanini, Schnabel, Horowitz, Casals and others (Signora Passigli was related to Casals's wife). Alberto Passigli founded the *Maggio Musicale* and the *Amici della Musica*, the most important Florentine music society, which brought all the great performers to Florence. His daughter, Vanda, was herself a pianist of professional standard, though she never became a professional. In 1940 she was to marry Marchese Luigi Scaravelli. He too was a fine musician but after becoming a medical doctor, he turned to science, mathematics and philosophy and became Professor of Philosophy at the University in Rome.

Vanda had been to the Ommen camp in 1930 but the gathering at Contessa Rafoni's was the first time she met K personally. After the gathering the Passiglis invited K and Rajagopal to visit them at their house above Fiesole, Il Leccio. Signor Passigli booked them into the Grand Hotel in Florence and they went up to Il Leccio for all their meals. After the war K constantly stayed with Vanda Scaravelli at this simple beautiful Tuscan house (which she and her brother were to inherit from her father), approached by an avenue of cypresses and commanding heavenly views over vineyards, olive groves and neighbouring hills. The large bedroom on the first floor which K always occupied when he was there looked on to the giant ilex tree from which the house derived its name.

*　　　*　　　*　　　*

From Ommen in the middle of April K was writing to Lady Emily that he and Rajagopal were 'dead tired', having been on the move for seven months, so they were going to Chesières-sur-Ollon in Switzerland for a rest. This was followed by a week in London where K stayed again with Lady Emily; then back to Ommen for a gathering for the whole of June. Although K spoke every morning for an hour and a half during the gathering, he was suffering from hay fever and bronchitis which sent him to bed in the afternoons. 'Rather awful, it doesn't give me much sleep,' he told Lady Emily. This is the first mention of the hay fever, often accompanied by bronchitis, from which he still suffers.

After the Ommen camp following the gathering, K went back to London for a week, staying with Lady Emily as usual. This visit was evidently not a happy one. He had had a convérsation with one of Lady Emily's daughters, Ursula Ridley, who was going through an unhappy time—a conversation which, it seems, had been totally misunderstood by Lady Emily, for back at Ommen K was writing to her on August 26:

I am very sorry that we separated with irritation but these psychological conversations or talks can't be disposed of in a few minutes. They have to mature into one; one has to think about them, not now and then but constantly. You said I was advising Ursie to be analytical, introspective, but I wasn't doing that. I was inferring that analysis and psychological dissection lead nowhere. Only the immediate perception of the futility of analysis, one part baring the other part of the mind, lead to 'somewhere'. To see the futility of self-analysis, one must be aware of the process of dissection. This is what I was trying to convey but all this demands more than a casual talk after tea. I am really sorry if I irritated you, mum, and please forgive me. I hope when we shall meet next I will explain myself better.

K challenged, and still challenges, the whole concept of the subconscious mind, maintaining that there is only one consciousness. The dividing of consciousness into different layers causes friction and conflict. 'When you become aware of your conditioning you will understand the whole of your consciousness,' he has said more than once in his talks.

K spent a quiet winter in 1937–38 at Ojai. He loved it there.

Ojai is particularly lovely now [he wrote to Lady Emily on January 31, 1938]. It has been raining which has made the earth green. There are soft changing shadows across the mountains. Mimosa is coming out and there's an occasional whiff of orange blossom for it's not yet the season. The orange trees look so artificial with their dark green leaves and bright golden oranges. The mountains against the soft blue sky, I am reminded of Taormina, its marvellous sea and distant Etna. What a lot of things have happened since we were there together [in 1914]. The changes have been so dramatic that one has become accustomed completely to them. The whole thing is fantastic.

K went on to tell Lady Emily that he was seeing hardly anyone except the Rajagopals, holding no meetings, giving no interviews. Rajagopal was mostly in Hollywood. Radha went to a little day school in the valley.

I am thinking a great deal [he continued] and am deeply thrilled with the unexpected and amazing discoveries within oneself. It's very good to be quiet like this; there are many ideas and I am slowly trying to find suitable words and expressions for them. There is a deep ecstasy. There is a maturity which is not to be forced, not to be artificially stimulated. It alone can bring about abundant fullness and reality to life. I am really glad for this quietness and apparently purposeless meditation.

'Making unexpected and amazing discoveries within oneself' without any direction or purpose is what K means by meditation. He does not approve of those systems of meditation which dull and tranquilise the mind by the repetition of a word or by concentrating on one object or idea. For him the mind is at its keenest, its most alive and most probing during meditation.

*   *   *   *

At the beginning of February 1938 K met the English writer, Gerald Heard, who was living in Hollywood and had written to ask if he might see him. Heard was invited to Arya Vihara where he spent the day. 'He seems a nice man and we all had interesting talk. He is well up in scientific knowledge,' was K's comment. Heard had arrived in America in April 1937 with Aldous Huxley and Huxley's Belgian wife, Maria Nys, and their son, and they had all motored across the States to California. Huxley was now in hospital with bronchial pneumonia but he sent a message by Heard to say how much he would like to meet K when he returned to his house in Hollywood. At this time both Heard and Huxley were pupils of Swami Prabhavananda, head of the Ramakrishna Order in Los Angeles, whose ashram was called the Vedanta Center because Ramakrishna's teaching had been derived from the ancient Hindu scriptures, the Vedas.

It was not until the middle of April that the meeting between K and Huxley took place. K went with Rajagopal to see him.

Pacifism and Aldous Huxley

Gerald Heard was there also [K told Lady Emily on May 9]. We liked them both very much. Of course Huxley is what is called an intellectual but I don't think he's merely that. We talked about almost everything—the difficulty of communication with propaganda, how people are mucking about with their minds, how difficult it is to create or form a group without vested interests, Yoga etc. Both Rajagopal and I liked them very much and it would be nice to continue further friendship with them. Huxley suffers from his eye-sight; one eye is blind and the other is weak and recently he has been ill. They are coming with Mrs Huxley to spend the day here next week.

Rajagopal was away when the Huxleys came—he had left for Europe on April 19—but Rosalind was there. 'Mr and Mrs Huxley and Mr Heard came the other day to spend the day here,' K wrote on May 30. 'We talked about meetings, groups, communities, discipline. Both of them were so well informed and highly intellectual. I think they saw some of the points I was explaining. I believe they are coming again. I like them.'

It was the beginning of a close friendship with the Huxleys. In November that year Huxley started treatment for his eyes by a method of eye exercises introduced by the American doctor, W. H. Bates.* K was later to practise this treatment himself, not because there was anything wrong with his eyes but in order to avoid wearing glasses as he grew older. As a result he can now, at eighty-six, see to read perfectly without glasses. He still keeps up these exercises regularly for ten minutes a day.

When Christopher Isherwood came to California in 1939 he was introduced by his friend Gerald Heard to Swami Prabhavananda and soon became his disciple. Meditation on a given word or mantra was central to the Swami's teaching, and puja took place every day in the small temple adjoining the Vedanta Center. Isherwood would prostrate before the Swami and take the dust from his shoes. Heard also introduced Isherwood to Huxley but their relationship was never an easy one.

That Aldous and I were both officially disciples of Prabhavananda didn't strengthen the bond between us as far as I was concerned [Isherwood was to write]. I was beginning to realize that Aldous and

---

* Dr Bates had contributed two articles to the *Herald of the Star* in March and October 1924.

Prabhavananda were temperamentally far apart. Prabhavananda was strongly devotional. Aldous was much more akin to his friend Krishnamurti, who was then living at Ojai, a couple of hours' drive from Los Angeles. Krishnamurti expounded a philosophy of discrimination between the real and the unreal; as a Hindu who had broken away from Hinduism he was repelled by devotional religion and its rituals. He also greatly disapproved of the guru-disciple relationship. According to my diary (July 31) [1940], I must have told Aldous at least something about Prabhavananda's latest instructions to me, thus prompting Aldous to tell me that Krishnamurti never meditated on 'objects'— such as lotuses, lights, gods and goddesses—and even believed that doing so might lead to insanity.[10]

Although the Swami claimed that Huxley had been 'initiated' by him, it seems that Huxley did little more than flirt with the Ramakrishna teaching, and then only before he met K. There are a few references to K in Maria Huxley's letters quoted by Sybille Bedford in her biography of Aldous: 'He [K] is charming and amusing and so simple. How he must suffer when he is treated as a prophet.' He was counted among their 'dearest friends', yet Maria could write, 'She [the English actress Iris Tree] lives next to our friends the Krishnamurti bunch and you know the horror Brahmins have of dogs. But they forgave Iris for bringing the dogs and sitting all over the car, leaving trails of smell and white hairs . . . K has travelled everywhere and speaks all the languages which is so nice too.' Far from having a horror of dogs, K loves them, and apart from English he could speak only French at that time.

When Maria Huxley's twenty-one-year-old niece came to California in 1946 she felt shy at having to talk to Aldous during 'those marvellous family walks in the mountains—whereas with Krishnamurti I was terribly relieved at not having to say a word and feeling completely at my ease'.[11]

K never really wants to talk during a walk unless it is about nature; conversation distracts him from observing everything around him as he likes to do. His memory for natural scenes, if for nothing else, is remarkably exact. Referring to himself in the third person he has thus described walking with Huxley:

He [Huxley] was an extraordinary man. He could talk about music, the modern and the classical, he could explain in great detail science and its effects on modern civilization and of course he was quite familiar with the philosophies, Zen, Vedanta and naturally Buddhism. To go for a walk with him was a delight. He would discourse on the wayside flowers and, though he couldn't see properly, whenever we passed in the hills in California an animal close by, he would name it, and develop the destructive nature of modern civilization and its violence. Krishnamurti would help him to cross a stream or a pothole. Those two had a strange relationship with each other, affectionate, considerate and it seems non-verbal communication. They would often be sitting together without saying a word.[12]

Alone with Rosalind and Radha at Ojai during the spring of 1938, after Rajagopal had gone to Europe, K reported to Lady Emily that he had been reading *The House that Hitler Built* (by S. H. Roberts) and that he intended to read *The Evolution of Physics* by Einstein and Leopold Infell. He had just received *Insanity Fair* (by Douglas Reed) from Lady Emily. War in Europe seemed imminent. 'There's war in Spain, in China and they are trying to start it in Mexico,' he wrote in April. 'Slaughter and more slaughter. What for!! As I am a complete pacifist, more than that, all this bloodshed is so shocking and utterly barbarous. Violence does not produce peace, it only breeds more violence, more hate. Many Americans are cancelling their trips to Europe.'

There were no talks at Ojai that year, probably because Rajagopal was away. K sailed from New York to Rotterdam on July 2 and went straight to Ommen where Rajagopal awaited him. Rosalind did not go to Europe this year because money was short so this was the first time K had ever travelled alone. At Plymouth, where the ship put in, he had posted a letter to Lady Emily saying that it had been 'the usual kind of voyage. Reporters at Plymouth and one of them asked me to do some tricks as I was a Hindu mystic!! Miss Lilian Gish is aboard and I know her. We were having tea together when the reporters barged in. They wanted to know whether there was a romance between us!!' K had met Lilian Gish, the heroine of those early silent films, *Orphans of the Storm* and *The Birth of a Nation*, with John Barrymore, a friend of K's until his death in 1942. It was Barrymore who had asked K to take the part of Buddha in a film he wanted to make on the Buddha's life.

The Ommen Camp, the fifteenth, took place in August. It was the last ever to be held there. It was cancelled the following year because of the imminence of war, and in 1941 the site was turned into a concentration camp by the Germans.

After the Camp K begged Lady Emily to come and stay at Ommen—she could stay in his hut which had every comfort or at Heenan. When he realised how reluctant she was to make the journey, he and Rajagopal went to London to see her. They arrived on September 16, the day on which Neville Chamberlain returned triumphantly from Munich with his 'paper of peace'.

Rajagopal left next day for America, and K, after a night in Paris, joined the *SS. Strathallan* of the P & O Line at Marseilles on the 24th en route for Bombay. This was the line by which British officials always travelled to India. An Indian friend, V. Patwardhan, always called Pat, whom K had known for many years, travelled with him. K's visit to Lady Emily had been a much happier one than the year before when they had parted with irritation. It was just as well, for it was to be nine years before they met again.

I was really sorry to have left you, mum [K wrote from board-ship on September 27]. I felt sad when the train pulled out. You were so sweet and you know I love you. I think P & O boats are the worst; people are rather rude, bad food and the distinction between the natives and the whites is very distinct and marked. What's the good of fighting the Germans when it is the same the world over. They had the other day, prayers; Protestants in the 1st class saloon, Roman Catholics in the tourist or second class saloon. The altars were draped in Union Jack! Even God must be approached through national flags. What will it all lead to? Death and destruction. What a world. Life's strange. In oneself there must be love and beauty, otherwise the world is too much.

And from Aden on October 1:

The passengers on this boat represent the world. The racial prejudice between the English and the Indians is brutally obvious. It is rather cruel and so unnecessary but you know all this. Among the English passengers themselves there are differences of class, prestige and wealth. There are some French people and they are severely left alone, like the 'natives'. The Australians—the boat goes to Australia—are by themselves. So there it is and we talk about the brutal Germans, persecution and injustice!! It is really a cruel world and individuals are the only hope.

Pacifism and Aldous Huxley

K found his Indian friends in Bombay, where he landed on October 6, immersed in the 'petty jealousies' of politics. Many of them, who were followers of Gandhi, had been in prison, one of them four times. K had met Gandhi several times but had never become involved in politics. 'I seem to be out of joint in all this, as I am elsewhere,' he wrote; and from Vasanta Vihar, Adyar, he was writing again on October 19 about the degradation that almost destroyed the beauty of India, and then continued:

English papers howl at the horrors the Japanese are perpetrating in China and at the devastation that is taking place in Spain but the same papers and the same people shut their eyes to the imperial brutality that's going on in Palestine and India. Imperialism is the curse of this world, whether it's that of England or Germany. There seems no end to this form of cruelty. It makes one weep to walk through these villages. Oh, God, one must remain sane for hate is insanity and that is prevalent all over the world. Let's remain sane and affectionate.

K saw no difference between German aggression and British imperialism. Having 'grabbed half the earth' the British 'could afford to be less aggressive', though at heart they were as 'brutal and greedy' as any other nation. Nationalism, like imperialism, was one of the world's curses. K has no violence in him. If attacked I doubt whether he would defend himself, even as a physical reflex. He would probably become unconscious. It is dangerously easy for him to lose consciousness; his hold on life seems such a fine thread, however well he is in health. The cliché question, 'What would you do if you saw your wife or child being tortured?' has no validity for him. He might ask the attacker to stop, and possibly the brute, recognising an extraordinary authority, would do so, but it is extremely unlikely that he would attempt a rescue by force. Certainly there is no cowardice in him any more than there is violence. Most violence and cruelty arise from fear, and having no fear K is without aggression or retaliation.

*   *   *   *

K returned to Bombay from Madras on October 24 where he fell ill with influenza. He did not cancel the public talks arranged for him there; he merely cancelled two of the discussions being held at the home of Ratansi Moraji, a cotton merchant with whom he had always stayed in Bombay. At one time a very rich man, Ratansi was now almost ruined and had had to move from his beautiful large house on Malabar Hill to a small flat. 'Every time I go away there is a general flop,' K wrote from Bombay on November 7, 'and I hope it won't happen this time. I think we shall create a group of people who will know what it's all about and intelligently understand.'

Two days later K went to Poona where he gave two public talks and held discussion meetings every morning during the week he was there. 'The public meetings were crowded,' he reported to Lady Emily. 'People love to go to meetings!! They listen with amazed silence; I do not know whether they fully agree, and out of that act, but one or two are keen and come to discuss further.'

From Poona he went up to the hills with Pat and Ratansi to stay with Pat's brother, the Raja of Sangli, at Malabeleshwar, a three-hour drive. Lady Emily had evidently written to remind him of what the Jews were suffering under Hitler, for on November 21 he was writing from Malabeleshwar:

I quite agree with you that the poor Jews are having a horrible and degrading time. It's so utterly mad the whole thing. That human beings should behave in that bestial manner is revolting; the Kaffirs are treated most brutally and inhumanly; the Brahmins in the south in certain parts have lost all sense of humanity with regard to the untouchables; the white and brown bureaucratic rulers of the land are mostly machines carrying out a system that's brutal and stupid; the negroes in the south of U.S.A. have a bad time; one dominant race exploits another, as is shown all over the world. There's no reason, sanity, behind all this greed for power, wealth and position. It's difficult for the individual not to be sucked into the storm of hate and confusion. One must be an individual, sane and balanced, not belonging to any race, country or to any particular ideology. Then perhaps sanity and peace will come back to the world. Sorry I have written like a preacher.

Still accompanied by Pat and Ratansi, K returned to Bombay from where he went by sea to Karachi, then on by air to Lahore, where he stayed a week, followed by another week in New Delhi. Rajghat at Varanasi, Benares, came next. Rajghat was the second Krishnamurti school founded in India. In 1928 the Rishi Valley

Trust had managed to acquire from the British military authorities 200 acres of land on the banks of the Ganges, five miles north of the city of Benares and on the same side of the river. (This was land that K had wanted for a long time. 'At last!' he had written in 1928. 'Only all our spare capital will be spent on this. But can't be helped.'). The school was not officially opened until 1934. In '33 K had resigned from the Rishi Valley Trust because he did not want to be associated with any organisation, but he was, and still is, deeply involved with Rajghat as with the Rishi Valley school. Rajghat has a long river frontage at the confluence of the Ganges and Varuna rivers. Through the compound runs the pilgrim's path to Sarnath where the Buddha preached his first sermon after Enlightenment. Now, after nearly fifty years, Rajghat like Rishi Valley is one of the most flourishing and best known schools in India. In the compound is the Rajghat Besant School with about 300 boys and girls from the ages of seven to eighteen, a women's college with a hostel attached, a farm, an agricultural school, a rural primary school and a free hospital, catering for the needs of twenty surrounding villages.

The beauty of Rajghat—the sacred Ganga in all its moods, the fishermen on the river, the sunrise and sunset over the water and walks along the pilgrim's path—occur in K's writings as often as the beauties of the Rishi and Ojai valleys. One knows these places intimately from his books even if one has never been there. K does not mention them by name, but from his descriptions one can tell immediately what place he is writing about, as from this evocative description of the pilgrim's path:

We walked up the steep bank of the river and took a path that skirted the green wheat-fields. This path is a very ancient way; many thousands have trodden it, and it was rich in tradition and silence. It wandered among fields and mangoes, tamarinds and deserted shrines . . . A few chattering villagers passed by on their bicycles, and once again there was a deep silence and the peace which comes when all things are alone.[13]

From Rajghat, where K stayed a fortnight holding discussions with the teachers every day, he went back to Madras at the beginning of 1939 and thence to Rishi Valley, and finally to Colombo at the end of March from where he wrote that he was surprised that so many came to his talks and that the papers had shown a great deal of interest. He sailed with Pat for Australia on April 1. Most of the passengers were uprooted Jews going to Australia or New Zealand to start a new life. Many of them were learning English on board. 'It's really a most brutal world,' he wrote to Lady Emily from board-ship. 'It's so easy to curse Hitler and Mussolini and Co but this attitude of domination and craving for power is in the heart of almost everyone; so we have wars and class antagonism. Until the source is cleared there will always be confusion and hate.' The source is, of course, the human heart: this clearing of the source is the basis of K's philosophy.

K spoke in Fremantle, Adelaide and Melbourne. In Sydney he stayed again with the Mackays until the end of May when he went on to New Zealand. When he eventually returned to California, Pat went back to India. He was to die suddenly of a brain haemorrhage in December.

5

The War Years

K reached Ojai longing for a complete rest. It was a relief, therefore, when it was decided that he should not risk going to Europe that summer because of threatened war. Ojai became so hot in August, reaching a temperature of 115°, that he took advantage of an offer from Lady Berkeley of her house just outside Santa Barbara, overlooking the sea. Rosalind and Radha accompanied him while Rajagopal went to England and Holland. 'Radha, who's eight, is full of energy, play, and astonishingly intelligent and lovable,' K told Lady Emily on August 14. 'Thank God for children in this mad world.'

Rajagopal returned to California just before war in Europe broke out on September 3. K remained at Santa Barbara until the middle of October, writing to say that everyone he met was determined to keep out of the war; it was a European war which would not destroy civilisation because civilisation was not a European monopoly. His letters to Lady Emily were infrequent that winter, but in every one he reiterated his pacifism and enlarged on the beauty and peace of Ojai. He was seeing the Huxleys who came 'quite often' to Ojai for the week-end during the war years when they would talk 'of many things, war, economics, meditation, nationalism'.

In March 1940 K started giving group discussions twice a week at Ojai and twice a week in Hollywood. 'Some were very anxious to discuss the European situation, the Federation of Europe and general politics,' he wrote, 'but we brought it round to ultimate realities of life.'

After the Germans walked into Belgium and Holland on May 10, K received no more news from Ommen. France capitulated on June 22. The de Manziarlys managed to get away to the States, except Sacha who was with the Free French in London.

The Suarès had gone to Egypt. News from India was rare. K was relieved to hear that Lady Emily was in the country in England looking after some of her grandchildren. 'The whole thing is ghastly and nightmarish,' he wrote to her on July 9. 'I wonder where and if we shall meet again. What a tragedy it is; even though one is so far away from it all, there is a constant awareness of what is going on there and the appalling suffering. Words are so futile but one's love is always there. You are in my heart.'

At this time K was giving talks in the Oak Grove—eight talks between May 26 and July 14. He made no allowance for anti-German feeling among his audience and when he preached pacifism, saying, 'The war within you is the war you should be concerned with, not the war outside', many of his listeners left the meeting after creating a disturbance. At the end of August he was at Sarobia again, near Philadelphia, where the Logans had arranged a gathering. It was the last time he was to speak in public until 1944.

In October K went with Rosalind to Martha's Vineyard, an island about eight miles from the southernmost tip of Massachusetts. They stayed there with a friend at Seven Gates Farm, a large area running along the north shore of the thirty-mile-long island, divided among a number of owners who each had a site of several acres on which to build, almost every house looking out to sea. There was also the so-called farm land, held jointly and kept wild. K found the place 'really enchanting'. His room overlooked the sea which in the mornings was 'rough and brilliant'. Behind the house were 'miles and miles of woods with lovely walks. The leaves are turning and the landscape is like a lovely Persian carpet'. While he was writing this, bombs were falling on London.

K remained quietly at Ojai during the rest of 1940 and the first six months of '41, seeing only the Huxleys apart from the Rajagopals and, occasionally, Gerald Heard. Holding a British passport, he had to apply in April for a renewal of his visa. If it was refused he would have to go to India which, he gathered from the few letters he received, was on the brink of revolution. He did not seem at all perturbed at the prospect of having to leave Ojai—he seemed prepared to take it in his stride as he took every change in his life. Accustomed to so much travelling and to continually meeting new people, perhaps he wanted to get away from the rather claustrophobic atmosphere of the valley even though he loved it so well.

Because of his anti-war propaganda the authorities were hesitant about extending his visa and he had still not heard from them by the end of July. In the meantime he had been with the Rajagopals for a fortnight to the Sequoia National Park, 250 miles north of Ojai at an altitude of 6,000 feet. They had stayed in a cabin at Camp Kaweah where there were wild bears and tame deer, miles of forest, many streams and a view of snow-capped mountains. Some of the great sequoias were said to be 3,000 years old. Descriptions of this Park often appear in K's writings. Although he does not identify it, the location is obvious from his references to bears and the ancient giant trees.

Wherever he was, K took long solitary walks every day. At Ojai he walked countless miles by himself during those war years. At some time after making his application to stay on in America, a man from the FBI came to see him at Ojai and asked him a lot of questions, wanting to know in particular why he took so many walks and whom he met on those walks. K was mystified by the questions until, at the end of the interview, the man, apparently satisfied, told him that the FBI had been tipped off about a plot to assassinate Roosevelt in which K was involved. K himself recently told me this strange story, one of his few memories of those years. It was not until November that he heard he had been granted a long extension permit.

On December 7 the Japanese bombed Pearl Harbour. America's entry into the war strengthened K's pacifism if possible. For those in England who had been proud to stand alone against Nazi aggression, who had felt exalted by the Battle of Britain, who had thrilled to Churchill's words and somehow managed to contain their terror during the blitz, believing passionately that they were fighting the embodiment of evil, K's pacific outpourings from such paradises as Ojai, Martha's Vineyard and the Sequoia National Park were hard to take. Lady Emily evidently told him as much with some asperity and accused him of escaping from the horror, for he was writing to her on April 14, 1942:

I don't think any evil can be overcome by brutality, torture or enslavement; evil can be overcome by something that's not the outcome of evil. War is the result of our so-called peace which is a series of everyday brutalities, exploitations, narrowness and so on. Without changing our daily life we can't have peace, and war is a spectacular expression of our daily conduct. I do not think I have escaped from all this horror, but only there's no answer, no final answer, in violence, whoever wields it. I have found the answer to all this, not in the world but away from it. In being detached, the true detachment that comes from being or attempting to be more [word left out] to love and understand. This is very strenuous and not easily to be cultivated. Aldous Huxley and his wife are here for the week-end. We have long talks about all this and meditation which I have been doing a good deal lately.

If Aldous Huxley had a sore conscience about staying away from England during the war, K's presence and convictions must have been a salve to it. He and K felt exactly the same about war but it was harder for Huxley because he loved England and had friends and relations in the armed forces.

Lady Emily was incapable of feeling detached, though at a less emotional time she might have sympathised more with K's point of view. Others cannot do so even today. But death is a small matter to K: far better to die than to live with hate in one's heart. He goes so far now as to say that if we really loved our children there would be no wars. This statement needs examination before the truth of it can be grasped: it is human beings, you and I, who make wars; there is hate, confusion, conflict, jealousy, envy, greed in our daily lives; we bring up our children 'to become soldiers, to be nationalized, to worship the flag, educating them to enter into the trap of the modern world'.[14]

*   *   *   *

By 1942 there were food shortages in America, and a speed limit of thirty-five miles an hour had been imposed before petrol rationing was introduced. The cost of living had gone up. K and the Rajagopals were growing vegetables at Ojai and keeping chickens and a cow, which they milked in turn and from which they obtained a little milk and butter. They had also started keeping bees.

At the beginning of September 1942 they went up to the Sequoia National Park again. They stayed there together for three weeks and then, when the Rajagopals had to return to Ojai for the beginning of Radha's school term, K stayed on for another three weeks by himself. As always when he was completely alone he was completely happy. He stayed in a cabin with hot water laid on but in which no cooking was allowed, so what little cooking he needed he did on an open stove under the great trees. The restaurant in the Park was too expensive; he ate, therefore, mostly from tins bought at the Camp market. 'The bracken is turning golden yellow and the dogwood a red that is really indescribable.' So he wrote to Lady Emily on October 9, the day before returning to Ojai. 'I have not seen a paper for a month,' he went on. 'It's splendid and beautiful, a perfect place for meditation which I have been doing two or three hours a day.' He was also walking about ten miles a day without any sense of fatigue. Being rather late in the season there were few visitors and he met hardly anyone on his walks, though plenty of animals—bears, deer and thousands of squirrels. The Park keeper warned him to be careful of the bears.

Helping to look after the vegetable garden and the animals—there were two cows now—occupied a great deal of K's time during the next year or two. He was also seeing more people who came to Ojai from long distances to have interviews with him in spite of petrol rationing. He was 'leading an extraordinarily strenuous life inwardly,' he told Lady Emily on August 31, 1943, 'very creative and joyous'. He was meditating for at least two hours a day. He went on in this letter:

Right meditation is really the most extraordinary phenomenon that one can experience. It's both a creative discovery and a liberating process and the Highest is revealed. I have not talked for over three years and it is good to be quiet. During those years one has developed deeply and found many things and one has rediscovered the light and love of the Eternal. Only now, it is deeply established and imperishable. As I said, I meditate several hours a day and there are inexhaustible treasures. This love is like a spring well, ever overflowing.

Subsequently he has written and spoken a great deal about meditation. The passage below perhaps sums up better than any other his conception of 'right meditation':

Meditation is one of the greatest arts in life—perhaps *the* greatest, and one cannot possibly learn it from anybody. That is the beauty of it.

It has no technique and therefore no authority. When you learn about yourself, watch yourself, watch the way you walk, how you eat, what you say, the gossip, the hate, the jealousy—if you are aware of all that in yourself, without any choice, that is part of meditation. So meditation can take place when you are sitting in a bus or walking in the woods full of light and shadows, or listening to the singing of birds or looking at the face of your wife or child.[15]

And recently he has written, 'All effort to meditate is the denial of meditation.'[16]

K was also writing every morning in his notebook during the war. It was apparently Aldous Huxley who was encouraging him to write at this time. K remembers that once when he was staying with the Huxleys in the Mojave Desert, to where they had moved in 1942, Aldous had said to him, '"Why don't you write something?" So I did and showed it to him. He said, "It's marvellous. Keep going." He used the word marvellous. So I kept going. He said he had never seen any literature where there is a description and then dialogue.'[17] There seems little doubt but that these writings were what afterwards became *Commentaries on Living*, published in 1956. Most of the eighty-eight short pieces in this book begin either with a description of nature or of unnamed individuals who have come to seek K's help about their diverse problems. Two more volumes of the *Commentaries* came out in 1959 and 1960. To my mind the third volume contains the most beautiful pieces. K does not identify any of the places he describes but one can almost always identify them for oneself, and to make individuals doubly anonymous he scrambles them; thus we find sanyasis in Switzerland or California and obvious Europeans and Americans sitting cross-legged on the floor in India. All three volumes were expertly edited by Rajagopal.

*   *   *   *

K began giving public talks again in the Oak Grove at Ojai in 1944 on ten successive Sundays from May 14 to July 16. An Authentic Report of these ten talks, printed in India as usual, was published in 1945 by Krishnamurti Writings Inc. (KWINC) as the Star Publishing Trust had now become. In June 1946 K was to sign a statement to the effect that the 'central Foundation throughout the world would be Krishnamurti Writings Inc.' and that he and Rajagopal would be two of the trustees and that three other trustees would be appointed by the two of them. KWINC was a charitable organisation exempt from income tax as the Star Publishing Trust had been and existed for the sole purpose of publicising and disseminating Krishnamurti's teachings throughout the world. Again like the S.P.T. the KWINC publications were sold only at K's meetings and through the mailing list. Later on K ceased to be a trustee and Rajagopal became President of KWINC, a circumstance that was to have most unhappy consequences.

One of the people who heard K talk for the first time in the Oak Grove in the summer of 1944 was Mary Taylor, the attractive only daughter of parents distinguished in the New York business and social worlds. Mary, who was afterwards to marry Sam Zimbalist, the producer of *Ben Hur* and other well known films, is now, as a widow, closer to K than anyone else. She travels with him, acts as his secretary and generally takes care of him. Either directly after the Ojai talks or early the following year, she had her first private interview with him. She was unhappy at the time and was deeply moved by what he said to her. It was to be many years before she saw him again.

K was talking once more in the Oak Grove in part of May and June the following year, the year the war ended. These talks and three of the following year, much abridged, were published together by KWINC in 1947. For the first time K wrote a preface to this volume:

This book of talks, like our previous publications, contains reports of spontaneous discourses about life and reality, given at different times, and is not intended, therefore, to be read consecutively or hurriedly as a novel or as a systemized philosophical treatise.

These Talks were written down by me immediately after they were given and later I carefully revised them for publication. Unfortunately, a few individuals, unasked, circulated their own notes of these Talks but those reports should in no way be considered authentic or correct.

These were the last talks that K revised or helped to revise himself. As at most of his previous talks there were questions and answers at the end of each meeting. What had the years of silence during the war brought forth? Evidently in his hours of meditation

K had gone very deeply into himself, for the talks of 1944, '45 and '46 were concerned chiefly with self-knowing. In his third talk in '44 he had advised his audience to 'try to write down *every* thought-feeling, whenever you have a little time. If you try you will see how difficult it is'. The following year a questioner asked why it was that having written down every thought and feeling for several months, as suggested, he had 'got no further'? To this K replied:

To dig deeply you must have the right instrument, not merely the desire to dig . . . To cultivate the right instrument of perception, thought must cease to condemn, to deny, to compare and judge or seek comfort or security. If you condemn or are gratified by what you have written down then you will put an end to the flow of thought-feelings and to understanding . . . Understanding is ever in the immediate present.

There were several questions about the war, such as, 'What should be done with those who have perpetrated the horrors of the concentration camps? Should they not be punished?' K's answer to this was predictable:

Who is to punish them? Is not the judge often as guilty as the accused? Each one of us has built up this civilization, each one of us has contributed towards its misery; each one is responsible for its actions . . . The power to oppress is evil and every power that is large and well organized becomes a potential source of evil. By shouting loudly the cruelties of another country you think you can overlook those of your own. It is not only the vanquished but every country that is responsible for the horrors of war. War is one of the greatest catastrophes; the greatest evil is to kill another. Once you admit such an evil into your heart then you let loose countless minor disasters.

And to the questions, 'How can I be on defence against aggression without action? Does not morality demand that we should do something against evil?' K replied: 'To defend is to be aggressive. Through wrong means can right be established? Can there be peace in the world by murdering those who are murderers? As long as we divide ourselves into groups, nationals, different religions and ideologies there will be the aggressor and the defender.' An unusually practical question was: 'How is one to earn a decent living and yet withdraw from the wheels of exploitation and war?' K's answer to this was in part:

... Our means of livelihood are dictated, are they not, through tradition or greed or ambition? Generally we do not deliberately set about choosing the right means of livelihood. We are only too thankful to get what we can and blindly follow the economic system that is about us. But the questioner wants to know how to withdraw from exploitation and war. To withdraw from them he must not allow himself to be influenced, nor follow traditional occupation, nor must he be envious and ambitious ... But though it is important and beneficial, right occupation is not an end in itself. You may have a right means of livelihood but if you are inwardly insufficient and poor you will be a source of misery to yourself and to others; you will be thoughtless, violent and self-assertive.

(K was later to say that the aim of education should be to enable the young not to seek a profession but to discover their true vocation.)[18]

Another question: 'Is there any difference between awareness and that of which we are aware? Is the observer any different from his thoughts?' called forth an answer that has become a continuous theme in K's teaching:

The observer and the observed are one; the thinker and his thoughts are one. To experience the thinker and his thought as one is very arduous, for the thinker is ever taking shelter behind his thought; he separates himself from his thoughts to safeguard himself, to give himself continuity, permanency; he modifies or changes his thoughts, but he remains ... The thinker *is* his thought; the thinker and his thoughts are not two different processes; the observer is the observed. To experience this actual integrated fact is extremely difficult, and right meditation is the way to this integration.

K has never sought to bring comfort; his teaching is stern, and one sympathises with the questioner who said at one of the meetings: 'You are very depressing. I seek inspiration to carry on. You do not cheer us with words of courage and hope. Is it wrong to seek inspiration?' K's reply could scarcely have made him feel less depressed:

Why do you want to be inspired? Is it not because in yourself you are empty, uncreative, lonely? You want to fill this loneliness, this aching void; you must have tried different ways of filling it and you hope to escape from it again by coming here. This process of covering up the arid loneliness is called inspiration. Inspiration then becomes a mere stimulation and with all stimulation it soon brings its own boredom and insensitivity . . . Besides, who can give you cheer, courage and hope? If we rely on another, however great and noble, we are utterly lost, for dependence breeds possessiveness in which there is endless struggle and pain. Cheer and happiness are not ends in themselves; they are, as courage and hope, incidents in the search for something that is an end in itself. It is this end that must be sought after patiently and diligently, and only through its discovery will our turmoil and pain cease. The journey towards its discovery lies through oneself; every other journey is a distraction leading to ignorance and illusion. The journey within oneself must be undertaken not for a result, not to solve conflict and sorrow; for the search itself is devotion, inspiration. Then the journey itself is a revealing process, an experience that is constantly liberating and creative. Have you not noticed that inspiration comes when you are not seeking it? It comes when all experience has ceased, when the mind-heart is still. What is sought after is self-created and so is not the Real.

There is a contradiction here such as is often found in K's early pronouncements. He tells his listeners that the 'end must be sought after patiently and diligently' and then that 'What is sought after is self-created and so is not the Real'. The contradiction surely arises from words getting tangled in his unceasing efforts to express the inexpressible.

6

Illness and India

For many years K had wanted to start a school at Ojai. When Mrs Besant had stayed with him there in 1926–27 she had launched a world-wide appeal for $200,000 to buy land in the valley for the work of the World Teacher. A trust was formed called the Happy Valley Association and enough money subscribed to buy 450 acres for a school in the upper valley, not far from Arya Vihara, and a further 240 acres at the lower end, including the Oak Grove, for a camp such as at Ommen. As we have seen, the Camp was started in 1929 but it was to be nearly twenty years before the school became a reality. With K, Rosalind and Aldous Huxley as three of the original trustees, the Happy Valley School, a small, co-educational, vegetarian, secondary paying school, financed by the Association, opened in September 1946. Huxley, according to his biographer, took a great interest in it.

K had planned to leave Ojai in September for New Zealand, Australia and India—the first time he would have been away from California since 1940. All the arrangements had been made when a few days before he was due to set out, and just after the Happy Valley School opened, he fell seriously ill with a kidney infection. He was in bed with fever for two months (for the first month he was in great pain) and took more than six months after that to recover. During this illness he was moved from the cottage where he usually slept to Arya Vihara. He did not want to go to hospital, so Rosalind nursed him although she had a broken foot in plaster and was much occupied with the school of which, as K put it, she was 'the leading light'. K did not shave for six months and grew 'a good beard'. 'I mustn't fall ill again,' he wrote to Lady Emily on March 12, 1947, 'for it takes me too long to recover.' He was too weak to give any talks at Ojai that summer.

K now has only the vaguest recollection of this illness. It does not interest him. 'I was ill for a year and a half [his memory is at fault here]: tremendously ill. There was a doctor but they did not give me anything. Not even an aspirin.'[19] This may have been at his own insistence. He would have been afraid of the effects of a drug on his delicate system. Even when the agony in his head and spine had been at its fiercest in the twenties he had never taken any kind of pain-killer. Although his body is extraordinarily sensitive he is so detached from it that he seems to be able to bear a greater degree of pain than most people. True, he faints when the pain becomes too intense, but not until he has reached a stage long before which the majority would have resorted to pain-killers.

K's plans now depended upon whether he could get a further extension of his visa. After Indian independence was granted on August 15, 1947, he, like all Indians and Pakistanis, was given the option of retaining his British passport or of taking out an Indian one. Although he considered nationality a source of evil and deplored the necessity of having passports at all, he plumped without much thought for an Indian one. This decision he subsequently regretted for it has made travelling more difficult: with an Indian passport he has to have a visa for every country in Europe except England. At least now he does not have to have a visa for the States for he has recently been granted residential status there which will enable him in time to become an American citizen if he so wishes.

A further extension was granted and K was able to stay on at Ojai until September, gathering strength to travel. On September 9 he sailed with Rajagopal from New York to Southampton, en route for India. He stayed nearly three weeks in London. He had not seen Lady Emily for nine years. He was now fifty-two and she seventy-three. Her husband had died at the beginning of '44 but she had retained a flat at the top of the Mansfield Street house where K was able to stay with her.

On September 26 he came to spend a long week-end with me and my second husband at our cottage in West Sussex. My mother and Marcelle de Manziarly, who had come to England specially to see him since he was not going to Paris, also spent the week-end with us. My first marriage in 1930 had been the result of a strong reaction against my Theosophical upbringing, and, thereafter, during the thirties, I had avoided K as much as possible when he came to London. I knew he would not approve of my rather racketty existence. Seeing him made me feel ashamed and unclean. I was unhappy, but did not seek his help because I knew I had no intention of changing my way of life, yet frequently I had great yearnings after that time when I had been very close to him during 1926–28. In 1945 I had been divorced and immediately married again—a partnership of perfect compatibility.

K had been too long confined at Ojai. He had felt encircled there and imprisoned by the Rajagopals who were inclined to bully him and order him about. His only escape from them had been in his long solitary walks. Now he looked well and was evidently experiencing a great sense of release and seemed full of energy. If more mature he was just as beautiful. It was a joy to me to feel that he was happy and relaxed while staying with us; he said it was 'just like old times'. We sat a long time over breakfast in our dressing-gowns, chatting and laughing. It never occurred to me, though, that I might one day work for him. I would always love him but did not want, any more than my mother did, to understand what he was saying in his talks. Marcelle, on the other hand, had at least two long private conversations with him which she described as 'magnificent'. She was still a follower whereas I was content to be merely a friend and, since my husband got on well with him and my life was now in order, I could continue to enjoy his friendship.

*   *   *   *

Rajagopal did not go with K to India. The latter flew alone to Bombay on October 4. It was his first flight to India. He was to remain there for eighteen months. During that time he came to know two sisters who have ever since been closely associated with him and his work. They were the married daughters of Vinayah Naud-Shanker Mehta, a Brahmin from Gujarat, who had been a distinguished member of the Indian Civil Service and a Sanscrit and Persian scholar. He had died in 1940. His widow, Iravati Mehta, had been awarded the Kaiser-i-Hind Gold Medal for her long record of social service. The younger daughter, Nandini, was unhappily married to a son of Sir Chuminal Mehta, also a well known member of the Indian Civil Service though no relation. Sir Chuminal was a devotee of K's and took Nandini to meet him on his arrival in Bombay and to listen to his talks. Later on, after K had left India, Nandini filed a suit against her husband in the High Court of Bombay asking for a separation on the grounds of cruelty. Her husband defended the suit, pleading that his wife was immature and had been unduly influenced by Krishnamurti's teachings which she had misunderstood, particularly his concept of freedom. Long extracts from Krishnamurti's talks were read out in Court by Mr Mehta to prove his point. Nandini lost her case. She left her husband, nevertheless, but as a result was deprived of her children. Both Mehta families being very well known, the case received a great deal of publicity. In England a false rumour was circulated that K had been cited as co-respondent in a divorce case.

K did not meet the other sister, Mrs Pupul Jayakar, until January 1948. She has been a social worker since the early forties and largely responsible for the development of handwoven textiles and crafts in India, and Chairman of several Government boards set up for the purpose. These industries provide employment for five million people in India.

Muslims and Hindus were butchering each other in the north; nevertheless, K went to Karachi and New Delhi after some weeks at Vasanta Vihar, Adyar, but he had left Delhi before Gandhi was assassinated there on January 30, 1948. It has been written that 'When the light had gone out with Gandhi's assassination, it was to Krishnamurti that Jawaharlan Nehru brought, in secret, his solitary anguish.'[20] K confirms that this was more or less true. K had had a great affection for Nehru until he became immersed in politics.

K gave twelve public talks in Bombay between January 18 and March 28, followed by private discussion at Vasanta Vihar throughout most of April. He told Lady Emily that he had never worked so hard in his life. His Bombay talks had been attended by over three thousand people and, as usual, there were several questions at the end of each meeting. In each talk he had tried to approach the problem of existence from a different point of view, but, as one questioner observed, 'When I listen to you, all seems clear and new. At home, the old dull restlessness asserts itself. What is wrong with me?' Part of K's long answer to this was:

Here, for the moment, you cease to be a Brahmin, you cease to be high-caste, or whatever it is—you forget everything. You are just listening, absorbed, trying to find out. But, when you go out of this place, you become yourself—you are back in your caste, your system, your job, your family. That is, the new is always being absorbed into the old, into the old habits, customs, ideas, traditions, memories . . . It is only when the mind is free from the old that it meets everything anew, and in that there is joy.'

This is a fundamental principle of K's teaching. Until one can get rid of one's old self one cannot begin to see truth.

In May K went up to Ootacamund, the hill station for Madras, for a long rest, staying with some friends at a house called Sedgemoor. Pupul Jayakar and Nandini Mehta were also at Ooty at a nearby hotel. Mrs Jayakar has recorded some occurrences that took place at Sedgemoor which show that K's 'process' was still going on in much the same way as it had done at Ojai, Ehrwald and Pergine, though less intensely. It must have been a startling if not frightening experience for these sisters who did not as yet know him very well and who were, apparently, quite unaware of the past happenings. It also shows how much he trusted them already.

K had been out for a walk with them when he suddenly said he felt ill and must return to the house. He asked them to stay with him, not to be frightened by whatever happened and not to call a doctor. He said he had a pain in his head. After a time he told them he was 'going off'. (This 'going off' was what had always happened in the past during 'the process'. K left his body in charge of what we used to call 'the physical elemental'—a childish entity who regarded K with great reverence and awe.)* His face was 'weary and full of pain'. He asked them who they were and whether they knew Nitya. He then spoke of Nitya, told them that he was dead, that he had loved him and wept for him.† He asked

* When I was with him at Ojai in 1927 and he used to 'go off', the 'physical elemental' asked me the first time who I was, although K had known me since I was two. When I told him he said, 'Well, if you are a friend of Krishna and Nitya I suppose you are all right.'

† It was at Ooty at the beginning of 1925 that Nitya had nearly died. When K went back there a year later, after Nitya's death, he had written, 'I am staying in the same room as Nitya. I feel him, see him and talk to him but I miss him grievously.' Staying there again, although in a different house, may well have brought something of this back to K.

them whether they were nervous but did not appear at all interested in their reply. He stopped himself from calling for Krishna to come back: '"He has told me not to call him"'. He then spoke of death. He said it was so close—'"just a thread-line"'—how easy it would be for him to die, but he would not like to because he had work to do. Towards the end he said: '"He is coming back. Do you not see them all with him—spotless, untouched, pure—now that they are here he will come. I am so tired but he is like a bird—always fresh." Then suddenly it was Krishna again.'

The record of this episode is undated. The next is dated May 30, 1948:

Krishna was getting ready to go for a walk, when suddenly he said, he was feeling too weak and not all there. He said, 'What a pain I have' and caught the back of his head and lay down. Within a few minutes the K we knew was not there. For two hours we saw him go through intense pain. He suffered as I have never seen suffering. He said he had pain at the back of his neck. His tooth was troubling him, his stomach was swollen and hard and he groaned and pressed down. At times he would shout. He fainted a number of times. When he came to the first time he said: 'Close my mouth when I faint.' He kept on saying: 'Amma,* Oh, God give me peace. I know what they are up to. Call him back, I know when the limit of pain is reached—then they will return. They know how much the body can stand. If I become a lunatic look after me. Not that I'll become a lunatic. They are very careful with this body—I feel so old—only a bit of me is functioning. I am like an India rubber toy, which a child plays with. It is the child that gives it life.' His face throughout was worn and racked with pain. He kept clenching his fists and tears streamed from his eyes. 'I feel like an engine going up hill.' After two hours he fainted again. When he came to he said: 'The pain has disappeared. Deep inside me I know what has happened. I have been stocked with gasoline. The tank is full.'

He then started to talk and described some of the things he had seen on his travels; he spoke of love: '"Do you know what it is to love? You cannot hold a cloud in a gilded cage. That pain makes my body like steel and oh so flexible, so pliant, without a thought. It is like a polishing, an examining."' Pupul Jayakar

* Meaning Mother. This was how he had addressed me and others when we were alone with him during 'the process'. He had behaved to me at times as if I were his mother and he a child of about four.

asked him if he could not stop having the pain, to which he replied, '"You have had a child. Can you stop it coming once it starts?"'. He now sat up cross-legged, his body erect.

The pain had gone from his face [Mrs Jayakar noted]. It was timeless. His eyes were closed. His lips moved. He seemed to grow. We felt something tremendous pour into him. There was a throbbing in the atmosphere. It filled the room. Then he opened his eyes and said, 'Something happened—did you see anything?' We told him what we had felt. He said, 'My face will be different tomorrow.' He lay down and his hand went out in a gesture of fullness. He said, 'I will be like a raindrop—spotless.' After a few minutes he told us that he was all right and that we could go home.

Two other occurrences of the same nature took place in June. On the 17th K had been for a walk alone and had asked Pupul and Nandini to wait for him in his room. When he returned he was 'a stranger':

K had gone. He started saying he was hurt inside; that he had been burnt; that there was a pain right through his head. He said: 'Do you know, you would not have seen him tomorrow. He nearly did not return.' He kept on feeling his body to see if it was all there. He said: 'I must go back and find out what happened on the walk. Something happened and they rushed back but I do not know whether I returned. There may be bits of me lying in the road.'

The next evening Pupul and Nandini again waited for him in his room while he went for a solitary walk. When he returned at about seven he was 'the stranger' once more. He went to lie down. 'He said he felt burnt, completely burnt. He was crying. He said: "Do you know I found out what happened on that walk. He came fully and took complete charge. That is why I did not know if I had returned. I knew nothing. They have burnt me so that there can be more emptiness. They want to see how much of him can come."' Again Pupul and Nandini felt the same throbbing filling the room as on the evening of May 30.[21]

The fact that these sisters knew nothing of what had happened in the past with regard to K's 'process' gives this account a particular value in that there are so many similarities between it and those other accounts given in *The Years of Awakening*: the body calling out 'Amma', his frequent fainting with the pain, his awe of Krishna and fear of calling him back, his realisation that the pain would stop if Krishna did come back but so would the 'process'. Then the allusion to the closeness of death: at Ehrwald in 1923 when the church bells suddenly rang out while Krishna was 'off' they caused the body such a shock of agony that Krishna had to come back; he said afterwards, 'That was a very narrow shave. Those bells nearly tolled for my funeral.' Pupul Jayakar's notes tell us that, apart from Krishna, there were other presences, just as there had been on those other recorded occasions—the 'they' who were very careful of the body, presumably the same 'they' who had returned with Krishna on the first occasion mentioned by Pupul—'spotless, untouched, pure'. Then there was the 'he' who had come 'fully' during the walk on June 17 and 'taken complete charge'. The being lying in agony on the bed had been 'burnt' to create more emptiness so that more of this 'he' could enter into Krishna or the body. So now there appeared to be three entities apart from the unnamed number referred to as 'they':—the being left behind to bear the body's pain; Krishna, who goes away and comes back again, and the mysterious 'he'. Are all these entities different aspects of K's consciousness or are they separate beings? Alas, the one person who might be able to enlighten us, K himself, remembers nothing of these happenings at Ooty any more than he remembers anything about 'the process' at earlier times. Since he was out of his body this is not surprising. He has always been conscious of being 'protected' by something or someone outside himself, and he believes that whoever is travelling with him shares this same protection. But from where that protection emanates he cannot say. What then is the explanation? Who or what is Krishnamurti? It is the chief object of this book to try to find out.

7

The Ending of Thought

After the relaxation of Ooty K's talks in India continued—
Bangalore from the beginning of July until the middle of August,
Poona in September and October, New Delhi in November. On
November 6 he gave a talk in Delhi on the All-India radio. He
began by saying that although India had 'gained so-called freedom'
she was 'caught in the turmoil of exploitation, like every other
people', and ended with the words, 'Only the incorruptible
enrichment of the heart can bring peace to this mad and battling
world.' For most of January and February 1949 he was at Rajghat,
Banaras (as Benares has been called since Partition), giving talks.
He then went up to Rishi Valley.

On April 9 K arrived in London where he stayed three days
before returning to Ojai. He had been away from California for
nineteen months. Throughout July and August he gave talks in
the Oak Grove. His main theme in these talks was to discover 'if
peace, happiness, reality, God, or what you will, can be given to
us by someone else'. His answer was that it was only through the
understanding of oneself that one could reach truth or have a
right relationship with another human being. Knowledge and
learning were impediments to an understanding of the new;
nothing of any value could be learnt from books or the experience
of another. It was not, of course, technical or practical knowledge
that he was talking about but psychological knowledge. Thought
must cease before there could be understanding. This was one of
the most difficult of K's concepts to grasp. Thought was the
result of the past; thought was founded upon the reaction of
many, many yesterdays—that is, the response of memory, the
result of time; therefore, to have an intimation of the timeless,
the thought process must come to an end; to receive something

new the old must cease. Again he was not including such thought or memory as was necessary for everyday living.

At the beginning of October K came to London again where he gave five public talks at the Friends Meeting House, his first in London since before the war. These talks dealt with the solving of the problems of living. 'Is the solution different from the problem?' he asked, 'or does the solution lie in an understanding of the problem?' There were numerous ways of escaping from a problem, he went on, but the only way to approach it successfully was to be without the desire to find an answer: 'Then you are directly in relationship with the problem; the problem is no longer separate from yourself. I think that is the first thing one must realize, that the problem of existence, with all its complexities, is not different from ourselves; and as long as we regard the problem as something apart from us, our approach must inevitably result in failure.' Try it for yourselves, he counselled.

At the end of the third meeting a man asked a question that many of K's old followers might have echoed: 'Your teachings some years ago were understandable and inspiring. You then spoke earnestly about evolution, the path, discipleship, and the Masters. Now it is all different. I am utterly bewildered. I readily believed you then and would like to believe you now. Which is the truth—what you said then, or what you say now?' Part of K's reply was:

First of all it's not a question of belief. You don't have to believe what I say—far from it. If you believe what I say, then it is your misery not mine; then you will use me as another authority, and therefore take shelter, comfort . . . To have a Master in India, or in some mountain far away from your daily life, is very convenient, very encouraging because then you can say, 'Well, I'll be like him in my next life. It will take me a long time to be free of greed'—and that you call evolution. Surely, greed is not a thing to be postponed; either you are free from greed now or you will never be. To say you will be free of greed some day, is the continuation of greed.

Another question was, 'How is one to be free of the constant fear of death?' This called forth a long answer the gist of which was:

What is it that continues? Idea, thought, is it not? The idea of yourself as a name, as a particular identified individual—which is still an idea, which is memory, which means the word ... Surely most of us are clinging to that, aren't we? You are not afraid of leaving your family, your children; that is just an excuse. Actually you are afraid to come to an end. Now, that which continues, that which has continuity —can that be creative? Is there a renewal in that which continues? Surely there is renewal only in that which comes to an end. Where there is an ending there is a rebirth—but not in that which continues. If I continue as I am, as I have been in this life, with all my ignorance, prejudices, stupidities, illusions, memories and attachments—what have I? And yet it is *that*, we cling to tenaciously.

It may appear from this that K believes in reincarnation but he does not. He declares that he has no beliefs. The question of whether there is or is not reincarnation has no interest for him. What he is concerned with is dying every moment to the old so that every moment is a re-creation.

*   *   *   *

Rajagopal had come to England with K but returned to Ojai when K flew to India in November. In late November and early December K talked at Rajahmundy on the River Godavri, 360 miles north of Madras. At the end of the first of three talks the question was asked: 'You say that man is the measure of the world, and that when he transforms himself the world will be at peace. Has your own transformation shown this to be true?' K replied:

You and the world are not two different entities. You *are* the world, not as an ideal, but factually ... As the world is yourself, in the transformation of yourself you produce a transformation in society. The questioner implies that since there is no cessation of exploitation, what I am saying is futile. Is that true? I am going around the world trying to point out truth, not doing propaganda. Propaganda is a lie. You can propagate an idea, but you cannot propagate truth. I go around pointing out truth; and it is for you to recognize it or not. One man cannot change the world, but you and I can change the world together. You and I have to find out what is truth; for it is truth that dissolves the sorrows, the miseries of the world.

After Rajahmundy K gave one talk in Madras before going to Colombo where he gave five talks from December 25 until January 22, 1950. He also gave two broadcasts there. An Indian professor, writing many years later, recalled this time in Colombo when, according to him, K 'made one of the most moving and thrilling speeches of his life'.

It was to the students of University College, Colombo [the professor was to write]; the hall was packed to the full, and it was clear that they were bent on mischief. As we entered (for I was one of Krishnamurti's party) there were not only cheers of welcome but louder noises of stamping, shouting and cat-calls.

This continued even after Krishnaji started talking, and finding himself in opposition, he smiled and asked them what they had expected of him, why that unwelcome after he had been specially invited to address them, and what was really wrong with him?

He smiled and waited for an answer. 'Are you the Christ, tell us first?' shouted half-a-dozen students from different corners. He smiled again, which soon burst into sad sweet laughter, and the students were swept into it without their knowing, and there was a changed atmosphere.

He pulled himself up and said: 'All right, Sirs, I'll answer you;' and he told them the poignant but moving story of his early life, his education, his messiahhood, his struggles and sufferings, his loneliness and longings, his quest and realizations, in the simplest and sincerest language; and as they listened to him they visibly changed, they broke into applause, they cheered him, and some were in tears and in a repentent mood . . .

I have seen this phenomenon over and over again, in several places, where hard-boiled materialists, orthodox fanatics and cocksure communists start bullying from the first with silly stupid questions . . . Unperturbed and with infinite sympathy he listens to their harangues and tries to answer them in their own language and idiom, and gradually leads them step by step to see his point of view, to understand his approach to their problems; and in the end, invariably, they say to him: 'Well, Sir, we do not pretend to have understood you, but we feel you are right.'

A radiant spiritual personality like Krishnamurti is a rare phenomenon even in this land; he is indeed the efflorescence of an age. Great as are Sri Aurobindo and Ramana Maharshi, as liberated souls and men of wisdom, I prefer Krishnamurti, as friend and comrade; for his way is the simple direct way of all nature's magnificent phenomena that I understand, like the bursting into flower of a rose-bud, like the flight of the home coming bird, like the natural flow of the river into the sea.

No organisation, no ceremonies, no priest, no *pooja*, no *darshan*, no magic and mystery.[22]

The Ending of Thought

This account does not appear in K's published talks. The nearest anyone got to rudeness in his published talks, was to ask, 'Why do you waste your time preaching instead of helping the world in a practical way?' K replied to this:

You mean bringing about a change in the world, a better economic adjustment, a better distribution of wealth, a better relationship—or, to put it more brutally, helping you to find a better job. You want to see a change in the world, every intelligent man does; and you want a method to bring about that change, and therefore you ask me why I waste my time preaching instead of doing something about it. Now, is what I am actually doing a waste of time? It would be a waste of time, would it not? if I introduced a new set of ideas to replace the old ideology, the old pattern. Instead of pointing out a so-called practical way to act, to live, to get a better job, to create a better world, is it not important to find out what are the impediments which actually prevent a real revolution—not a revolution of the left or the right, but a fundamental, radical revolution not based on ideas? Because, as we have discussed it, ideals, beliefs, ideologies, dogmas prevent action.

K ended his second Colombo broadcast with the words:

There is only one fundamental revolution. This revolution is not of idea; it is not based on any pattern of action. This revolution comes into being when the need for using another ceases. This transformation is not an abstraction, a thing to be wished for, but an actuality which can be experienced as we begin to understand the way of our relationship. This fundamental revolution may be called love; it is the only creative factor in bringing about transformation in ourselves and so in society.

Back in Madras K gave two more talks followed by five talks in Bombay up till March 14. On March 17 he flew to Paris where Marcelle de Manziarly met him at the airport and where Rajagopal joined him. He stayed there with the Suarès until the beginning of May. It was the first time he had been to Paris since 1938 and he gave four talks there, one at the Sorbonne. He spoke no differently to a European audience than to an Indian or American one, and there was very little difference in the questions asked after the meetings. Human problems were the same the world over and it was the world problem that K was tackling. Self-knowledge was still at the root of his philosophy. As he said at the end of his last talk in Paris on May 7: 'When I understand myself, then there is quietness, then there is stillness of the mind. In that stillness, reality can come to me. That stillness is not stagnation, is not a denial of action. On the contrary it is the highest form of action. In that stillness there is creation—not the mere expression of a particular creative activity, but the feeling of creation itself.'

*   *   *   *

In May K returned to Ojai, but not for long, for by the beginning of June he was in New York where he gave five public talks while staying with an old friend, Frederick Pinter, and his wife, at 200 West 59th Street. 'The talks went off fairly well, I think,' he reported to Lady Emily on July 3. 'They said to have such large audiences for New York about such serious things is quite unheard of. And they didn't come out of curiosity either.' In one talk he had dealt with fear in answer to the question, 'How am I to get rid of fear, which influences all my activities?' Are we afraid of the fact or of an idea about the fact? K had countered, and he then gave as an example the fear of the ache and pain of loneliness. 'Surely that fear exists because one has never really looked at loneliness, one has never been in complete communion with it.' This is virtually the same as what he had said about the fear of death. It was the idea, the opinion, of something based not on the *fact* but on previous knowledge that created fear—all fear. 'How can there be fear of a fact?' he asked. 'When I am face to face with a fact there is no fear. What causes fear is my apprehension *about* the fact, what the fact might be or do.' Here again, of course, he was speaking of psychological fear.

At the end of another talk the question had been put to him: 'How can I fulfil the longing to love and be loved? For without it life has no meaning.' The essence of K's reply was that the question was based merely on thought, a reflexion of the mind—but *could* one think about love? One could think about the person one loved, cling to the person, try to possess the person and so create laws to protect the possession of what we love, whether it be a person, a piano, a piece of property, or an idea, a belief; because in possession with all its complications of jealousy, fear, suspicion, anxiety, we feel secure. So, we have made love into a thing of the mind; and with the things of the mind we fill the heart. Because the heart is

77

empty, the mind says, 'I must have love'; and we try to fulfil ourselves through the wife, through the husband. Through love we try to become something. That is, love becomes a useful thing, we use love as a means to an end ... As long as we are *seeking* love there must be a self-enclosing process ... Love can only be when the sense of the self is absent, and freedom from the self lies through self-knowledge. With self-knowledge there comes understanding; and when the total process of the mind is fully revealed and understood, then you will know what it is to love. Then you will see that love is not a means of fulfilment. Then love is by itself without any result. Love is a state of being.

On July 4 K flew with Rosalind and Radha to Seattle for yet more talks. Radha had just finished her first year at Swarthmore College. 'She is quite a young lady now,' K told Lady Emily.

On returning to Ojai in the middle of August, K decided to go into retreat for a year. He gave no interviews and spent much time alone, meditating, going for walks and 'pottering about the garden' in his own words to Lady Emily. It was not until February 1951, however, that a notice appeared in the *International Star Bulletin*, stating that after his 'strenuous and extensive travels for the last three years Krishnaji was taking a complete rest in California for a year.'

*   *   *   *

In November 1951 the round of travelling began again, though not the public speaking. On the 10th K arrived in London, Rajagopal having preceded him there. Lady Emily no longer had room for him in the smaller flat she had moved to so he stayed for the first time with Mrs Jean Bindley at 50 Sheffield Terrace, off Notting Hill Gate. He saw Lady Emily every day, however. It was probably during this visit that Mrs Bindley's son introduced him to his own tailor, Huntsman in Savile Row. Up till then K's tailors had been Myer & Mortimer in Conduit Street who had now closed down. Thereafter K was to patronise Huntsman exclusively.

Rajagopal flew to India with K this year, the first time he had been there for over fourteen years. From Bombay they went to Madras. Jinarajadasa, who had been President of the T.S. since George Arundale's death in 1945, met them at the station, looking very frail. Rajagopal saw him and other T.S. members several times, but K saw no one at first. He had had fever and continued his retreat at Vasanta Vihar until the beginning of 1952 when he began giving talks again in the garden of Vasanta Vihar after a public silence of sixteen months. Judging from these twelve talks on Saturday and Sunday mornings from January 5 to February 10, he had been trying during his retreat to find new words and expressions in which to convey his solutions to the complexities of living, though fundamentally he was not saying anything new. A man who wanted to find peace, who wanted to create a new and happy world, surely could not isolate himself through any form of belief, so the first thing was to stop belonging to any religion or nationality. 'Have a complete break with the past,' he urged, 'and see what happens. Sirs, do it and you will see delight. You will see vast expanses of love, understanding and freedom. When your heart is open then reality can come. Then the whisperings of your own prejudices, your own noises, are not heard.' Self-knowing was still the master-key to understanding, and understanding an essential for psychological transformation.

By March K and Rajagopal were back in London. K stayed again with Mrs Bindley though seeing Lady Emily frequently. Throughout April he gave a series of talks at the Friends Meeting House before flying back to California via New York at the beginning of May. In June he had hay fever so badly at Ojai that he went to stay with Rosalind at Santa Barbara where she had rented a house so as to be near Radha who was taking a summer course at the University of California. By the sea K was free from his allergy. He was there when there was a rather bad earthquake at five o'clock one morning which did a great deal of damage. Although the centre of it was 150 miles away, the house 'shook violently back and forth' but did not collapse because it was made of wood. 'It wasn't exactly frightening,' K told Lady Emily, 'but it was paralysing. I couldn't move.'

In July Radha was married to an American, James Sloss, whom she had known since childhood. After a civil wedding they had a party of 250 people at Ojai. K reported that the young couple seemed 'happy and gay'. In the autumn they would both be returning to College.

K talked every Saturday evening and Sunday morning in the Oak Grove throughout August. He was asked two pertinent questions during these talks. The first was: 'Great minds have never been able to agree as to what is the ultimate reality. What do you say? Does it exist at all?' Part of K's answer to this was: 'What do *you* say? Is not that much more important: what *you* think. You say that great minds have said there is and there is not. Of what value is that?' He went on to explain that only one's own mind was capable of finding out, 'But your mind is crammed with knowledge, with information, with experience, with memories; and with *that* mind you try to find out. Surely, it is only when the mind is creatively empty that it is capable of finding out whether there is an ultimate reality or not.'

The second question was: 'Does not the process of constant self-awareness lead to self-centredness?' It does, K replied in effect, as long as you are consciously or unconsciously concerned with a result, with success; you are miserable, frustrated, and feel there is a state in which you can be happy, fulfilled, complete, so you use awareness to get what you want. Through awareness, self-analysis, reading, studying, you hope to dissolve the ego and thereby become happy, enlightened, liberated—one of the elite. So the more you are concerned with gaining an end, the greater the self-centredness. But in understanding *why* the mind seeks a reward, a satisfying result, there is a possibility of going beyond the self-enclosing activities of thought.

*   *   *   *

By October K was back in London without Rajagopal before proceeding alone to India for the winter of 1952–53; then, after the usual round of talks, back to England in March '53 en route for Ojai where he intended taking another complete rest since he found 'all the journeying quite exhausting'. Radha had a baby girl in April, born a few weeks prematurely due to a fall. But K's rest was only for two months this time because from the middle of June until the middle of July he was giving talks on Saturdays and Sundays in the Oak Grove. There were 'large crowds,' he told Lady Emily, 'and hundreds of cars.' He also had the usual interviews and discussions during the week. He tried to get to Santa Barbara every ten days or so to alleviate his hay fever which was still troubling him badly.

8

The First and Last Freedom

1953 saw the publication of K's first book brought out by a commercial publisher, Harper & Row in America and Gollancz in England, who have remained his publishers ever since. Called *Education and the Significance of Life* this little book, only 125 pages long, clearly states K's views on what he considers to be right education. The jacket material described the author as 'One of the most thorough and conscientious thinkers of our time . . . a work of superlative and complete honesty.' Already by then K had been deeply concerned with education for twenty-five years. The child should be taught not what to think but how to think; he should be stripped of his conditioning and 'resist being turned out in a mould of mediocrity'.

If we are being educated merely to achieve distinction [he wrote on p. 11], to get a better job, to be more efficient, to have wider domination over others, then our lives will be shallow and empty . . . Though there is a higher and wider significance to life, of what value is education if we never discover it? We may be highly educated but if we are without deep integration of thought and feeling, our lives are incomplete, contradictory and torn with many fears; and as long as education does not cultivate an integrated outlook on life, it has very little significance. In our present civilization we have divided life into so many compartments that education has very little meaning, except in learning a particular technique or profession. Instead of awakening the integrated intelligence of the individual, education is encouraging him to conform to a pattern and so hindering his comprehension of himself as a total person.

He advocated small schools. 'Nothing of value can be accomplished through mass instruction, but only through the careful study and understanding of the difficulties, tendencies and capacities of each child.' (P. 85.) He maintained that parents who believed in this should come together to start a school: 'To start such a school they need not wait until they have the necessary means. One can be a true teacher at home, and opportunities will come to the earnest.' (P. 86.) K has never believed in waiting for the means. By this time he had ceased to be a trustee of the Happy Valley School. It was a successful school and Rosalind was still its 'leading light' but Krishnamurti's teaching was no longer its mainspring.

*   *   *   *

K had hoped that Jinarajadasa, who was in America this year, would be coming to Ojai where K looked forward to having 'a good long talk with him', but he died suddenly in Chicago on June 18. 'Raja [Jinarajadasa] was the connecting link with the T.S.,' K wrote to Lady Emily, 'and now that he has gone a great deal of the past has gone with him. I was thinking the other day that you and I had known each other since 1910 [actually 1911] and what's still more strange we have loved each other all those forty years!! I still love you mum.'

Lady Emily was now writing an account of her life in Theosophy in which, of course, K had played the star role. She had already written an autobiographical book—*A Blessed Girl*—an exchange of letters between herself, from the age of fourteen, and an old clergyman, Whitwell Elwin, who had at one time been editor of the *Quarterly Review*. An intimate record of a Victorian girlhood, this book had been eagerly accepted by Rupert Hart-Davis, who was now encouraging her to write this second book. (*A Blessed Girl* when it was published in October '53 was a great success. It had splendid reviews and sold some 10,000 copies.)

K knew that Lady Emily was now writing this book about her life in Theosophy and had given her permission to quote his letters to her and also his and Nitya's accounts of his experience at Ojai in 1922. He had commented on it in a letter of August 17:

I am glad that the second book is coming along and it must be quite a job sorting, choosing etc. You have Mary to help you so that's something [I had been a professional writer since 1930]. I am not ashamed of the past but you know how strange all that has been and I hope what you are going to say won't cause too much animosity among the T.S. crowd but that of course can't be helped.

He added that Rajagopal had left for Europe and that he, K, was to meet him in Amsterdam on September 23; he would not be going to England that winter. On September 25 I went with my husband to Amsterdam to see K. We spent two happy days with him and Rajagopal at the Hague. As K told my mother, 'We had most of our meals together, went about together. It was quite like old times and what a lot of things have happened since then.' Rajagopal and I had always been very good friends since he first went to Cambridge where I used to visit him. I was extremely fond of him.

From Holland K and Rajagopal went to Rome where they stayed for a few days with Vanda Scaravelli, née Passigli, and her husband, Marchese Scaravelli, who was teaching philosophy at the University. They then went with Signora Scaravelli (she seldom uses her title) to Il Leccio above Fiesole, the house K had first visited in 1937 as has already been described. The Signora had arranged a fortnight's gathering for him there from October 4. A bus ferried about forty people of different nationalities every day from Florence to Il Leccio. Among those who attended by special invitation were Marcelle de Manziarly, Carlo and Nadine Suarès and Mrs Bindley. According to Marcelle's diary K spoke one morning about conditioning, how it came into being and how it could come to an end by the perception of all conditioning. And another morning he spoke about thought: 'Can thought come to a stop? Of course it can.' This theme of thought coming to a stop was by now an integral part of K's philosophy which will be developed later.

'It is lovely here,' K wrote to Lady Emily from Il Leccio on October 14, 'amidst olives, cypresses and hills. What a beautiful country this is. The village people and peasants are so friendly; they are so poor but cheerful.' He added as a postscript: 'Rajagopal said he had a letter from you in which you said that Mr Agar [one of Lady Emily's sons-in-law and a partner in Hart-Davis] thought highly of your new book. I hope before it's finished that we can look at it! Please.'

Thereafter, for many years, K would usually stop in Rome on his way to and from India and go with Vanda Scaravelli to Il Leccio. He loved it there, loved walking along the cypress avenue leading to the house or in the fields where the peasants became very fond of him and felt somehow protective towards him. In the *Commentaries on Living* (Third Series) he describes his walks while staying at Il Leccio, although he does not mention where he is, and the train journey from Rome to Florence which he came to know so well—how he went along by himself through the restaurant car and the luggage van to the engine-driver's cabin; no one stopped him and the two drivers of the electric train not only welcomed him but apologised for not speaking English and rejoiced that he could understand their beautiful language. He does not give any place names, but for those who know the country this journey is instantly recognisable.

*   *   *   *

K and Rajagopal flew to India on October 24. From Bombay they went on by train to Bangalore and then by car to the Rishi Valley School. Torrential rains had just come to the valley after years of drought. As K wrote to Lady Emily on November 8:

You can imagine what it has been like, starvation, no water in the wells, cattle dying. It has been terrible. But now the land is smiling, rich in green and it is very beautiful.* There are talks to children and long discussions with teachers so we are fairly busy. We leave here for Adyar [Vasanta Vihar] towards the end of the month. I am glad we shall be able to see the manuscript before it is printed.

Lady Emily sent the typescript of her book to Rajagopal, saying that she wanted it back as soon as possible. It arrived at Vasanta Vihar on December 24 at a time when K, according to Rajagopal, replying on the same day, was 'quite worn out' after 'eight weeks of steadily talking' and a few days before they left for Rajghat at Benares, but after glancing through it he, Rajagopal, felt it to be a most important record, intensely interesting, but that when it was published there would be many stirring reactions and to some people the story would be deeply disillusioning, even shattering; he would have many suggestions to make, impossible to write down then and there or at Rajghat where they were going for daily discussions with teachers and endless interviews; nor was it advisable to show it to K at Vasanta Vihar, or at Rajghat where he

---

* Mrs Gandhi paid a visit to K at Rishi Valley in December 1980, and afterwards ordered a dam to be built to give permanent irrigation to the valley.

would be even more fatigued. K had said to him casually when he saw him reading it that one or two things should be omitted although he had not even looked at it. Rajagopal had replied to K that unless he himself read it through carefully it would not be fair to say what should be cut out; whereupon K had said that he would neither approve nor disapprove; he only wanted certain things eliminated—but, Rajagopal asked, how could he know *what* unless he had read it? Could it not wait until they came to London in April when Rajagopal would give her every help he could?

This answer was most unsatisfactory to Lady Emily, for it was obvious that Rajagopal did not want the book published without a good deal of alteration. K *did* read the typescript at Rajghat, though she was not to know this for three months. In the meantime she worked on the manuscript with my help. Her editor at Hart-Davis, Milton Waldman, felt that there was not enough of her in the book.

From Rajghat K went to Bombay in February 1954 for public meetings twice a week for a month, talking to children on some other mornings and giving innumerable interviews. This year a free school for poor children was started in Bombay by the Foundation for New Education as the Rishi Valley Trust had become the year before. Nandini Mehta was, and still is, the Director of this school, Bal Anand at Malabar Hill, for 130 children from the ages of four to fourteen who are admitted irrespective of caste or creed.

On March 5 K and Rajagopal flew to Athens for a fortnight. I had evidently written to K enclosing a letter from my brother-in-law, Herbert Agar, praising my mother's book, for he wrote from Athens on March 23:

Thank you very much for your letter enclosing Mr Agar's letter. It was nice of you to have taken the trouble to write at length about Mum's new book. I read it very carefully in Benares [this was the first time we had heard that he had read it] and my general impression of it was that it was good and read well. You see Mary I really wanted to talk it over with Mum and you, before it should appear in print. I am not, if I may say so, saying whether it should be published or not for that is Mum's and your responsibility; only I wanted to talk it over with you both to see if it was a wise thing to publish. I do not say it is not but by talking it over leisurely, we might come to some understanding which might be valid. Please do not think that I am suggesting that you should not publish it but if it had been possible, I really would have liked to have talked it over with you both. If you won't misunderstand me it's up to you both to decide.

I also received a letter from Rajagopal saying that he had refrained from discussing the book with K so that we could have a decision from him which was *his own* but that as I would see from his letter to me he had made no such decision. Rajagopal had come to the conclusion that K would like us to come to the same decision as he had without telling us what that decision was. There was now nothing that my mother or I could do until K came to London.

After Athens and five days of discussion in Rome, K went to Il Leccio again for three weeks to stay with Vanda Scaravelli while Rajagopal went to Munich, Zurich and Paris to see about translations of K's books. K and Rajagopal both came to London for a fortnight at the beginning of May before flying back to America. K stayed with Mrs Bindley again but, as usual, saw Lady Emily every day. I also saw him several times. Of course we talked about the book but he seemed to have no wish to discuss it; he made no more objections to it *at all* and my mother and I both became so convinced that he was happy, even eager, for us to publish it that I delivered the final typescript to Hart-Davis while he was still in London. Rajagopal said afterwards that *his* opinion had not been asked. K knew that the book contained not only quotations from his letters to my mother but the full accounts written by him and Nitya of his 1922 experience. These accounts had never before been made public. Only a few typed copies of them were in existence which had been sent to Mrs Besant, Leadbeater, Lady Emily, Miss Dodge and one or two others. It was Rajagopal who had originally typed the manuscripts. K also approved the title we had chosen for the book—*Candles in the Sun*. The meaning behind this title was that the light of all those who had proclaimed the coming of the World Teacher had been dimmed when the sun himself appeared.

*   *   *   *

In May 1954 K's second book was published by Gollancz (it had appeared earlier that year in America)—*The First and Last*

Freedom. It was a much more substantial book than *Education and the Significance of Life*, with a ten-page foreword by Aldous Huxley. It was an immediate success and by the end of the year was in its sixth impression. The first part of the book consists of twenty-one chapters on such themes as What are We Seeking?, Individual and Society, Self-Knowledge, Fear, Desire, Can Thinking Solve our Problems?, Self-Deception. The second half is made up of Questions and Answers taken from various talks. In his foreword Huxley wrote: 'In this volume of selections from the writings and recorded talks of Krishnamurti, the reader will find a clear contemporary statement of the fundamental human problem, together with an invitation to solve it in the only way in which it can be solved—for and by himself.' Huxley then quoted some passages integral to Krishnamurti's way of thought: 'There is life in men, not in society, not in organized religious systems, but in you and me.' 'Belief invariably separates. If you have a belief, or when you seek security in your particular belief, you become separated from those who seek security in some other form of belief. All organized beliefs are based on separation, though they may preach brotherhood.' It was to 'protect himself from beliefs' that Krishnamurti had not read 'any sacred literature'.

The *Observer* reviewer wrote about the book, '. . . for those who wish to listen, it will have a value beyond words', and the critic of *The Times Literary Supplement:* 'He is an artist both in vision and analysis', while Anne Morrow Lindbergh had written of the American edition, '. . . the sheer simplicity of what he has to say is breathtaking. The reader is given in one paragraph, even one sentence, enough to keep him exploring, questioning, thinking for days.'

*   *   *   *

A week of talks and discussions in New York at the Washington Irving High School, beginning on May 22, followed K's return to the States. They attracted large crowds, many new people having become interested since the publication of *The First and Last Freedom*. K stayed in New York with Frederick Pinter again. In writing to Lady Emily from there he made no mention of her book, only expressed his happiness that they had seen so much of each other in London. Nor did he mention his own book. He never refers to his own books and seems to take little interest in them; he has virtually never read them after publication, and now, for many years, has not read any book derived from his own talks or writings before publication. He carefully considers the titles, however, while leaving the editing in the hands of a team he trusts.

K remained quietly at Ojai for the summer. There were no talks there that year. Lady Emily's book was in page proof by the end of August, scheduled for publication in the autumn. Having sent an early proof copy to Rajagopal at Ojai, she was stunned with dismay when on September 3 she received a brief letter from K telling her that the book must on no account be published. She immediately sent a cable to him: 'Your sudden and unexpected opposition to publication most distressing after your often expressed willingness to leave decision to me. Physical difficulties and vast expense of withdrawal now probably insuperable at this stage.' K's answer to this was a longer letter written on the same day:

My dearest Mother,

A few days ago I wrote saying that your new book should in no circumstances be published. It will really do a great deal of damage to the work I am doing; it will bring unnecessary and unimportant things into prominence; it will upset a great many people, causing bitterness etc. This is not what you want to do and certainly will *not* aid in what I am doing and I am certain of that. It will create a great deal of superficial and temporary interest and sensation, which is the last thing one wants.

I have been thinking a great deal about it and I am deeply convinced it should not come out at all. You may also accept my conviction and if you do you must persuade Mary too. Please, I am *very* serious about this, Mum, and the book will do perhaps irreparable harm. I say perhaps not that I am uncertain about it but you and Mary may feel different. But as the book is unfortunately concerned about me, what I say must be fully taken into account. So please, mum, out of love and respect for everything, do stop it. Don't hesitate about it. It is not too late.

Do please listen to what I have written.

We shall have to consider the financial side of it but please I beg of you, do not let that consideration stop the book from [not] being published and sold.

This is much too serious to let our personal feelings spoil something very real. So, Mum, I beg you and Mary to stop it, without hesitation.

With love as usual

Krishna

The whole tone of this letter was so unlike K in its definiteness that we at once thought that some influence had been brought to bear on him and, without the slightest justification, suspected Aldous Huxley; yet no one but Rajagopal could have had time to read the proof copy; it is doubtful whether K himself could have had time to do more than glance at it. K, when tackled on this point by letter, denied that anyone had influenced him—it was 'quite untrue and unfair to suggest such a thing'. Rajagopal when appealed to disclaimed all responsibility, financial or otherwise, for K's decision; he could not possibly spend money, he wrote, subscribed for K's work for such a purpose. One might have thought the money well spent if the publication of the book was going to damage K's work. Some miserable days followed for my mother as we tried to get the book stopped. One of the things that hurt her most was that the partners in Hart-Davis, who had formerly felt that K had come out so magnificently in the book, were now angry and disillusioned with him.

Fortunately Rupert Hart-Davis, my mother's devoted friend, released her from her contract when he saw how unhappy she was, but, of course, the firm had to be reimbursed, not only for the cost of production but for overheads. My mother could not afford to do this. K offered to pay the whole sum himself in instalments out of his income from Miss Dodge. This we would not allow, and, anyway, it would have been no security, for the income would stop at his death. In the end my husband and I found the necessary money. From the draft of a letter, I find that I was able to assure K on September 21 that the matter was settled:

Mother looks about ten years older and is very shaky since the bomb-shell of your letter came. She has hardly been able to sleep and can think of nothing else. She is of course at the moment very unhappy and feeling deeply humiliated over all the trouble she has caused to the firm of Hart-Davis, but that is nothing, I know, to what she would have felt if she had not been able to comply with your wishes. That she would never have got over; this I hope will pass in time.

K wrote back on September 28 to say how profoundly sorry he was to have caused such unhappiness. 'I am really thankful that the publishers have behaved so generously. Thank goodness the book was stopped in time. If it could not be, and knowing I wanted it stopped, it would have been an impossible position for Mum.'

K was not far behind this letter. On October 16 he came to London without Rajagopal. He stayed with Mrs Bindley and saw my mother and me together the next morning. She asked him at once, 'What would you have done if I had not been able to stop the book? Would you ever have spoken to me again?' to which he replied with his usual sweetness, 'Really, Mum, as if it would have made any difference.' He sat holding her hand for a long time. It was difficult to reconcile this with the uncompromising firmness of his recent letters. My rather unfriendly feelings towards him were entirely dissipated and my mother looked happy for the first time for weeks. She and I both gained the strange impression that he would not really have minded very much if the book *had* been published, and we could not help suspecting again that there had indeed been some pressure put on him to get it stopped and that now he was alone in London that pressure had been lifted.

9

Commentaries on Living

Rajagopal joined K in Rome at the end of October and flew with him to India where K stayed until April 1955, speaking in all the usual places. He had bronchitis rather badly at Rajghat in February and after giving eight talks in Bombay between February 16 and March 13 he went up to the northern hill station of Ranikhet by himself because he was not feeling well. Rajagopal meanwhile went on ahead of him to Europe. On April 27 K flew to Rome and then moved up to Il Leccio where he remained resting until the middle of May. He then joined Rajagopal in Holland. A house had been taken for him at Laren, not far from Amsterdam, by the *Stichting* (Dutch Committee) of KWINC. He was looked after there by a Dutch friend of long standing, Miss Anneke Korndorffer, a professional speech therapist and the chief representative of the *Stichting*. He gave five talks in Amsterdam from May 17 at the Bellevue Hotel.

In June K was in London again, with Rajagopal this time, for six talks at the Friends Meeting House and several discussion meetings. A phrase he used during his third talk on June 19 particularly struck Marcelle de Manziarly who had come to London to hear him: 'One can enter alive into death.' This pronouncement, though not quite in those words, had come in answer to the question: 'I'm afraid of death. Can you give me any reassurance?' K's answer was in part:

. . . The fact is, there is death; the organism comes to an end. And the fact is, there may or may not be a continuity. But I want to know *now*, while I am healthy, vital, and alive, what it is to live richly; and I also want to find out now what it means to die—not wait for an accident or a disease to carry me off. I want to know what it means to die—living to enter the house of death. Not theoretically but actually,

I want to experience the extraordinary thing it must be—to enter into the unknown, cutting off all the known.

Not to meet with the known, not to meet a friend on the other side—*that* is what is frightening us. I am afraid to let go of all the things I have known, the family, the virtue that I have cultivated, the property, the position, the power, the sorrow, the joy, everything that I have gathered, which is all the known—I am afraid to let all that go, totally, deep down, right from the depths of my being, and to be with the unknown—which is, after all, death . . . So the question is, can I put away all the known? I cannot put away the known by will, by volition, because that entails a maker of the will, an entity who says, 'This is right and this is wrong', 'This I want and this I do not want'. Such a mind is acting from the known, is it not? It says, 'I want to enter the extraordinary thing which is death, the unknowable, and so I must relinquish the known'. Such a person then searches the various corners of the mind, in order to push aside the known. This action allows the entity who deliberately pushed away the known, to remain. But as that entity is itself the result of the known, it can never experience or enter that extraordinary state . . . Can I, who am the result of the known, enter into the unknown which is death? If I want to do it, it must be done while living, surely, not at the last moment . . . While living, to enter the house of death is not just a morbid idea; it is the only solution. While living a rich, full life—whatever that means—or while living a miserable, impoverished life, can we not know that which is not measurable, that which is only glimpsed by the experiencer in rare moments? . . . Can the mind die from moment to moment to *everything* that it experiences, and never accumulate?

K was to express the same idea very simply in one of his books: 'How necessary it is to die each day, to die each minute to everything, to the many yesterdays and to the moment that has just gone by! Without death there is no renewing, without death there is no creation. The burden of the past gives rise to its own continuity, and the worries of yesterday give new life to the worry of today.'[23]

Before leaving London K again brought up the subject of my mother's book and asked for my assurance that it would never be published, not even after his and my mother's death. Apparently I did not give him a satisfactory promise, for on September 27 he was writing from Ojai asking once more for this assurance, and when I did not answer this letter he wrote again on October 22 to know whether I had ever received it, repeating what he had said and hoping to have an answer before he and Rajagopal flew from San Francisco to Sydney in the first week of November. In reply to this I argued that he was a public figure, that after his death people were certain to write things about him which would not necessarily be true, whereas my mother and I had written as authentic an account of his early life as possible and that it should be preserved. He answered from Sydney:

I feel very strongly that Nitya's and my account of Ojai happenings should not be published. Very few have Nitya's or my account; one or two people to whom they were sent have returned them. Future biographies may or may not be written but Nitya's or my account cannot be included without my permission. I am not trying to tie you up; I understand if I may say so your point of view nor am I 'bullying' you to accept what I feel [I had never suggested he was]. But what I feel is clear and definite. I would not have bothered you or upset Mum so much, if I had not felt strongly against Nitya's and my account being made public. If Rajagopal has given permission to Mum to make public Nitya's or my account of the events at Ojai, then I withdraw that permission also. Rajagopal is in sole charge of all these things and as you know, he has in the archives all my papers, manuscripts etc and I have given him complete permission to deal with them according to his judgment, now or after my death. I am giving him a copy of this letter.

I naturally had no alternative now but to bow to K's prohibition. In 1957 my mother published *Candles in the Sun*, leaving out K's letters to her and the accounts of the Ojai experience and putting more emphasis on her own life and family difficulties.

*   *   *   *

Rosalind joined K in Sydney at the end of November after his talks there and went with him to India while Rajagopal returned to Ojai. K's programme that winter of 1955–56 took him to Rajghat, New Delhi, Rishi Valley, Madras and, for the whole of March '56, to Bombay. Then at the beginning of April he went to New Delhi again where my husband and I happened to be after a visit to Kashmir. K was staying with his very old friend, B. Shiva Rao, and his Austrian wife, with whom he usually stayed in Delhi. We all had a delicious Indian meal together in Shiva Rao's house, 16 Tughlak Road. Shiva Rao had remained a close friend of mine since my visits to India in the twenties.

K and Rosalind left for Europe on April 15 via Cairo. They spent a week there with the Suarès at Alexandria before proceeding to Athens and thence to Rome. When K went up to Il Leccio, Rosalind returned to Ojai. K kept his friends more or less in separate compartments. Even after ten years of friendship with Vanda Scaravelli he had never mentioned her by name to Lady Emily. He wrote from Rome on May 8, 'I have been in Florence staying in the country with some friends and am back here before flying to Stockholm for some talks there'. Rajagopal joined him in Stockholm. They went next to Brussels in June for yet more talks and then on to Laren again near Amsterdam in July. K's allergy and bronchitis were very bad there.

After a few days in Paris K was driven down to a place called Cuzorn, near Périgueux, where he stayed at a house, Roudignon, with a farm attached to it. His hosts were Monsieur Léon de Vidas, who had a textile business in Paris, and his wife, whom K had known for some time. He found the country round Cuzorn wonderfully beautiful. No English was spoken and he was glad of this opportunity to polish his French. He remained there for over a month. It was his 'holiday', he wrote; he was recovering from his bronchitis and doing nothing but resting and going for walks. He was never hungry now, he said, but 'forced' himself to eat 'to gain energy'.

September this year saw the publication of *Commentaries on Living*, admirably edited by Rajagopal. This was the book that Aldous Huxley had encouraged K to write. It is to my mind the easiest to read of all his books. The first line of the first piece captures one instantly: 'The other day three pious egotists came to see me.' The descriptions of nature with which many of the pieces begin quieten the mind to receive the teaching which is imparted almost imperceptibly. When the American edition of the book came out, Francis Hacket, the well-known journalist and author, wrote in the *New Republic:* 'I feel that he has hold of a major secret . . . He is no other than he seems—a free man, one of the first quality, growing older as do diamonds but with the gem-like flame not dating and ever alive'; and the reviewer of the *Times Literary Supplement*: 'The insight, spiritual and poetical, of these commentaries is as simply expressed as it is searching in its demand.'

*   *   *   *

K left Cuzorn on September 22 for talks in Brussels, Hamburg and Athens. Rajagopal was with him on this tour. In October K flew alone from Athens to Delhi via Istanbul and Karachi. The usual round followed after Delhi—Rajghat, Rishi Valley, Madras. Wherever he went he was escorted by a small group of followers. In Madras he fell ill with a high fever and had to postpone some of his talks; this necessitated postponing his first talks at his next port of call, Colombo, where he stayed from January 11, 1957, until the 28th. The Government of Ceylon allowed all five of his public talks to be broadcast. 'It is extraordinary and I don't quite know why they did it,' he wrote to Miss Doris Pratt in London, secretary and agent of K W I N C in England who had worked for him since the early twenties. He was in Bombay for the whole of February and the first week in March, giving talks.

K's last talk in Bombay was on March 3. It so happened that from this date until September 1958 he gave no more talks. This was not a decision taken at the time; circumstances dictated it. He was approaching a great change in his outward life.

K flew to Rome on March 6 from where he went to Il Leccio. His intention was to stay there until the end of the month, then go to Rome for a week and on to Helsinki with Rajagopal for a gathering. In the event he got no further than Rome where Rajagopal met him and where a small gathering of only ten people had been arranged for him. On April 2 he wrote to Doris Pratt from Rome, 'I was quite seriously ill in India but I hoped to carry on with all the arrangements that have been made but I cannot carry on with any of them. So I have been obliged to cancel the talks in Finland and in London and the gathering at Biarritz. Also I have to cancel Ojai, New Zealand and Australia.' He returned without Rajagopal to Il Leccio where he remained for weeks, doing nothing, hardly even writing any letters. He told Lady Emily that it would have been 'stupid' to go on with talks all round the world in his state of health.

Vanda Scaravelli's husband died in Florence early in May while K was still at Il Leccio, eight miles away. K left Il Leccio on

95

May 26, met Rajagopal in Zurich and went on with him to Gstaad in the Bernese Oberland where they had been invited to stay by Madame Nora Safra who had a house there. This was K's first introduction to Gstaad which he was to come to know so intimately. It may have been during this visit that he conceived the idea of starting an annual gathering in Europe on the lines of the Ommen camp which would save him from having to travel so much. Gstaad or some village near it seemed an ideal centre. He felt he could never return to Ommen since it had been a concentration camp.

On June 11 K and Rajagopal proceeded to Villars, staying at the Hotel Montesano where K had stayed several times before. After a fortnight Rajagopal returned to California leaving K alone at Villars with only just enough money to pay the hotel bill. There had been some kind of crisis in K's relationship with Rajagopal in Rome in April. As I have said, there had never been any natural affinity between them; they were too far apart temperamentally. For a long time now there had been a strain, constant irritations and bickerings. They must have got very much on each other's nerves when travelling together. Rajagopal was parsimonious and dictatorial while K's passivity made him an easy victim for bullying. Tension had in fact been growing between them all through the war years when they had been thrown so much together at Ojai. The frailty of an already frayed relationship was exposed when Rajagopal, who had made all the arrangements for K's talks in Europe and elsewhere, suddenly had to cancel everything. It seems that he told K in Rome or at Villars that he was sick of being his courier and travel agent and that in future his travel arrangements could be made by Doris Pratt in London.

K's expenses in London and journeys from London were defrayed by a simple arrangement: an old follower of K's from the Theosophical days and a great friend of Doris Pratt, Charles Burdick, had been anxious in 1947 to make a gift of money and shares in his company to KWINC for K's work. Because the exchange control at that time made it impossible to send money to America, Mr Burdick, at Rajagopal's suggestion, gave the money and shares personally to Doris Pratt, a British resident. In March '47 she opened a separate account with £2,000 from

Mr Burdick. Rajagopal instructed her to send all bank statements to him and keep an account of every penny she paid out for K. She also drew on this account for Rajagopal's expenses when he came to England. Mr Burdick had invented a paint-spraying pump, and the shares he gave Miss Pratt were in the Aerograph Company he had started to promote his invention. They brought in an annual average dividend of £600. Rajagopal sent funds from America for K's expenses in India, but for the past ten years all expenses in England had come from the Burdick account.

Whatever it was that had happened between K and Rajagopal in Rome had made K reluctant to return to Ojai. He remained, therefore, quite alone at Villars from June 19 until July 20. He made no reference to Rajagopal in the only letter he wrote to Lady Emily from there on July 2. (He had never said a derogatory word about Rajagopal in any of his letters to her.) He seemed perfectly happy: 'I am in retreat. I see nobody and the only conversation is with the waiter. It's nice to be doing nothing but doing other things. There are splendid walks here and hardly anybody on them. Please don't tell anyone where I am.' By 'doing other things' he no doubt meant the meditation that went on inside him whenever he was quiet. On leaving him at Villars Rajagopal had told him that he would learn what it was to be lonely, but K is never lonely, especially when he is alone.

Doris Pratt knew where he was. She forwarded letters to him which he returned after reading, telling her that he was not going to reply to any of them since he wished 'to take a long and complete rest even though I am well'. He sent her detailed instructions how to answer them impersonally without her reading them.

On July 20 Léon de Vidas found K at Villars with no money and took him down to his new house at Tournon d'Agenais in the Dordogne. K was to remain there until November. 'It is very quiet here and I see no one except my two hosts,' he told Lady Emily on October 31. 'It's right away in the country, miles away from any town. It has been a complete retirement, walks and solitude. It has been very good. I shall do the same in India.'

Rajagopal went with K to India that winter for the last time. In November they flew together from Zurich to Bombay, Doris

Pratt having made all the arrangements. Rajagopal stayed in India only until January 17, 1958, and for much of that time he was not with K. He had many business matters to attend to at Vasanta Vihar. His right-hand man in India was R. Madhavachari, the Secretary of KWINC, who held Rajagopal's power of attorney. It was Mr Madhavachari who made arrangements for K's talks and travels in India, edited his Indian talks and saw through the press all the talks published in India.

K was to remain in India for sixteen months, the longest he had ever stayed there since he left in 1912. Until September 1958 he was in complete retirement, first at Rishi Valley, then at Rajghat and then at the northern hill station of Ranikhet. From Rajghat he had written to Lady Emily in February '58: 'As I am in retirement people leave me alone, but plenty of things to observe, both inwardly and outwardly'; and in June, from Ranikhet, he was asking Doris Pratt to send him by air a Sanscrit grammar, for although Sanscrit text-books were compiled in India, the Indian scholars did not know how to teach beginners. When a Sanscrit primer by E. D. Perry arrived, published by Columbia University Press, K proclaimed it 'excellent . . . If I can get through this it will be a little miracle'. He reckoned it would take him sixteen or seventeen weeks. I doubt whether the little miracle occurred. (Now, at eighty-six, K is studying Sanscrit again.) For a whole month he was alone at Ranikhet, apart from two servants, at a house outside the town that had been taken for him, No 1 Bungalow, Chanbattia—'good walks, plenty of solitude' and stupendous views of the Himalayas.

K left Ranikhet reluctantly at the end of July to go to Poona via Delhi and Bombay. Towards the end of August he started holding private group discussions twice a week at Poona. 'Surprisingly there are quite a lot of young people,' he told Lady Emily. 'Poona is supposed to be an intellectual centre.' He now resumed his public talks—in Poona during September, in Madras in October and November, and in Bombay in December. He had also been to Rishi Valley again and to Rajghat, talking to teachers and students. While he was at Vasanta Vihar in November he had signed on the 13th the document given below which was attested by the Notary Public, High Court of Jurisdiction, Madras, and sent to Rajagopal on the same day:

I hereby give the proprietorship of the copyright in all my writings previous to this date as well as from this date forward to Krishnamurti Writings, Inc., Ojai, California, U.S.A.; London, England; and Madras, India.

Further I authorize Mr D. Rajagopal, President of Krishnamurti Writings, Inc., to make any arrangements that may be necessary with regard to the publication of all books and articles that I have written or may write. He has my full authorization to make contracts or agreements on my behalf or to authorize contracts or agreements to be made on my behalf in connection with the publication of my writings.

Made in duplicate and good faith.

It seems strange that K should have made this declaration at a time when his relationship with Rajagopal was, to say the least, strained. Perhaps it was the very fact that there was friction between them that had induced Rajagopal to put pressure on K to make his position legal. K had told me in his letter from Sydney in 1955 that Rajagopal had all his papers and manuscripts and permission to deal with them according to his judgement; he had not said, however, that there was any *legal* agreement to that effect. One can hardly see K taking the trouble to legalize Rajagopal's position unless he had been pressed to do so. At some time before this K had ceased to be a trustee of KWINC. He cannot remember himself when this was or whether he had consciously resigned because he did not want to be bothered with business matters or whether he had signed a paper presented to him by Rajagopal without realising what he was signing. Rajagopal had probably become President of KWINC at the time K had ceased to be a trustee.

*   *   *   *

In February and March 1959 K was giving talks in Delhi. The heat was so intense there that he was delighted when in April a house was taken for him at Srinagar in Kashmir. The house turned out to be so dirty and rat-infested that in June he moved to Achabal, also in Kashmir. At the beginning of July he moved again to Pahalgam, a valley in Kashmir 7,200 feet up, surrounded by snow peaks and miles of pine woods, where he stayed in a Government hut, 'not at all luxurious', but with intoxicatingly beautiful surroundings. Mr Madhavachari had been with him at

Srinagar and Achabal, and Pupul Jayakar had also been with him for a time, but at Pahalgam he was alone with Parameshwaran, the cook who is now head cook at Rishi Valley. Pahalgam is a centre from which a great annual pilgrimage starts to Amarnath, about forty miles away. 15,000 pilgrims were expected by August 20. 'What a stink there will be,' K commented in a letter to Lady Emily of July 20. He was not feeling well enough to do much walking: 'There's nothing wrong but I feel washed out.'

K had imagined that he would still be at Pahalgam when the pilgrims arrived; instead he fell ill in the middle of August with a kidney infection and was taken down to Srinagar with very high fever, and then moved to Delhi where he was given antibiotics for the first time in his life—'too strong as the infection was very serious,' he wrote afterwards. The antibiotics had the effect of temporarily paralysing his legs and he was so weak that Parameshwaran had to feed him like a baby. Since his condition remained unsatisfactory he went to Bombay to be x-rayed. On September 11 he wrote from there to Doris Pratt, 'I came here from Kashmir as I had severe infection of the kidneys. Keep this to yourself as otherwise people will write.' Back at Srinagar he was able to report to Lady Emily on October 1: 'With proper medication it's all under control and I am gradually getting back to the normal. Have been in bed for nearly seven weeks but everything is all right. It is stupid to fall ill and it is a great nuisance to others. I will have to see that it doesn't happen again.' However, the fever returned at Srinagar and he had to go back to Bombay to be re-examined.

From Bombay K went to Rishi Valley at the end of October and after recuperating there for a few weeks, resumed talking in Madras, Bombay, Rajghat and New Delhi from November 22 to March 6, 1960. At last, on March 11, he flew to Rome where Vanda Scaravelli met him and took him to Il Leccio. Doris Pratt assumed that Rajagopal at Ojai knew all about his plans as usual but Rajagopal wrote to her on March 5 to say that he had only just heard from K that he was to stay with Vanda Scaravelli for some weeks and then going perhaps to the Bircher-Benner Clinic at Zurich. He, Rajagopal, did not know whether K intended to go to Ojai that summer or not. Rajagopal had written to Vanda Scaravelli three times in the last three months but had had no reply from her. (It seems likely that K had told her not to disclose his plans to anyone.) Rajagopal was anxious that Doris Pratt should send funds to K from the Burdick account in case he went to the Clinic. This she was unable to do owing to the exchange control but when she passed this on to K he told her not to worry about it; the money would be forthcoming from friends who had been with him in India and who could be reimbursed in London. (These friends were an elderly couple from South America, Enrique and Isabel Biascoechea, who had been devoted to K for years. They insisted that the money for the Clinic should be a gift.)

K entered the Bircher-Benner Clinic on April 11. That day he wrote to Doris Pratt to say that when the doctors had finished with him he would be flying to California via London; he had obtained his visa in Zurich without any difficulty. 'The doctors here are making a thorough and complete check-up,' he added, 'and it's a long and tiresome affair. The treatment will start as soon as the diagnosis is made.'

K left the Clinic and flew to London on May 1. Doris Pratt met him at Heathrow and was shocked to see how tired and haggard he looked. He had been impressed by the treatment at the Clinic and said that the doctors wanted him to go back there after Ojai. They had put him on a strict diet and had impressed on him the need for a complete rest after every bout of activity. He would, therefore, have to rest in New York before flying on to Los Angeles. He stayed with Mrs Bindley for the few days he was in London, saw Lady Emily two or three times and did some shopping. He had to order new shoes because his feet had become so much thinner. (He always went to Lobb's for his shoes.) 'Despite his lack of reserve of strength he positively *refused* to travel first class by air,' Doris Pratt reported to Rajagopal on May 2. The day he left London, May 9, to stay with Frederick Pinter in New York, Miss Pratt was writing again to Rajagopal:

I went with him to the airport and I must tell you, very, .very privately, that I feel him to be a very sick man. He seems *to me* to be not at all in a fit state to give talks at Ojai, but he seems determined to do so. I have observed him very closely and though I have had no 'personal' talk with him whatever, I have been very aware of a great change in him, physically at any rate, and maybe more than physical.

His strength is extremely limited and his reserve of strength nil. It has been said that he nearly died in Delhi, and I can believe it from his present state. I should think it highly important that the utmost and most loving and gentle care be taken of him at Ojai, as in my view his health is affected even by the people and circumstances of the moment. He has returned a good portion of the money I gave him [£44].

It was while K was staying in New York this time that Frederick Pinter, who knew Rajagopal well, warned him that unless he took some steps he would soon find that he had no say whatever in the affairs of KWINC, for Rajagopal had complete control of all its assets. Mr Pinter urged K to make inquiries and take more responsibility since the large sums donated to the Trust were given for *his* work.

Nothing bored K more than routine business; nevertheless, Mr Pinter must have impressed upon him so strongly what his duty was to the people who had given donations that when he got to Ojai he asked Rajagopal for information about KWINC's financial position. After thirty-five years of running the practical side of K's life without any interference, Rajagopal saw no reason for this sudden interest. True, he had a vice-president and a board of trustees but all the real work had been left to him and his assistant, Byron Casselberry. Rajagopal had become an autocrat. 'Rajagopal *is* KWINC and KWINC is Rajagopal,' one of the trustees was to say. Unfortunately Rajagopal declined to give K the information he asked for, maintaining that it was none of his business since he was not a trustee. K then asked to be put back on the Board but this request was also refused. Such secrecy and lack of co-operation bred mistrust in a partnership that could only work when there was complete confidence.

On May 21, a week after arriving at Ojai, K gave the first of what were to have been eight talks in the Oak Grove on four consecutive week-ends, but at the third talk on May 28, he opened the meeting by announcing: 'When I came to give this series of talks, I had the full intention of going through with eight talks; but unfortunately I can't do it. I can only give these four—and so the last talk will be tomorrow morning. As many of you have come from great distances to listen to them, I regret very much that physically I can't go on with all the talks. I am sorry.' He then proceeded to give a superb talk on the need for a radical transformation in human consciousness and how the mind could be 'made innocent through death of the known'. Only such a mind 'could discover that which was everlasting'.

Rajagopal, writing to Doris Pratt a month later, sounded aggrieved: the cancellation of the last four talks had created a turmoil, and K had not cancelled them because he was ill but because he did not feel he had enough energy to go on with them, and in spite of the cancellation he had 'given three days to interviews of several hours duration'.

One of those who had attended the talks was Mrs Zimbalist, formerly Mary Taylor, who, as has already been related, had heard K speak in 1944. She was living in a house on the coast at Malibu, some sixty miles from Ojai. Her husband had died suddenly of a heart attack in 1958. K's 1944 talks and the interview she had had with him afterwards had made a profound impression on her, and a desire to hear him again had been one of her chief motives for going on living. She was granted a private interview with him and he spoke to her of death in a way she was able fully to respond to, having herself reached the realisation that one could not run away from death by the usual routes of escape, that the fact of death had to be understood, that it was the escapes from loneliness that brought sorrow, not the *fact* of loneliness, of death; grief was self-pity not love.

K was sleeping at Pine Cottage and having his meals at Arya Vihara, keeping to the strict diet of the Clinic. He had intended to return to London on about June 20 and then go back to the Clinic, but he suddenly decided to postpone his departure. He postponed it several times again, to Rajagopal's exasperation. He was giving no interviews now and not answering any letters, hundreds of which had piled up. He was having tests made at a laboratory in Santa Barbara and going regularly to the dentist. In July he went with Rosalind for a holiday to Carmel. Rajagopal told Doris Pratt at the end of the summer that if K had no plans it was simply because he did not want to make any. One senses Rajagopal's intense irritation. There is no doubt that there was a great deal of friction between him and K at this time and probably open quarrels.

There are no letters from K to Lady Emily during this long stay at Ojai, nor did he write to Mrs Bindley nor even to

Vanda Scaravelli, for all three were telephoning to Doris Pratt for news of him of which she had had none directly. Lady Emily was 'having nightmares about his departing forever' and wondering whether he was having another 'initiatory experience'.

K had made up his mind by September not to go back to the Clinic since he now felt quite well; he would stay on at Ojai until he went to India in November. He did not leave Ojai, therefore, until the beginning of that month and then broke his journey to Bombay in New York, London and Rome. In London he told Doris Pratt that when he returned from India, probably in March, he would like to have a gathering in England and then later on, in July or August, after he had been back to Ojai, talks arranged for him somewhere in Europe.

K arrived in India on November 17 and went straight to Vasanta Vihar at Adyar. At about the same time Rajagopal left Ojai for Switzerland and London, intending to be away for quite a long time. K evidently wrote to him, asking him to arrange the gathering in England the following year, for towards the end of December he received a cable from Rajagopal from London saying, 'Received your letters. Unable now personally arrange anything. Have discussed with Doris Pratt who will help. Kindly write her. Happy new year.' Rajagopal had presumably washed his hands of anything to do with K's travels and meetings in Europe, though KWINC continued to publish verbatim reports of all his talks after he began public speaking again.

K, who was now at Rajghat, wrote to Doris Pratt after receiving Rajagopal's cable:

1. Till July 1961 I cannot give any public talks. I am not giving any public talks here in India at present.
2. As I cannot give public talks, only gatherings are possible.
3. I shall be leaving India by the middle of March, shall take a rest in Italy or elsewhere and will be ready for gatherings about the end of April, till about the first week in June, about 5 or 6 weeks, when I shall be leaving for California.
4. So the gatherings will have to be arranged between end of April and beginning of June.
5. Suggest these gatherings be held in England, preferably not in London but just outside London. What do you say about it?

6. Can you undertake to arrange such a gathering? Later on, when I come back from California, we can have a gathering and perhaps talks in Europe before I return to India.

Miss Pratt undertook to do what he asked although it was a great responsibility for her. Two years before, with Rajagopal's blessing, she had asked someone else to take over the KWINC office in London which she had been running single-handed from her house in Harrow. This was a young woman, Mary Cadogan, who with her husband, had been interested in K's teaching for several years. A first class secretary, Mrs Cadogan had before her marriage worked for the BBC. She had a young baby but had agreed to take over the office at a very small salary provided she could work from home. This was perfectly acceptable and in July 1958 all the office equipment and stocks of books had been transferred to the Cadogans' house in Clapham. The work consisted of sending out notices to the mailing list, taking and sending out orders for books, acknowledging donations and, when K gave public talks in London, making all the arrangements. Any profits from the sale of books, all donations and accounts were sent to Rajagopal with whom Mary Cadogan was on very cordial terms. Her salary was paid out of the Burdick account.*

*   *   *   *

Doris Pratt had found Rajagopal in a very unhappy state while he was in London in December. She described him in a letter to K of January 11, 1961, as being 'a mixture of love, clear acumen, and great violence'. She had told him that she would no longer send him copies of K's letters to her and hers to him as she had always done in the past, but would 'inform him of any fait accompli as regards the coming gatherings'. She added in her letter to K, 'We had several violent and bitter exchanges', but they had parted 'with love uppermost and I hope we shall be able to keep it so'.

I myself saw Rajagopal once at the Athenaeum Court Hotel in Piccadilly where he was staying. Knowing nothing about the

---

* Mary Cadogan has since written three very successful books in collaboration with Patricia Craig, published by Gollancz—*You're a Brick, Angela!* (1976), *Women and Children First* (1978) and *The Lady Investigates* (1981).

change in his relationship with K, I was deeply shocked and dismayed when he started abusing K, though giving no reason for his hostility. I told him that feeling as he did he ought to give up working for K—it must be bad for them both. At the same time I felt great compassion for him, particularly as I was extremely fond of him. He was nearly sixty and what else could he do? I believed his trouble was that, being deeply affectionate himself, he had never felt sufficiently loved. I gathered that his marriage was not happy; indeed he and Rosalind were soon to be divorced.

Rajagopal also abused K to my mother during this visit which distressed her as much as it did me because she too was devoted to Rajagopal. Neither of us breathed a word of the matter to K, feeling that it could only cause mischief; we prayed that Rajagopal's attitude was a temporary phase.

10

Krishnamurti's Notebook

K started holding small gatherings in New Delhi in January 1961, followed by gatherings in Bombay in February and March. On March 16 he left India for Rome where Vanda Scaravelli met him as had become habitual and took him to Il Leccio for a few weeks. For his stay in London in May and the first half of June, Doris Pratt had rented a small furnished house at Wimbledon, 19 Inner Park Road (now demolished). K had enjoyed walking on Wimbledon Common since the days when he had stayed with Miss Dodge at West Side House. Miss Pratt stayed with him at Inner Park Road and Anneke Korndorffer came over from Holland to do the housekeeping. Another follower, Joan Wright, came daily to motor him wherever he wanted to go. Doris had hired the Kenneth Black Memorial Hall in Wimbledon for twelve small meetings and sent personal invitations to about 150 people. Several of K's old friends came from abroad, including Léon de Vidas, Carlo Suarès and Madame Safra, with all of whom K had many discussions about the gatherings he wanted to hold in July and August in Switzerland and Paris.

At the Wimbledon meetings K agreed for the first time to use a microphone and to allow his talks to be recorded. At Rajagopal's request, K took the tapes with him when he flew to America in the middle of June. The day after he left, Doris Pratt wrote to tell Rajagopal that although she had found K better in health than the previous year

there were some very strange and difficult times when all life and energy seemed to be drained from his body and when he became 'weak and ill' to an alarming degree. These occasions only lasted a few moments in their essence, but necessitated rest afterwards. On quite a few occasions he cried out aloud at night and on one or two occasions Anneke heard him and was very troubled. On other occasions he would mention at breakfast that he had been calling out and that he hoped he had not disturbed us. Similarly on several occasions at meal times he suddenly dropped his knife and fork and appeared to be kind of transfixed for a moment or two, and then to go limp and faint so that one thought he might drop to the floor. I questioned him about it because I wanted to know whether there was anything at all the onlooker could do. He replied there was nothing we could do except keep quiet, relaxed and not worry, but also *not* touch him at all. I pressed him a bit, and he said while he himself knew exactly what was happening, he was unable to explain it to us. He said it was linked with the happenings which were alluded to in the *un*expurgated book by Lady Emily [the unpublished version of *Candles in the Sun*]. During the eight weeks I was living in the same house I felt on many occasions that I was an onlooker at a most profound and tremendous mystery. Here was a man who, on the platform, looking at first hand into the human mind and heart, built a magnificent scaffolding, girder by girder, which towered dizzily into the very heavens, stretching the capacity of every person present, so that many felt they had put one hand into the hand of God. Then there was the man who rapped out concise and strict instructions about meetings, the tape recordings etc., and who would stand no nonsense. There was the man tender as a mother with someone in real distress. There was also the man deeply concerned about food, right diet and health, frantically and conscientiously trying—it seemed to me—to combat the physical disabilities which seem to beset him. At times the hay fever was truly appalling. Then there was the incessant traveller, grumbling to himself about the nightmare of travelling, packing and the boring necessity of having suitable clothes for varying climates. Then again there was the man who during his own morning meditation period, spread a mantle of intense quietude over the house which even a rhinoceros like myself could feel. Then there were those mysterious attacks and some equally mysterious healings. It seems right that you should know what a deeply serious problem all this travel, seeing people, giving meetings, and keeping going physically, seems to be. He really *needs* all your help because things are going to get harder and harder for him.

Mrs Bindley was also aware of the 'mysterious attacks' when K stayed with her for a few days before leaving London. What they were experiencing, of course, was something of 'the process'. He flew from Heathrow on June 14, breaking his journey in New York where he stayed as usual with the Pinters before flying to Los Angeles. The day after his departure from London Doris

Pratt was writing to 'Signora Vanda', as K referred to her: 'I think he was dreading his journey and the occasion of his visit there [Ojai], but I gather there is something to be faced there. He is tremendously appreciative of all you do for him and could not stop talking about your generosity and support. I really think he would be utterly lost in Europe if you had not stepped in to help him and his work.' He had said that he might return very quickly.

Strangely enough it was on June 18, the day before he flew to Los Angeles from New York, that K began suddenly to write an extraordinary record of his inner states of consciousness. Written clearly in pencil with hardly any erasures, in ordinary exercise books, he kept up this journal for seven months.[24] He had never kept such a record before and has no recollection of what, if anything, prompted him to start it. One gleans from it something of what it must be like to be inside the consciousness of this extraordinary being. It is probably the nearest one will ever get to him. It begins abruptly: 'In the evening it was there, filling the room, a great sense of beauty, power and gentleness. Others noticed it.'

The 'immensity', the 'sacredness', the 'benediction', the 'otherness', the 'vastness' were all names by which K referred in the course of the journal to the mysterious 'it' which was suddenly there, filling the room—which could not be sought but which came to him every day so strongly that sometimes others noticed it. He wrote at the same time of 'the process' which was both a part and yet apart from 'it'. 'The process' was intense pain in his head and spine.

On June 19 he was writing: 'All night it was there whenever I woke up. The head was bad going to the plane [to fly to Los Angeles]. The purification of the brain is necessary. Only when the brain has cleansed itself of its conditioning, greed, envy, ambition, then only can it comprehend that which is complete. Love is this completeness.' And on the 21st at Ojai:

Woke up about two and there was a peculiar pressure and the pain was more acute, more in the centre of the head. It lasted over an hour and one woke up several times with the intensity of the pressure. Each time there was a great expanding ecstasy; the joy continued. Again, sitting in the dentist's chair, waiting, suddenly the pressure began . . .

The strength and the beauty of a tender leaf is its vulnerability to destruction. Like a blade of grass that comes up through the pavement, it has the power that can withstand casual death.

And on the 30th: 'Yesterday afternoon it was pretty bad, almost unbearable . . . Walking, surrounded by these violet, bare, rocky mountains, suddenly there was solitude; it had great unfathomable richness; it had that beauty which is beyond thought and feeling.' Although K remained nineteen days at Ojai and wrote every day in his notebook he records nothing of what he did there beyond mentioning his visit to the dentist and this walk. On July 7 he wrote, 'Woke up several times shouting. Again there was that intense stillness of the brain and a feeling of vastness. There had been pressure and strain. Success is brutality. Success in every form, political and religious, art and business. To be successful implies ruthlessness.' And on the last day at Ojai, the 8th: 'Before going to sleep, or just going off to sleep, several times there were groans and shouts. The body is too disturbed on account of travelling, as one leaves tonight for London.' Since he was staying alone in his cottage his groans and shouts would not have been heard. Rosalind was still at Arya Vihara where K had said she might remain for her lifetime. She was now independent, for Robert Logan when he died (his wife had died before him) had left her money and property. Ever since its opening her chief concern had been with the Happy Valley School. Rajagopal had moved to a house at the west end of the valley, not far from the Oak Grove, where he also had his office.

Even on the plane (he was flying direct to London) K was recording:

. . . amidst all the noise, smoking and loud talking, most unexpectedly, the sense of immensity and the extraordinary benediction which was felt at *il L* [Il Leccio], that imminent feeling of sacredness, began to take place. The body was nervously tense because of the crowd, noise etc. but in spite of all that, it was there. The pressure and the strain were intense and there was acute pain at the back of the head . . . The whole body was wholly in it and the feeling of sacredness was so intense that a groan escaped from the body and the passengers were sitting in the next seats. It went on for several hours, late into the night. It was as though one was looking, not with eyes only but with a thousand centuries; it was altogether a strange occurrence. The brain was completely empty, all reaction had stopped; during all those hours, one was not aware of this emptiness but only in writing it is the thing known, but this knowledge is only descriptive and not real. That the brain could empty itself is an odd phenomenon. As the eyes were closed, the body, the brain seemed to plunge into unfathomable depths, into states of incredible sensitivity and beauty.

K stayed in London with Mrs Bindley for three nights before flying off to join Vanda Scaravelli at Geneva and then on to Gstaad where she had rented a large furnished house for the summer, Chalet Tannegg, which she was thereafter to take for him every summer. A small gathering had been arranged for him at the Landhaus (the Town Hall) in the neighbouring village of Saanen. Doris Pratt, who had met K at Heathrow, reported to the Signora that she had found him 'absolutely exhausted', and that he had said to her, 'You don't know what it is like to have some-one like Signora Vanda to go to. I have never been treated so wonderfully before. She is *so* kind.' Doris continued:

I do not think he has had at all a happy time at Ojai. He would not gossip about it all, but said he would answer any questions I wanted to ask. So I asked whether Rajagopal had changed his recent destructive attitude, and he replied, 'No'. I asked if Rajagopal is going to continue with the work, and he replied, 'Yes'. I said I supposed it would be in a limited kind of way, concerned with publications only, and he said 'Yes'. He added, 'I shall be writing him a letter'.

K asked Doris not to send Rajagopal any further information about money spent on his behalf. His expenses in London in May and June, including the rent of the Wimbledon house and hire of the hall, had come to £477 while donations had amounted to £650 in the same period.

K did write to Rajagopal asking again to be informed of the financial position of KWINC and insisting that his letter should be shown to the other trustees; he said that he had as much responsibility for the Trust as Rajagopal had, and he reiterated that he wanted to be reinstated on the Board. To this he received no reply, though at some time later on while he was in India, Rajagopal sent him a balance sheet which, of course, he was unable to make head or tail of.

Nine meetings were held at this first Saanen gathering between July 25 and August 13. The Landhaus, holding about 350 people, was full at each meeting and nineteen different nationalities were represented. K had had nearly a fortnight at Chalet Tannegg before the meetings began. The day after his arrival, July 13, he wrote in his notebook: 'The body is completely relaxed and at rest here. Last night, after the long and lovely drive through the mountainous country [from the Geneva airport], on entering the room, the strange, sacred blessing was there. The other [the Signora] also felt it.' And the next day: 'Last night the sacred feeling filled the room . . . The urge for the repetition of experience however pleasant, beautiful, fruitful is the soil in which sorrow grows.' Four days later Vanda Scaravelli had her first experience of K's 'process' which she recorded:

We were talking after lunch, No one was in the house. Suddenly K. fainted. What happened then is impossible to describe, as there are no words that can come close to it; but it is also something that is too serious, too extraordinary, too important to be kept in the dark, buried in silence or not mentioned. There was a change in K.'s face. His eyes became larger and wider and deeper, and there was a tremendous look, beyond any possible state. It was as if there were a powerful presence which belonged to another dimension. There was an inexplicable feeling of emptiness and fullness at the same time.

K had evidently 'gone off', for Vanda jotted down the remarks made by the being left behind: '"Don't leave me till he comes back. He must love you if he lets you touch me, as he is very particular in this. Don't let anyone near me until he returns".' Vanda then added, 'I could not understand at all what was taking place, and I was very astonished.'

The next day, the 19th, at the same hour K 'went off' again, and again Vanda noted down what 'the body' said while he was 'away': '"I feel very strange. Where am I? Don't leave me. Could you kindly stay with me until he returns? Are you comfortable? Take a chair. Do you know him well? Will you look after him?" I still could not fathom what was happening, it was all too unexpected, too incomprehensible. When K regained consciousness, he asked me to tell him what had happened, and so I wrote these notes in an attempt to convey some faint idea of what I had seen and felt.'

Vanda had already had experience of his fainting. The first time it had happened was when she was driving him to Gstaad on July 12. Without warning he had slipped down in his seat and folded over like a piece of cloth. He told her afterwards that he never fainted unless somebody was there. Another time when they were walking at Gstaad he went down backwards like a felled tree; fortunately she was behind him and he landed in her arms. Strangely, she was not alarmed or concerned by his fainting although it could have been dangerous. He would recover completely after a few moments. He said he always felt better after fainting.

On July 20 K was writing in his notebook:

The process was particularly intense yesterday afternoon. In the car, waiting, one was almost oblivious of what was going on around one. The intensity increased and it was almost unbearable so that one was forced to lie down. Fortunately there was someone in the room [Vanda].

The room became full of that benediction. Now what followed is almost impossible to put down in words; words are such dead things, with definite set meanings and what took place was beyond all words and description. It was the centre of all creation; it was a purifying seriousness that cleansed the brain of every thought, and feeling; its seriousness was as lightning which destroys and burns up; the profundity of it was not measurable, it was there immovable, impenetrable, a solidity that was as light as the heavens. It was in the eye, in the breath. It was in the eyes and the eyes could see. The eyes that saw, that looked were wholly different from the eyes of the organ and yet they were the same eyes. There was only seeing, the eyes that saw beyond time-space. There was impenetrable dignity and a peace that was the essence of all movement, action. No virtue touched it for it was beyond all virtue and sanctions of man. There was love that was utterly perishable and so it had the delicacy of all new things, vulnerable, destructible and yet it was beyond all this. It was there imperishable, unnameable, the unknowing. No thought could ever touch it. It was 'pure', untouched so ever dyingly beautiful.

All this seemed to affect the brain; it was not as it was before. (Thought is such a trivial thing, necessary but trivial.) Because of it, relationship seems to have changed. As a terrific storm, a destructive earthquake gives a new course to the rivers, changes the landscape, digs deep into the earth, so it has levelled the contours of thought, changed the shape of the heart.

On July 27 Aldous Huxley and his second wife, Laura Archera (his first wife had died of cancer in 1955), arrived at Gstaad and stayed at the Palace Hotel for ten days. They went several times to hear K speak,—

... among the most impressive things I ever heard [Huxley wrote]. It was like listening to a discourse of the Buddha—such power, such intrinsic authority, such an uncompromising refusal to allow the *homme moyen sensuel* any escapes or surrogates, any *gurus*, saviours, *führers*, churches. 'I show you sorrow and the ending of sorrow'—and if you don't choose to fulfil the conditions for ending sorrow, be prepared, whatever gurus, churches etc you may believe in, for the indefinite continuance of sorrow.[25]

Huxley was evidently writing about K's sixth talk on August 6 wherein he dealt with sorrow. 'Time does not wipe away sorrow,' he had said in the course of it. 'We may forget a particular suffering, but sorrow is always there, deep down. And I think it is possible to wipe away sorrow in its entirety, not tomorrow, not in the course of time, but to see the reality in the present, and go beyond.'

At the first talk on July 25 he had spoken with an unusually stern authority:

What we are concerned with is the shattering of the mind so that a new thing can take place. And that is what we are going to discuss at all these meetings; how to bring about a revolution in the mind. There must be a revolution; there must be a total destruction of all the yesterdays, otherwise we shall not be able to meet the new. And life is always new, like love. Love has no yesterday or tomorrow; it is ever new ... So, if you are willing, if it is your intention also, we will go into the question of how to transform the dull, weary, frightened mind, the mind that is ridden with sorrow, that has known so many struggles, so many despairs, so many pleasures, the mind that has become so old and has never known what it is to be young. If you will, we will go into that. At least, I am going to go into it, whether you will or will not. The door is open and you are free to come and go. This is not a captive audience; so if you do not like it, it is better not to hear it; because what you hear, if you do not want to hear, becomes your despair, your poison. So you know from the very beginning what is the intention of the speaker: that we are not going to leave one stone unturned, that all the secret recesses of the mind are to be explored, opened up and the contents destroyed, and that out of that destruction there is to be the creation of something new, something totally different from any creation of the mind.

After the last talk on August 15, K wrote in his notebook: 'On waking this morning, there was again that impenetrable strength whose power is the benediction . . . During the talk it was there, untouchable and pure.' To read in print this talk is not as powerful as the others. Often people have felt when listening to K that a talk has been particularly revealing and inspiring; then, when they come to read it afterwards, they are somewhat disappointed. It is probable that during such special talks K has been experiencing this strange power, this benediction, and has conveyed it to his audience who have been inspired by the power rather than by his words.

*   *   *   *

On August 11 at Chalet Tannegg, an official committee had been formed for the purpose of inviting Krishnamurti to speak at Saanen in 1962 and subsequent years and making all arrangements for these gatherings which would be much larger in future. Doris Pratt, Léon de Vidas and Madame Nora Safra were among those who became members. Madame Safra, who lived at Chalet Isabelle at Gstaad, where K had stayed with her in 1957, supplied the necessary Swiss address for legalizing the Committee under Swiss law. It was intended that the Committee should function under the aegis of KWINC. K hoped that Saanen would become another Ommen as, indeed it has, with the difference that instead of staying in tents or huts, the ever-increasing numbers attending each year find accommodation at Saanen or other villages nearby. Those who wish to camp do so in the official Saanen camping ground.

When Doris Pratt wrote to tell Rajagopal about the formation of the Saanen Gatherings Committee it caused 'a strong reaction' in him. He feared that K was going to cut out Ojai altogether. This was not the intention, though in the event K did not return to Ojai until 1966. The tape-recordings of the Saanen meetings in '61, and those of K's earlier talks in London and subsequent talks in Paris, were sent to Rajagopal for publication by KWINC.

The editing, at Rajagopal's request, was done by Doris Pratt. Rajagopal still had complete control over all publication matters.

*   *   *   *

After the Gathering, K remained quietly at Chalet Tannegg for three weeks with Vanda Scaravelli. Throughout this time Vanda herself was constantly aware of 'the benediction', 'the otherness', whose presence K described every day in his notebook, and her account of it in her diary tallied very much with his, though seen from outside. For instance, in one entry she wrote, 'Just as we were sitting down, a different look came into his eyes for a few seconds. It was a look of strange immensity and such overwhelming strength that one felt out of breath.' And on another day: 'We were talking and suddenly that look spread out again. It was tremendous with the fire of destruction in it, and a flash of something incredibly strong, as if the essence of power and of all powers were focused in it.' And again:

In the late morning we had gone out for a drive in the car. An instant after K. had sat down next to me and was looking at the hills in front of us, a short shout came out of him and all his being became alive and intensely intent: the look in his eyes, his head, his hands, the whole body and with it, the whole mind, were a single thing focused in only one point; like a horse held still the moment before a race, when every part of it is in full tension and completely alert.

On August 1 she had written, 'This morning it was there, deeply pervading and invading each part of our being. It was there with softness and vigour, with immense largeness and generosity. Although very powerful it was gentle too, and easy to receive, like grace.'

K's entry for the same day—a very short one—reads: 'It was a beautiful day and driving in the beautiful valley there was that which was not to be denied; it was there as the air, the sky, the mountains. Woke up early, shouting, for the process was intense but during the day, in spite of the talk [his fourth talk at Saanen], it was going on with mildness.' Three days later he mentioned that 'the process' was acute but that it was not necessary to refer to it every day. Thereafter he did not refer to it at all, which did not mean that he did not continue to have the pain. The pain, 'the

116

process', seems to have been an integral part of 'the benediction'. He mentioned once in the journal that the pain did not exhaust him.

*   *   *   *

On September 4 K flew alone to Paris and stayed as usual with the Suarès in their eighth-floor apartment. He wrote on the day of his arrival that it was a violent change to be in the noisy town after the beauty of the villages and high mountains, yet, 'Sitting quietly in the afternoon, looking over the roof-tops . . . most un-expectedly, that benediction, that strength, that otherness came with gentle clarity; it filled the room and remained. It is here as this is being written.'

K gave nine talks in Paris between September 5 and 24. It was a trying time because there was a good deal of friction between Carlo Suarès and Léon de Vidas who each considered himself the chief organiser of the meetings. K was glad to get to Rome on the 25th where Vanda Scaravelli met him; after a visit with her to Circeno, near the sea between Rome and Naples, they returned to Rome and thence by train to Florence and on to Il Leccio. In his notebook K described the train journey without mentioning his destination, and how 'the drivers of the electric train welcomed us and asked us to come into their cabin for we had met several times in several years', and at Il Leccio on October 4 he was writing, 'There is a huge tall tree in the garden, it has an enormous trunk and during the night its dry leaves were noisy in the autumn wind.' This was the great ilex outside his window.

On October 18 K flew from Rome to Bombay; he then went on to Rishi Valley were he stayed a month. I have never been to Rishi Valley but I feel I know it intimately from K's lovely descriptions of it in his journal. While he was there he was corresponding with Doris Pratt about having his talks in London, Saanen and Paris translated into French, an idea he was very enthusiastic about. He was also greatly interested in plans for his talks in London and Saanen in 1962 which had been left to·Doris and Léon de Vidas to arrange. In December Doris wrote to Rajagopal asking for £1,000 to ensure the success of the next Saanen Gathering. Rajagopal replied that since he was being 'kept in the dark' about what was happening in Europe he could not concern himself with it.

In the third week in November K motored to Vasanta Vihar to give talks in Madras until December 17. The day after the last talk he wrote to Doris Pratt to say that Rajagopal had allowed Mr Madhavachari to record the talks on tape instead of taking them down in shorthand, but that he had only a very bad recorder, so would it be possible for someone in England to give a better one? A donation of £75 enabled a new recorder to be bought and sent to India. The fact that Rajagopal's permission had to be asked to record the talks is an example of the tight control he still exercised over some of K's affairs.

From Madras K went to Rajghat where he gave talks until January 14, 1962. Again, one gets to know Rajghat intimately from the journal. On January 20 he flew to Delhi where he stayed with his old friend Shiva Rao. He was to give eight talks there. On January 23 his journal stopped as abruptly as it had begun, possibly because it was so intensely cold in Delhi that he could hardly hold his pencil. On the 22nd he had written:

The mind is always occupied with something or other, however silly or supposedly important. It is like that monkey always restless, always chattering, moving from one thing to another... To be empty, completely empty, is not a fearsome thing; it is absolutely essential for the mind to be unoccupied, to be empty, unenforced, for then only can it move into unknown depths.

Part of the last entry reads:

... of a sudden that unknowable immensity was there, not only in the room and beyond but also deep, in the innermost recesses, which was once the mind... that immensity left no mark, it was there, clear, strong, impenetrable and unapproachable whose intensity was fire which left no ash. With it was bliss... The past and the unknown do not meet at any point; they cannot be brought together by any act whatsoever; there is no bridge to cross over nor a path that leads to it. The two have never met and will never meet. The past has to cease for the unknowable, for that immensity to be.

The publication of this extraordinary document in 1976 passed unnoticed by the press both in England and America except for a paragraph in the American *Publishers Weekly*, concluding, 'Krishnamurti's teaching is austere, in a sense annihilating.' One or two people among the handful who read the manuscript were

averse to its publication. They feared it would dishearten K's
followers. He maintains that human beings can transform themselves radically, not in time, not by evolution, but by immediate
perception, whereas the *Notebook* shows that Krishnamurti is not
an ordinary man transformed but a unique being existing in a
different dimension from ordinary humanity. It was a valid point
and I put it to him. His reply was, 'We do not all have to be
Edisons to turn on the electric light.' Later he was to say to a
journalist in Rome, who suggested that he had been born as he
was and that therefore others could not attain to his state of
consciousness, 'Christopher Columbus went to America in a
sailing ship; we can go by jet.' What he was trying to convey in
both these metaphors was, of course, that he had discovered
arduously how to free men from sorrow so that now anyone
could benefit from his discovery without having to go through
all that he had gone through.

11

Saanen and Chalet Tannegg

K gave twenty-three public talks altogether in India that winter as well as holding dozens of discussion meetings and giving innumerable private interviews. Over 4,000 people turned up for every talk. It was not perhaps surprising, therefore, that he was exhausted when he arrived in Rome on March 15. Vanda Scaravelli, who met him there, recorded that soon after his arrival he went down with fever:

His eyes were closed or half closed. This incident is not related to any of the previous accounts. There was no transformation in his face, he did not faint, and it was not at all similar to the things which had happened in Switzerland. The words came out simply and easily, and the way he spoke seemed rather natural: 'Don't leave me. He has gone far away, very far away. It has been told to you to look after him. He should not have gone out. You should have told him. At table he is not all there. You must tell him with a look so that other people don't see it, and he will understand. Nice face to look at. Those eyelashes are wasted for a man. Why don't you take them? That face has been very carefully worked out. They have worked and worked for so long, so many centuries, to produce such a body. Do you know him? You cannot know him. How can you know the running water? You listen. Don't ask questions. He must love you if he lets you come so near him. He is very careful not to allow his body to be touched by other people. You know how he treats you. He wants that nothing should happen to you. Don't do anything extravagant. All that travelling was too much for him. And those people in the plane, smoking, and all that packing all the time, arriving and going, it has been too much for the body. He wanted to arrive in Rome for that lady [Vanda]. Do you know her? He wanted to come quickly for her. He gets affected if she is not well. All that travelling—no, I am not complaining. You see how pure he is. He allows nothing for himself. The body has been all this time on the edge of a precipice. It has been held, it has been watched

K in 1900, aged five

K's mother, Jiddu Sanjeevamma

K in 1910 after his first Initiation

Rajagopal, Nitya and K at Ehrwald, Austria, 1923
K and Mrs Besant opening the Ommen Camp, 1926

C. Jinarajadasa, Bishop Leadbeater, Koos van der Leeuw, Rajagopal
and Rosalind Rajagopal at Castle Eerde, early thirties

The banyan tree theatre at Rishi Valley School

K in 1936

Lady Emily Lutyens
in old age

K in 1978

Rishi Valley

Brockwood Park, Hampshire, the south side

The Pavilion, the first building of the Oak Grove School, Ojai

J. G. Links, K, Mary Zimbalist and Mary Lutyens
at Deventer, Holland, 1981

K and Mary Lutyens, Deventer, 1981

K speaking at the Brockwood Park Gathering, 1972

K speaking at the Rishi Valley School, 1972

like mad all these months and if it lets go, he will go very far. Death is near. I told him it was too much. When he is in those airports he is by himself. He is not quite there. All that poverty in India, and the people die. Terrible. This body too would have died had it not been found [by Leadbeater]. And all that dirt everywhere. He is so clean. His body is kept so clean. He washes it with so much care. This morning he wanted to convey something to you. Don't stop him. He must love you. Tell him. Take a pencil, tell him: 'Death is always there, very close to you, to protect you. And when you take shelter you will die.'

When the fever left him they went up to Il Leccio where he soon fell very ill. He seems to have had a recurrence of his kidney trouble, complicated by a severe attack of mumps. He was so ill that for several nights Vanda slept on the floor outside his door. When he was better he asked Doris Pratt to keep very quiet about his illness because people 'worried too easily'.

Two months after leaving India he came to London where Doris Pratt had rented another furnished house for him at Wimbledon, 'Casa Romagna', 36 Ridgway Place (now replaced by Lantern House). Doris stayed with him there, Anneke Korndorffer came again to do the housekeeping and Joan Wright to drive him about. Public talks had been arranged at the Friends Meeting House and the Wimbledon Town Hall, and some meetings at the Community Centre, Wimbledon, for small invited groups for May and June.

Lady Emily was eighty-seven now and her memory was failing; nevertheless, K often went to see her and would sit holding her hand, quietly chanting to her, which she loved. He also visited Mrs Bindley. I drove him down a few times to Sussex to walk in our bluebell woods. During the drive he would ask after various members of my family and I would ask him about mutual friends in India. We never spoke of anything important in those days, and while walking in the woods we hardly talked at all. He delighted in the beauty of the woods, in the bird-song, the young beech leaves and the scent and sight of the thick mist of bluebells. He would frequently stop and look backwards through his legs at the blue carpet. I felt it was a relief to him not having to make conversation.

It was over thirty years since I had heard K speak, but on an impulse I went to his first evening talk at the Friends Meeting

House on June 7. While I seemed to understand what he was saying while he was actually talking I could not afterwards have given any coherent idea of it to someone who had never heard him. Even now I find I understand him with that sense, that intuition, which grasps the meaning of difficult poetry rather than through my intellect. But on this occasion I was watching him far more intently than I was listening. The hall was packed; people were standing at the back. I did not see him come on to the platform; at one moment the solitary hard chair placed in the centre of the platform was empty; the next moment he was sitting there on his hands, having made no sound on entering, a very slight figure, impeccably dressed in a dark suit, white shirt, dark tie, feet in highly polished brown shoes placed neatly side by side. He was alone on the platform. (He is never introduced and he never has any notes.) There was complete silence in the hall as a strong vibration of expectancy ran through the audience. He sat there quite silent, his body still, assessing his audience with slight movements of his head from side to side. One minute; two minutes; I began to panic for him. Had he broken down altogether? I was prickling all over in an anguish of concern for him when he suddenly began, unhurriedly in his rather lilting voice with its faint Indian accent, startling the silence.

This long silence at the beginning of a talk still disconcerts me. It is immensely impressive. But the reason for it is not to impress. He only rarely knows what he is going to say before he starts speaking and seems to look to his audience for guidance. This is why a talk frequently begins lamely: 'I wonder what the purpose is of a gathering such as this?' he may say, or, 'What do you expect from this?' Or he may begin a series of talks, 'I think it would be as well if we could establish a true relationship between the speaker and the audience.' At other times he knows exactly what he is going to say: 'I would like this evening to talk about knowledge, experience and time', but the talk that follows does not necessarily confine itself to those subjects. He is always insistent that he is not talking didactically, that he and the audience are taking part together in an investigation. He will remind the audience of this two or three times in the course of a talk.

On this particular evening at the Friends Meeting House he knew just what he wanted to say:

To understand what we are going to consider this evening and on succeeding evenings, needs a clear mind, a mind that is capable of direct perception. Understanding is not something mysterious. It requires a mind that is capable of looking at things directly, without prejudice, without personal inclinations, without opinions. What I want to say this evening concerns a total inward revolution, a destruction of the psychological structure of society, which we are. But the destruction of this psychological structure of society, which is you and me, does not come about through effort; and I think that is one of the most difficult things for most of us to understand.

Reading an authentic report of a talk, listening to it on cassette, even viewing him on video-tape, can never be the same as listening to him and seeing him in the flesh. The meaning behind the words comes through the physical presence of the man himself—there is an emanation that flashes a meaning direct to one's understanding, by-passing the mind, and whether one finds a talk more or less meaningful depends, I think, more on one's own state of receptivity than on what he says. I hate it when people ask me what Krishnamurti's teaching is all about. I want to snap back, 'What it's all about is what *you* are all about.' Instead I try to put my small understanding into words and fail utterly. How can I succeed when he has been trying for nearly sixty years to find words in which to convey an understanding of what to him is truth? I find all interpretations of his teaching hopelessly inadequate.

Although K sits on his hands when he first comes on to a platform, he gesticulates with one or both of them most expressively in the course of a talk, often spreading his fingers wide. His hands are a joy to watch. At the end of a talk he will slip away as unobtrusively as he entered. His audiences in India have always been far more demonstrative than in the West. He is acutely embarrassed by the demonstrative devotion he receives in India, by prostrations and efforts to touch him or his clothes. As he drives away from a meeting in India, hands reach out to take hold of his hands through the open car window. Recently he was horrified when a man seized his hand and engulfed it in his mouth.

*   *   *   *

On June 21 K left London for Paris, and after two nights flew to

Geneva where he was met by Vanda Scaravelli and motored up to Chalet Tannegg at Gstaad. In July the second gathering was held at Saanen—in a tent this year with a pre-fabricated dome invented by Buckminster Fuller, the American architect-designer. Holding about 900 people it was erected on a Swiss military air-strip and hired for ten meetings from July 22 to August 12. There were also some small discussion meetings after the talks in the Bellevue Hotel at Saanen.

K was not at all well after the meetings at the end of August so he decided to cancel his visit to India that winter and remain at Chalet Tannegg. He was consulting a urologist in Geneva and having treatment for a tooth. Rajagopal came over in October to see him in the hope of re-establishing their old relationship, but since Rajagopal wanted the reconciliation to be on his own terms and K still insisted on being put back on the Board of KWINC it did not take place. When Rajagopal left, though, he gave K enough money to pay his doctor's and dentist's bills.

From Gstaad Rajagopal went to Amsterdam where he put his point of view to Anneke Korndorffer who had worked for him and K since the early Ommen days. Anneke wrote to Doris Pratt on October 15:

It has been the strangest and yet the best meeting I ever remember having had with Raja. All the same I can hardly say a word about it; I feel dumb-founded, moved and deeply stirred.

Yet there is one picture that vividly remains with me. Krishnaji is a phenomenon—like a whirling fire, and everyone who attempts to get near him is bound to get scorched. That may be the very meaning of his appearance in this world.

When I carefully listen to Raja—without any thought or reaction of my own and with that deep feeling of warmth that has always been there—every word he says sounds true and right. He seems to have an excellent, exceptional mind, a very subtle and intelligent mind; he is also a courageous man. About *myself*, the only thing I can know is that I am very serious and just as keen to find out for myself what is true. Yet we all seem to walk on the edge of a precipice. I hope and pray that you and Rajagopal will both be able to say *everything*, and yet look at it all without saying 'yes' or 'no', and without losing the existing mutual affection. Krishnaji can drop any of us at any time. I think we all know that. The fact and method of *our* approaching *him* is nobody else's concern but our own. If we burn to death or break our necks, that is also our own concern and responsibility, and Krishnaji does not seem to care. He will let us clash; we are probably meant to do so. Krishnaji's outward appearances seem to be full of contradictions and discrepancies; yet what he says is Truth itself. A comet, a whirling flame of fire, always seems to have a lot of smoke all round its appearance.

Maybe one day I shall refrain altogether from coming near to him but go back to the happy ranks of those who only read his books.

Anneke is today one of K's staunchest adherents. She has not been dropped or burnt and continues to do valuable work for him. K does not drop people; they drop him. If they become possessive or feel they are essential to him or have an exclusive relationship with him, they are hurt when they discover that emotionally and psychologically he is not in the least dependent on them and that they can easily be supplanted. Disillusioned and jealous they then drift away from him. To expect gratitude from him for the work they have done is to court disappointment; he never asks or expects them to work for him personally, only for that truth to which his life is consecrated, and if new people come along who are able to contribute more in any way to the fulfilment of his teaching, they are 'taken up' and the old ones feel they have been 'dropped'. He is held by nothing and no one. He cannot be bought or flattered.

From Amsterdam Rajagopal came to London. Mrs Bindley, with whom he lunched, found him 'sincere, mellowed and kind'. I wish I could have said the same. I saw him on October 24 at Mount Royal, Oxford Street, where he was staying, and he was even more abusive of K than he had been the year before. I still had no idea what their quarrel was about. His main charges against K were that he was a hypocrite and cared too much about his appearance before he went on to a platform, making sure in a mirror that every hair was in place. Rajagopal offered no evidence of hypocrisy and it seemed to me that to care about his appearance before a public meeting merely showed respect for his audience; besides, Rajagopal must have known as well as I did that K has always cared very much for outward appearance, both his own and that of others. I urged Rajagopal more strongly than ever to leave K; it was not right for either of them that he should continue to work for him feeling as he did. I argued that he was entitled to a substantial pension after all the work he had done for KWINC and asked whether he could not leave Ojai and settle somewhere in Europe where he had many friends. I gathered that money was not a consideration. His real trouble seemed to be that he was completely obsessed by K and could not let go. It appeared to be a classic example of a love-hate relationship. I still felt great compassion for him. With his brains, education and organising ability he might have risen to a high position in India. I was delighted when I heard soon afterwards that he had married again. I felt so sure that domestic happiness would break his obsession.

*   *   *   *

K remained at Chalet Tannegg until Christmas. He then went with Vanda Scaravelli to Rome where he was introduced by her in the winter of 1963 to many prominent people—film directors, writers and musicians, including Fellini, Pontecorvo, Alberto Moravia, Carlo Levi, Segovia and Casals who played for him. Aldous Huxley came to Rome in March and saw K several times. This was their last meeting. Huxley died on November 22 in Los Angeles. A month after his death K wrote to me: 'Aldous Huxley told me a couple of years ago that he had cancer of the tongue; he told me he had told no one not even his wife. I saw him in Rome this spring and he looked fairly well and so it was a shock when I knew that he had gone. I hope he didn't suffer.'

In February it had been announced through the Krishnamurti mailing lists that in future K was to concentrate all his talks in Europe in one place—Saanen. When he came to London, therefore, in May there were no public meetings; instead he held ten small discussion groups for about eighty people at the Marlborough Hall, Wimbledon. Doris Pratt had rented for him the same house at Wimbledon as in 1961—19 Inner Park Road. Anneke Korndorffer was there again and Joan Wright. K was rather ill most of the time he was there. He visited Mrs Bindley and my mother. My mother had now completely lost her memory, yet her face would light up radiantly when she saw him and he would stay just as long with her, holding her hand and chanting to her. She never lost her joy in seeing him, even though she was not sure who he was.

On May 28 he left London for Gstaad. In June my husband and I stopped a night at Gstaad on our way to Venice by car. We went up to Tannegg to see K who was all alone there except for the Signora's Italian cook. He was most welcoming, seemed pleased to show us over the chalet and then took us for a drive in the mountains in the Mercedes owned by the Saanen Committee. We had the impression that the car was cherished, seldom used, and cleaned and polished by him every time it returned from even the shortest run. Continuing into Italy we stopped at the castle-hotel at Pergine where we had all been together with Nitya in the summer of 1924 and where K's 'process' had been so agonising. I sent him a post-card of the round tower where he had stayed. He replied, 'I can't remember a thing about it; it might be of any other castle. It's so completely blotted out of my mind.'

The Saanen Gathering was in July. K gave ten talks in the same domed tent, but situated now by the side of the Saanen river, the site where the Saanen Gatherings were to be held thereafter, though the land had not yet been bought. The only disadvantage of this site was that it was close to a railway and K had to pause three times during an hour's talk while the noisy little local train went by. The talks, which ended on July 28, were again followed by a week of daily discussions with a small group at the Bellevue Hotel. K was feeling much better in health. Marcelle de Manziarly and the Suarès were among those who attended all the talks and discussions. The Yehudi Menuhins and their children, who were staying at Gstaad, came to lunch one day at Tannegg, and another day the Charles Lindberghs lunched there. Doris Pratt could not be at Saanen this year because she had shingles, so Mary Cadogan, who ran the London office, took her place in helping K with his correspondence and with arranging the private interviews he gave. She recalls:

It was an interesting experience to see how Krishnaji dealt with his correspondence. I remember sitting in the room with him at Chalet Tannegg confronted with a pile of letters that had not been opened. Krishnaji said, 'How shall we deal with them?' I suggested that we should open the letters and that then they should be sorted into three piles—those requiring interviews; those requiring some other kind of answers; and those which were really simply letters or poems of adulation which did not require answering. He thought this was a very good idea, but I realised, when trying to sort them out, that he did not have sufficient interest in the sorting process to put them on the right piles. He was, however, very sympathetic about the way in which the interviews were organized. It was extremely moving to see him sometimes just before and just after he had seen certain people who came to him with very serious problems.

A newcomer was at Saanen this summer who, not long afterwards, was to play for a time a considerable part in K's life. This was the thirty-five-year old Alain Naudé, a South African of Huguenot descent. A professional pianist, who had studied in Paris and Siena and given concerts in Europe, Naudé was at this time a lecturer at the University of Pretoria. Drawn since boyhood to the spiritual life and having read of Krishnamurti, he had come to Saanen during the vacation to hear him speak. He met K personally and went to India that winter while K was there but did not see much of him. When he returned to Pretoria early in 1964 he resigned his position at the University in order to devote himself entirely to the religious life, though at that time there was no question of his working for K. He played at his last public concert in May '64.

In September 1963 K had come to London for a few days before going to India in October. It was the last time he saw my mother. She died of an aneurism on January 3, 1964. I cabled the news to K and he replied from Madras on January 16:

Life's a strange business. One could not have wished for Mum to go on living but all the same, London won't be the same. It has been a long friendship, more than that, for nearly fifty-two years, almost one's whole life. What we have all been through! It will be very strange, all the same, not to see her. I loved her.

K has not forgotten her. Often, now I am old, I remind him of her. He will say with pleasure, 'You looked just like Mum then.' He remembers in particular a turquoise and diamond ring she always wore which I inherited. I wear it now whenever I see him because I know he likes it. Occasionally I have asked him to wear it for me while we are lunching together in London. He puts it on his little finger and when he gives it back the diamonds are sparkling brilliantly. This is not imagination. The first time it happened I saw one of my grand-daughters just after lunch and she exclaimed, 'You have had your ring cleaned! How lovely it looks!'

*   *   *   *

K gave talks in the usual places in India between October and March '64. There is a particularly memorable passage in the fourth talk he gave in Bombay on February 16:

> I am going to describe a scene that took place [at Rajghat]. It actually happened. We [meaning himself] were sitting on the bank of a river, very wide, of an evening. The crows were coming back from across the river, and the moon was just coming over the trees. And there was a man sitting beside us. He was a sanyasi. He did not notice the water and the moon on the water. He did not notice the song of that village man, he did not notice the crows coming back; he was so absorbed in his own problem. And he began to talk quietly with a tremendous sense of sorrow. He was a lustful man, he said, brutal in his demands, never satisfied, always demanding, asking, pushing, driving; and he was striving and he was driven for many years to conquer it. And at last he did the most brutal thing to himself; and from that day he was no longer a man. And as you listened you felt an extraordinary sorrow, a tremendous shock, that a man in search of God could mutilate himself for ever. He had lost all feeling, all sense of beauty. All that he was concerned with was to reach God. He tortured himself, butchered himself, destroyed himself, in order to find that thing which he called God. And as it got dark, the stars came out full, wide, with immense space; and he was totally unaware. And most of us live that way. We have brutalized ourselves through different ways, so completely. We have formed ideas, we live with formulas. All our actions, all our feelings, all our activities are shaped, controlled, subjugated, dominated by the formulas which society, the saints, the religious, the experiences that one has had, have established. These formulas shape our lives, our activity, our being.

K stopped in Rome on his way back from India and then came to London on April 20. Yet another house was taken for him in Wimbledon, 27a St Mary's Road, and Doris Pratt, Anneke Korndorffer and Joan Wright were with him there again. He gave several talks in the first two weeks of May at the Kenneth Black Memorial Hall, Wimbledon, from which many people were turned away disappointed because it was full. I took him down to see our bluebells as usual. My mother's death had made no difference to our friendship one way or another; it was an impersonal relationship. I had no problems of a kind I wanted to talk over with him and he did not mention to me anything about Rajagopal or any other troubles. It made me happy to think that he could be completely relaxed with me. We always seemed to have perfect weather for these bluebell outings.

K went on to Paris in the middle of May where he stayed with the Suarès for a fortnight and gave some talks. He then flew to Geneva and motored from there with Vanda Scaravelli to Chalet Tannegg. The Saanen Gathering, which began on July 10 that year, brought Alain Naudé to Gstaad again. It also brought Mary Zimbalist who was soon to make an incalculable difference to K's outward life. Still living at Malibu, Mrs Zimbalist had hoped to hear K speak again at Ojai as she had done in 1960, but when it seemed unlikely that he would speak there again she decided to go to Saanen to hear him. She went to all the talks, met Vanda Scaravelli and, when the talks were over, arranged an appointment through another Italian for an interview with K at Tannegg on August 5. The interview lasted an hour and a half. Afterwards K asked her to stay on at Gstaad to attend some small private discussions he was to hold from August 15. At one of these meetings she met Alain Naudé and they became friends. When she returned to Malibu she got in touch with Rajagopal and went to Ojai at his invitation to listen to tape-recordings of the discussions she had heard at Gstaad.

The land on which the tent was erected for the Saanen Gatherings could no longer be rented after this summer because the owner wanted to sell. 1¾ acres, with a river flowing by and woods on two sides, it was the only completely flat land at Saanen; consequently the Saanen Committee, a legally independent body from KWINC, decided to buy it. Rajagopal agreed to put up the purchase price of $50,000 on the understanding that after K's death the land should revert to KWINC.

Mr Burdick was now dead and his Aerograph Company had ceased to pay dividends. The shares, now considered practically worthless, had been given by Rajagopal to Doris Pratt (they were already held in her name it may be remembered).* Since there

* The Company was afterwards taken over by an American organisation and Doris received a considerable sum for her shares, which she has used for K's work.

was no money left in the Burdick account, other financial arrangements had to be made for K. While at Saanen that August, Doris, as a member of the Saanen Committee, sent a memorandum to Rajagopal with the following suggestions:—that the Saanen Committee should pay all K's personal expenses while he was anywhere in Europe (this would free K from having to account to Rajagopal for every penny he spent on himself as he had had to do in the past and which he now strongly objected to doing); that all expenses connected with his work in England and his travelling in Europe should come from KWINC funds raised in England, and that his fares to and from India and America and his expenses in those countries should be paid by KWINC, Ojai. It was also urged that for reasons of health K must in future travel first class by air. Rajagopal returned the memorandum without comment but with initialled agreement to all these points except the one about K travelling first class which he left blank.

12

New Friends

K was back again in India in October after a stop in Rome. He spoke in Madras, Bombay, New Delhi and Rajghat as usual. Alain Naudé went to India again independently and it was while he was there this time that K invited him to work for him as 'a kind of secretary' for a small salary, and travel with him wherever he went. Naudé accepted the offer and returned with K to Rome in February 1965 where Vanda Scaravelli was very welcoming and gracious to him. Naudé's appointment only became official, however, after Rajagopal gave his approval of it. K asked Doris Pratt to approach Rajagopal in the matter, fearing that the request would be refused if he asked Rajagopal himself. The latter agreed to pay Naudé's salary and travelling expenses out of Ojai funds.

In April Naudé accompanied K to London and stayed with him at the same house in Wimbledon as had been rented the year before, 27a St Mary's Road; Anneke Korndorffer was there again as well as Doris Pratt. K gave six talks in April and May at the Kenneth Black Memorial Hall. Naudé was now in charge of the tape-recording. As usual the tapes were sent by air to Rajagopal.

One morning at the end of April when I joined K at Huntsman, his tailor in Savile Row, I met Alain Naudé for the first time. There was an immediate rapport between us. I had not known of his existence until that meeting. When on May 5 I drove K down to Sussex for our customary bluebell walk I asked about him. K, who was in high spirits, spoke with enthusiasm of Naudé's having given up his musical career to lead a religious life. It was evidently a great joy to K to have someone so congenial to travel with him, and give him the help he needed in so many practical ways. K felt naturally drawn to Alain who, though serious minded, was lighthearted, energetic and fun to be with. K could laugh with him as he laughed with Sacha de Manziarly. K has a particularly infectious laugh. I have frequently seen him laugh till he cries at some silly joke.

Mary Zimbalist had also come to London in April but I did not meet her on this visit. She went to all K's talks at Wimbledon and hired a car to take him and Naudé for drives to Boxhill and Wisley Gardens. When K and Alain flew to Paris she went too, and hired a Mercedes to take them for drives to Versailles, St Germain, Chartres and Rambouillet—pleasures normally denied to K in his outwardly dull existence. She also went to his five talks at the Salle Adyar in Paris between May 16 and 30.

When K and Alain arrived at Gstaad from Paris on June 5 Mary Zimbalist was already installed there, at K's suggestion, in part of a chalet, Les Caprices. Vanda Scaravelli was in America where her married daughter was living and did not arrive until July 4; meanwhile, she had opened up Tannegg for K and Alain and sent her cook to look after them. A new Mercedes had just been given by a generous friend to the Saanen Committee, though it was intended for K's use. After driving Mary in it to Château d'Oex—its first outing—K washed and polished it with infinite care.

After the talks and discussions which lasted until August 29, Mary flew back to California while K and Naudé remained at Gstaad until the middle of September when they went to stay with Vanda at Il Leccio. Mary rejoined them in Rome at the end of October and flew with them to Delhi on November 1. She travelled round with them to all the usual places where K gave talks. In December K received an unexpected invitation from Rajagopal to speak at Ojai in October '66. This he accepted.

The Indian Prime Minister, Lal Bahadur Shastri, died on January 11, 1966, and Indira Gandhi, a great friend of Pupul Jayakar, became Prime Minister on January 22. By that time K was at Rishi Valley, still with Mary and Alain. It was not until March 6, after public talks in Bombay and many private discussions, that they flew back to Rome. There Mary left them to return to California while they went to Il Leccio again.

K arrived in England with Alain on April 22. This time Doris Pratt had taken a house for them at 4 Ullswater Close, Kingston Vale; as usual Anneke Korndorffer came to keep house and Joan Wright to do the shopping. K could now take his regular long afternoon walks in Richmond Park instead of on Wimbledon Common. Mary Zimbalist arrived in London on the 25th and took delivery of a new Jaguar she had ordered in which she drove K somewhere every day during the three weeks he was at Kingston Vale—weeks in which he gave five talks at the Friends Meeting House as well as many private interviews. He also recorded a broadcast which was later in the year transmitted on the Third Programme of the BBC, and he made his first flexible gramophone record, *The Ending of Sorrow*.

My husband and I were at our Sussex house one week-end in May when, returning from an afternoon walk, we saw three figures approaching us along the lane. They turned out to be K, Alain Naudé and Mary Zimbalist who had come to see us unexpectedly after picnicking in the car. The new Jaguar looked incongruously grand outside our cottage door. This was my first meeting with Mary Zimbalist. What struck me most about her was her extreme elegance and quiet voice with the gentlest possible American accent. She had spent a great deal of her life in Europe and had many friends in England. She was truly cosmopolitan, speaking French and Italian fluently. K seemed extremely happy and on the spot with these new companions. From that time onwards my friendship with Mary and Alain grew steadily, though with Alain more rapidly because we corresponded.

Anneke Korndorffer had a hard time running the household at Ullswater Close, for there were always people to lunch and tea. 'Needless to say,' Doris Pratt reported to Rajagopal a few days after K's departure from London, 'Krishnaji himself was always helpful, considerate and deeply solicitous. Naudé also was always thoughtful and happily humorous. He goes everywhere with Krishnaji and being young, strong and very sensitive, he is quite invaluable.' Doris Pratt went on to say that she did not think she could go on any longer making all the arrangements for K in England but that Mary Cadogan, with K's approval, had consented to carry on in her place. She added, 'It seems to me the time has come when I can rightly and happily resign as Agent from KWINC. At the moment I can still manage the Saanen Committee work but I feel that Mary should be responsible direct to you in future, legally as well as morally.' Rajgopal merely replied that he would consider the situation, and there the matter rested for almost two years.

*   *   *   *

K with Naudé and Mary Zimbalist left London on May 12. They took the car over by air ferry from Lydd to Le Touquet and after two nights in Normandy drove to Paris where K gave talks until May 29. This was the last time he stayed with Carlo and Nadine Suarès. On May 31 Mary drove him and Alain to Geneva. K had warned her that he was liable to faint in the car; she must take no notice and just drive on. Sure enough, on the autoroute soon after leaving Paris, he fainted quietly and slowly into her lap. After a few seconds he came to with a cry and was at once perfectly normal. This was to happen quite frequently in the future when she was driving him.

A month's holiday followed, staying alternatively at the Hotel du Rhone in Geneva and Les Caprices at Gstaad which Mary had rented again that year. They went for many expeditions, saw a number of films and did a great deal of walking. A Volkswagen was bought for Alain so that he could drive K when Mary was not there and take most of the luggage when the three of them travelled together. A young yoga teacher, Desikachar, nephew of Iyenger and son of Krishnamacharya, the best-known yoga guru in south India, had been invited to Gstaad that year to teach K new exercises and was there for most of the summer. For years K has done yoga every morning for the sake of his health, not as a spiritual practice to awaken higher energies. The yoga he does is Raja Yoga, king of yoga. K has explained it himself as 'part of a highly moral life—not to hurt, drink or drug yourself'. 'You will never awaken spiritual insight by exercises,' he maintains.

When Vanda Scaravelli arrived at Tannegg K moved up there from Les Caprices. The Saanen Gathering started on July 10 and lasted until August 9. K's bronchitis was troubling him again at this time and he became a patient of the homoeopathic doctor, Pierre Schmidt, in Geneva.

Frederick Pinter had recently died and K was very anxious when he went to New York before going to Ojai in October to stay there with Mary and Alain; Mary, therefore, cabled to the brother who agreed to lend them his apartment in New York for the visit. K also wanted to stay with Mary and Alain when he went to Paris the following spring, preferably somewhere outside the city. Mary promised to look for accommodation for them. She was able to reassure K completely when he worried about her spending too much money on his comfort. But the most important plan discussed that summer was the possibility of starting a Krishnamurti school somewhere in Europe. An American friend had offered K a large sum with which to buy a permanent home for himself if and when he retired. Not intending ever to retire, he asked if he might use the money to start a school, a request which was at once granted. It was an exciting project. Switzerland, Holland, France: where should it be? Lunching with me the next time he came to London, K asked me where I would live for preference. When I told him that there was nowhere I wanted to live except England he thought I was joking. Until that moment I do not think he had considered the possibility of having the school in England. In spite of being brought up there it was not a country he was at all fond of.

On September 1 Mary Zimbalist left the Jaguar at Thun to be stored for the winter and flew back to California while K and Alain drove to Rome where K held some discussion meetings until the 20th. They then flew to New York and stayed with Mary in her brother's apartment on Fifth Avenue at 93rd Street. On the 26th K was to give the first of six talks at the New School for Social Research in New York, continuing until October 7. During this time in New York he met Ralph Ingersol, journalist and author, Tim Leary, the psychologist, and Allen Ginsberg, the poet, who had collaborated with Leary in anti-war propaganda in 1961. K also met two men he already knew quite well who happened to be in New York and who were soon to become more closely associated with him—Count Hughes van der Straten, a Belgian industrialist, and Gérard Blitz, founder of the Club Méditerranée.

Alain Naudé, who was eager for K to come in contact with more young people, had arranged for him to speak at Harvard, so on October 16 he flew to Boston with Alain and Mary for discussions with students at Lowell House. Two days later the three of them flew to Los Angeles and for the first time K went to stay at Mary's beautiful house at Malibu on a cliff overlooking the ocean.

On the 28th they moved to Ojai. K, who had not been there for over five years, stayed in Pine Cottage; Alain slept in a room which had been added to it, and Mary in the office flat which Rajagopal had offered to her if she would drive K during the period of his talks. Although they all had meals with Rosalind at Arya Vihara, K's friendship with her was no longer a close one after his long absence and was soon to cease altogether.

On October 29 K held the first of six talks in the Oak Grove. He had not spoken there since May 1960. Before the third talk on November 3, a television crew was set up and for the first time a talk of his was filmed. This talk was concerned, as were all his talks fundamentally, with how to bring about a radical revolution in the human mind. Without such a revolution there could be no real change in society, no real joy, no peace in the world. His words should be a mirror, he said, in which his listeners could see what was actually taking place within themselves.

The expected and hoped for reconciliation between K and Rajagopal resulting from the invitation to speak at Ojai did not take place although they met alone two or three times. K also saw James Vigeveno, the Vice-President of KWINC, and Mima Manziarly Porter, one of the trustees, both of whom he had known for years, but they seemed unable or unwilling to help. K insisted again that he was responsible for KWINC and wanted to be informed and consulted about its affairs and re-instated on the Board. Rajagopal adamantly denied that K had any responsibility for it. K also asked for the return of the journal he had written in 1961–62 which had been sent to Ojai and was now in the archives there; this Rajagopal refused to give up. When K returned to Malibu on November 18 the split between them was even more painfully ragged than before. Distrust of, and resentment against, K's new friends had not helped the situation. The next day K and Alain flew to Rome while Mary remained at Malibu.

*　　　　*　　　　*　　　　*

When K flew from Rome to Delhi on December 11 Alain flew to Pretoria to see his parents. K's programme in India followed its traditional round. The 1967 talks in India were the last ever to be published by KWINC.

On March 6, 1967, K was back in Rome again where he stayed with Vanda Scaravelli and gave three public talks at the Istituto Pedagogia. Alain Naudé and Mary Zimbalist joined him there and the three of them moved on April 11 to the house near Paris which Mary had taken for K, 11 rue de Verdun, Boulogne-Billancourt. Although there was a part-time maid who went with the house, Mary did most of the cooking. During the month they stayed there K gave talks in the Salle de la Chimie. He saw the Suarès frequently and also Marcelle de Manziarly and her brother Sacha.

K left Paris with Mary on May 10 in the Jaguar she had fetched from Thun, and with Alain following in the Volkswagen, they drove to Huizen, near Amsterdam, where Anneke Korndorffer had rented a thatched farmhouse for them. K was not to go to London that spring; instead he gave five talks at the great RAI Hall in Amsterdam where he had not spoken since 1956. Students from the University of Utrecht came one day to the farmhouse to hold a discussion with him, and sixty other young Dutch people came on another day.

My husband and I, who happened to be in Holland, went to Huizen on May 20 to have tea with K and the others. Just as we were leaving, K asked me out of the blue if I would do a book for him. To my amazement I heard myself saying 'Yes'. Then I asked, 'What kind of book?' 'Something based on the talks? I leave it to you,' he replied. The rest of my summer was overshadowed by the enormity of what I had let myself in for. I did not consider going back on my undertaking but I could not for the life of me think what kind of book it was going to be. The first thing obviously was to read some of K's talks which I had not done for nearly forty years. When I returned to London I asked Doris Pratt what she considered to be the best talks of recent years. She recommended those of 1963–64 and in due course sent me the four volumes of authentic reports of talks in India and Europe for those years. I did not so much as open them for several months.

* * * *

K and his two friends left Huizen on June 2 in the two cars and drove to Gstaad, spending three nights in Germany on the way. They all stayed at Les Caprices until July 1 when Vanda Scaravelli arrived and K moved up to Tannegg. A few days before this move he had been in bed with fever. Mary believed he was delirious when he became childish in voice and manner, looked at her without recognition and spoke of 'Krishna going away'. .He asked her whether she had 'questioned Krishna', adding, 'He doesn't like to be questioned. After all these years I'm not used to him.' This was not delirium, of course, but part of 'the process' which Mary did not as yet seem to know about.

Desikachar, the young yoga teacher, was at Gstaad again by invitation, and Nandini Mehta came for a visit with her daughter. Gérard Blitz, whom it may be remembered K had seen in New York the previous year, was also there and was elected a member of the Saanen Gatherings Committee. Sacha de Manziarly, who was now French Consul in Geneva, came frequently to Tannegg, and K also saw the Walter Lippmans several times that summer. Rajagopal rang up twice from Ojai at the end of July but the conversations were unsatisfactory.

During the time the Saanen talks were going on in July there was much discussion about the school K wanted to start in Europe. He had now met the person who above all others was to make the dream possible—Dorothy Simmons, a sculptor, who had exhibited in London and New York. Mrs Simmons had first become interested in K from reading *The First and Last Freedom*; her husband, Montague, had recently retired from running a Government school for eighteen years so they were free and eager to meet a new challenge. Mrs Simmons's enthusiasm for the new school was only matched by K's own. Gérard Blitz, who was also keenly interested in the prospect of a school, was ready with financial advice. There were several meetings at Tannegg for all those concerned with the school project, and a School Committee was formed.

Before K flew from Geneva to Paris on September 5, he had persuaded Mary Zimbalist to exchange her Jaguar for a Mercedes, his favourite make of car, to be delivered the following year. Mary had motored ahead of him to Paris. They stayed a few days at the Westminster Hotel before going on to London where the house in Ullswater Close, Kingston Vale, had been rented again. Alain Naudé, driving direct from Gstaad, joined them there. This year Mary did the housekeeping with the help of an Italian maid. It was decided during this visit that the new school was to be in

England, chiefly because Mrs Simmons, who was to be the Principal, would not be able to run it so efficiently in a foreign country.

I went to two of K's small discussion groups at Ullswater Close. During one of them K asked, 'What is it that we want for our children?' I piped up with, 'Happiness.' It was, apparently, the wrong answer and I was badly snubbed by K. Evidently I did not begin to understand him. When he asked me how I was getting on with the book, I replied evasively that I had not yet quite decided how to tackle it.

There is no better way, of course, to understand a subject than to have to write about it. It seems incredible to me now that I had had the cheek to agree to write this book when I was so completely ignorant of K's teaching (he could not have realised just how ignorant); more incredible still perhaps that having undertaken the task I should have delayed almost six months before reading a word of his. Some time that winter of '67 I began reading the talks Doris Pratt had sent me. I am a compulsive worker, anyway, but never have I worked with such concentrated avidity and excitement as I did on that first book for K. I found that pronouncements of his, such as 'Ideals are brutal things' and 'I will try, is the most dreadful statement one can make', revolutionized my thinking. The subjects he spoke about were inextricably mingled in each talk and there was necessarily a great deal of repetition, for he was speaking to different audiences in many different places. The repetitions, though, were never in quite the same words; some were more clearly or more beautifully expressed than others. I made an index from the four volumes of what I considered to be the best expressions of his ideas under such headings as Awareness, Conditioning, Consciousness, Death, Fear, Freedom, God, Love, Meditation etc. It was a long business; there were over a hundred headings. I then wove them into a book of 124 pages divided into sixteen chapters, giving them, I hoped, a sequence, a build-up, for better understanding. Every word was K's own; I did not add so much as a conjunction; all I was responsible for was the selection and arrangement. Since I was learning as I went along, I consider this book a Krishnamurti primer. It was published in 1969. The title, *Freedom from the Known*, was chosen by K himself.

The chapter on love is the one I find the most beautiful and the most shattering:

The demand to be safe in relationship inevitably breeds sorrow and fear. This seeking for security is inviting insecurity. Have you ever found security in any of your relationships? Have you? Most of us want the security of loving and being loved, but is there love when each one is seeking his own security, his own particular path? We are not loved because we don't know how to love . . . When you say you love God what does it mean? It means that you love a projection of yourself clothed in certain forms of respectability according to what you think is noble and holy; so to say, 'I love God', is absolute nonsense. When you worship God you are worshipping yourself—and that is not love . . . This belonging to another, being psychologically nourished by another, depending on another—in all this there must be anxiety, fear, jealousy, guilt, and so long as there is fear there is no love; a mind ridden with sorrow will never know what love is . . . Don't you know what it really means to love somebody—to love without hate, without jealousy, without anger, without wanting to interfere with what he is doing or thinking, without condemning, without comparing—don't you know what it means? When you love someone with all your heart, with all your mind, with all your body, with your entire being, is there comparison? . . . Sorrow and love cannot go together . . . So when you ask what love is you may be frightened to know the answer.[26]

Another passage in this book spoke very directly to me: 'To be free of all authority, of your own and that of another, is to die to everything of yesterday, so that your mind is always fresh, always young, innocent, full of vigour and passion.'

I found one of the most difficult concepts to grasp, central to K's teaching, was that of the observer being no different from what was observed, the thinker no different from his thought. The mind creates images:

One image, as the observer, observes dozens of other images around himself and inside himself . . . there is a central image put together by all the other images, and this central image, the observer, is the censor, the experiencer, the evaluator, the judge who wants to conquer or subjugate the other images or destroy them altogether. But other images are the results of judgments, opinions and conclusions of the observer, and the observer is the result of all the other images— therefore the observer *is* the observed.

I was intoxicated during the three months or so it took me to compile this book—working often nine hours a day with an absorption that shut out all other duties. I could now understand the people who had told me that Krishnamurti had changed their lives. My thinking would never be the same again. It so happened at this time that a great friend of mine was devastated with misery because her lover of many years had fallen in love with a younger woman. I wrote to her frequently, expounding K's conception of love. There is no doubt it helped her, and she in her turn was able to help the lover when the younger woman deserted him. My friend won through to a devoted friendship with him which lasted until her death.

13

The New Foundation

Mary Zimbalist flew back to California early in October when K and Alain went from London to Rome on their way to India where they stayed from October 21 until the following February 1968. Gérard Blitz, who had to be in California in December, had offered to look into the affairs of KWINC while he was there and to go and see Rajagopal in an effort to break the deadlock. The result of his enquiries, as outlined by K in the statement below, written in Bombay on January 25, 1968, was most disturbing, though it did explain Rajagopal's reiterated assertion that K had no responsibility for the finances of KWINC.

Mr Blitz, whom I have known for several years, asked if he could help me in any way. I considered this offer carefully and then asked him, since he goes to California so often on business, if he would see Rajagopal and see what could be done. I gave him a brief resumé of the situation with Rajagopal, but told him that I did not under any circumstances want to go to court or hurt Rajagopal. So later that year he saw Rajagopal [he had a fruitless seven-hour conversation with him at Ojai on December 17, 1967]. From his lawyers' inquiry the following was revealed.

There were for a number of years two parallel organisations, each legally independent of each other: there was first of all the Star Publishing Trust, founded in 1923 or 1924 by me, and over which I had complete control, and then there was the Ojai Star Institute, founded in 1928 or 1929 by Rajagopal and a small committee of his own, over which he had complete control. The Star Publishing Trust which I founded in Holland was later changed to Krishnamurti Writings Incorporated. Now as I was not interested in the administrative details of KWINC, and as Rajagopal was extremely secretive about administrative matters, I always naturally signed everything he asked me to sign. I had complete confidence in his integrity. That is how I signed a paper, apparently, transferring all the assets of KWINC Holland to the Star Institute, over which Rajagopal had complete control. This happened in 1956. Of course I had no idea that I was doing this, as Rajagopal did not explain to me what I was signing. So he is now in complete control of all the assets of KWINC, which are considerable, which run into millions of dollars. Also I have signed away to this body which he now controls completely the copyright of everything published under my name. This is what had been revealed to Mr Blitz in his investigations and subsequent conversation with Rajagopal.

So this is the situation as it now stands. When I see Mr Blitz in the Spring I shall decide definitely what is to be done. I shall certainly not go to court whatever happens, for it is an unthinkable thing for me ever to go to court over anything. Rajagopal knows this as I told him so repeatedly in Ojai in 1966.

After receiving Monsieur Blitz's report in Bombay, K asked Alain Naudé to write on his behalf to Mr Vigeveno, the Vice-President of KWINC, to say that he would have nothing more to do with KWINC as long as Rajagopal was at the head of it and therefore would accept no more money from it, and neither would Naudé. On February 14, K and Alain flew to Rome and five weeks later went to London where they stayed at the White House, comfortable service flats with a restaurant attached, near Regent's Park. Mary Zimbalist had been in London since March 10 and had booked the flat for them and herself. Their reason for coming to London was to see a solicitor, Michael Rubinstein, of Rubinstein, Nash & Co, an expert on copyright law. Gérard Blitz was also in London and several discussions were held with him and Mr Rubinstein about the KWINC situation.

Early in April, K, Mary and Alain went to Paris where Mary had rented the same house as the year before at Boulogne-Billancourt. This time she had engaged a French chef because so many people came to meals. As well as giving talks in Paris at the Maison de la Chimie and many interviews, K found time to go to several cinemas. Mima Porter happened to be in Paris on a visit, K asked her to lunch on April 11 and told her that he had received no answer from Rajagopal to his many letters. Apparently Rajagopal had not shown K's letters to the other trustees as K had requested him to do. K further told Mrs Porter that if he did not hear from Rajagopal by a certain date he would be forced to disassociate himself altogether from KWINC. Mrs Porter said that as soon as she returned to Ojai she would see Rajagopal and try to resolve matters.

While he was in London K had informed Doris Pratt and Mary Cadogan about the situation with Rajagopal and had asked Mrs Cadogan not to send any more information about his work to Ojai. When, therefore, Mary Cadogan was asked by Rajagopal to send him the quarterly accounts and statements from the London office as she had been doing for the past ten years, she wrote to him on April 17 telling him frankly that K had told her that he did not want to have anything more to do with KWINC while he, Rajagopal, was at the head of it. She ended this letter:

> For me the present situation is an extremely sad one . . . It is not easy to write this letter to you, as we have always had a good working and personal relationship in the past. But it seems to me that the most important thing is for Krishnaji's work to be able to continue, freely and fully, all over the world. Therefore I wish to do all I can to help with this work, which as I see it must mean respecting Krishnaji's wishes about how the work should be carried out.

It was Byron Casselberry, Rajagopal's assistant, not Rajagopal himself, who replied to this on April 24. He said that Rajagopal had been very shocked by her letter; he respected her freedom to help or not help whoever she chose but the question was not whether she preferred to work with Krishnaji or with Rajagopal; she was the assistant of Doris Pratt, legal Agent of KWINC, Ojai, and as such it was an obligation on her to send the requested statements. If she and Doris Pratt wished to resign their responsibility to KWINC, Ojai, she should immediately take steps to account for all the property of KWINC now in her possession. He added that he was sending a copy of this letter to Doris Pratt.

Mary Cadogan replied direct to Rajagopal, '. . . you will I feel sure understand that my obligation, moral, and probably legal too, must be to the work as defined by Krishnaji himself.' Doris Pratt also answered Casselberry's letter direct to Rajagopal:

> As you know, dear Raja, our association—yours and mine, Mary's and yours, and mine and Mary's—has never been primarily a legal one. The whole basis of our relationship, both business and personal, has been founded not merely on mutual respect, trust and affection but much more fundamentally and deeply on our desire to help Krishnaji

in his tremendous work. That has been the only imperative, and it has kept me going now for some 45 years.

Rightly or wrongly, I have always felt that in working for KWINC, Ojai, I was helping, in however tiny a measure, to forward the work of Krishnaji and naturally I have never doubted—until comparatively recently, that you as the President of KWINC, Ojai, had also the sole aim of interpreting and fulfilling the wishes of Krishnaji himself.

I cannot convey the grief I felt, and the shock, when I came face to face with what appears to be the actual fact,—that for many years you have not only neglected to share the basic running of the KWINC organization with your Board of colleagues, but that you have even refused to allow Krishnaji himself—for whose sake the whole thing was founded—to participate.

If this is not accurate, then for God's sake tell me so, and make clear what your attitude is and has been. I feel you owe that much to me, Raja, for it seems to me that it is the functioning of the KWINC, Ojai, which may be illegal all this time, and which will now force Mary to confine her activities to acting as custodian of the funds, books and documents at Horsham [where the Cadogans were now living] until such time as she can again discuss the matter with Krishnaji himself and with others who feel concerned.

The work at Horsham will continue and must continue. Letters and books are being sent out daily, and the stock and funds are needed for this purpose. This is an unhappy state of affairs, to say the least of it. But I am confident that none of us wants to harm the other personally; far, far from it. Perhaps all that Mary and I can do for the moment is to face with all the humility and affection we have, the situation as it arises from day to day, and act as best we can.

It was Byron Casselberry again who answered this on May 6. (Doris Pratt knew Casselberry well from the days when he had lived at Ommen.) He began by telling her that he was writing as a trustee of KWINC, which he had recently become; he and Rajagopal did not wish to get into any controversy over the matter, either by correspondence or otherwise, and preferred to let things take their course and see what happened.

Doris answered Casselberry on the 17th:

In reply to your letter of the 6th of May, written partly on Raja's behalf and partly also from your own heart, I want you to know that I am not in a position to accuse anybody of anything. I merely wanted you and Rajagopal to know how shocked and hurt I felt when I heard— not only from Krishnaji—that there had been no real consultation, communion and sharing in the basic running of the KWINC, for some considerable time, and that Raja had refused Krishnaji's request to be put on the Board. If, as you imply in your letter, there was no need for me to be shocked—because of certain other facts in your possession—then surely you would not be 'entering into any controversy' by just telling me, your friend and colleague, what those other facts are; it is your duty to tell me.

You say you are now a *Trustee* of KWINC. That, in this connection, is almost a sacred word, Byron, as you must know. You cannot be a *Trustee* of KWINC, without having a direct responsibility to Krishnaji himself, for whose sake it was founded. And Krishnaji has said that he cannot regard the KWINC as working for him while Rajagopal remains the dominating force on it or behind it. You may feel this is a desperately sad situation, as we all do, but you cannot evade your own relationship with Krishnaji and your responsibility to him for funds, properties etc., raised in his name and for the proper democratic working of the organization.

If you just 'let things take their course' you will be evading your responsibility to Krishnaji and to all of us who are concerned. This would be a highly dangerous situation for us all, not least for Raja himself. So, as a friend, I beg you deeply to consider your position as trustee.

In a short letter dated May 24 Casselberry replied that he quite understood how Doris felt and why she wrote as she did but that there was much more to the whole situation than she and others had any idea of, as Krishnaji himself knew very well. It was no business of his, Casselberry's, to explain it or talk about it; it was something that could only be settled by Krishnaji and Rajagopal dealing directly with each other. Meanwhile he, Casselberry, would continue to do what he had been doing all these years, co-operating as whole-heartedly as he could with Rajagopal in his dedicated life's work of making the teachings widely available. Casselberry ended with the quotation, 'Let a man do what seemeth to him to be right'.

As soon as she received this letter Doris telephoned to K, who had just arrived at Gstaad, and had a long conversation with him from her house at Harrow. She then wrote off an appeal to Casselberry:

I feel that you and I and Raja must make one great final effort to sort this thing out, because if we three life-long friends cannot somehow come to the truth together, then we might as well give up the ghost.

And this is not heroics. I feel more deeply than I can say that the truth, however terrible, can help and heal us all three.

I want to go through your letter step by step, if you will allow me. Most important of all is your statement: 'As Krishnaji himself knows, there is much more to the whole situation than you and others know.' This statement implies that you as well as Raja, know of some hidden, secret, personal issue between Krishnaji and Raja, or concerning Krishnaji's functioning, of which we lesser fry can know nothing. I have ventured this very day to question Krishnaji about this, as I felt it only right to do so, and Krishnaji categorically and immediately replied that what you say and suggest is not the truth. The *only* issue that has brought about the present disastrous state of affairs has been the almost total usurpation by Raja of K's own responsibilities. It's as simple, open and fundamental as that; and there are no other hidden issues or personal and private implications of any kind involved—at any rate, Krishnaji says, as far as he himself is concerned. Krishnaji told me, Byron, that for ten years now he has been asking Raja to keep him informed and consult him about the work, without result. He has asked Raja who is on the Board, and why his own name was removed from it, and he has asked to be put back on the Board,—all without result. Telegrams from Krishnaji, letters, long telephone calls, personal conversations, all extending over a period of many years now, have been stone-walled and ignored by Raja. In the end Krishnaji asked a friend, Mr Blitz, to investigate the Ojai affairs and from this investigation it appears that long ago Krishnaji innocently and trustfully signed a document transferring all the assets of the original Star Publishing Trust (of which *he* was the founder) over to the Ojai Star Institute, of which Rajagopal was the founder. It has never been Krishnaji's wish to be totally absolved from any responsibility for the funds etc., raised in his name, but for the last ten years (and right back to the ending of the S.P.T.) Raja has constituted himself the sole arbiter of the affairs of KWINC—even to the extent of denying Krishnaji money he has specifically asked for.

You must believe all this, Byron, however much it shocks, for it is the truth. Whether we,—you and I—can help turn the tide of events at this late stage, I really don't know. But it is imperative that we try, because as I see it we have been partly responsible for this whole situation, calamitous as it is. Our very unquestioning acceptance of Raja's supreme authority may have caused harm to the work, to us and to Raja; our very feeling of dedication—without being crystal clear as to what we were feeling dedicated to, or about—must have befogged the real issue.

After all, looking back, the feeling that one has dedicated one's whole life to making a few books widely available and keeping some excellent archives, hardly makes sense—especially when one manages at the same time to cherish the feeling that the author of the books can be very unfair and unjust! This is akin to that other feeling which perhaps one harbours (in company with many theosophists), that somehow Krishnaji is two different people,—in part totally unconditioned and in part somewhat immature! This, frankly, is ludicrous, and would seem as such by thousands of people who have talked often and very intimately with Krishnaji and who have followed his talks and noted their totally pure quality all these long years. The 'dual personality' gambit can be highly damaging and a sinister cloak for one's own lack of understanding.

I am telling you, Byron, that Raja has tried to 'manage' Krishnaji and in the process has usurped complete authority,—even if he has done so under the guise or illusion of pure motives and protecting Krishnaji. In view of all this you cannot say: 'It's no business of mine; and I'm merely going to go on doing what I've been doing all these years.' It is *our* business; you and I are deeply involved in all this because perhaps what we've been so blithely doing all these years has been basically a false thing. We certainly cannot afford to take refuge in what I hope you will forgive me for calling a slick phrase: 'Let a man do what seemeth to him right'. Such a phrase must have comforted Herod, Pilate and Hitler. Isn't it better, if more uncomfortable, to say: 'Let me question always, and doubt deeply,—especially my own motives.' Read all this to Raja, Byron, and beg him on behalf of both of us to keep the issue simple and not to still suggest that there are hidden, personal issues between him and Krishnaji. Beg him, from me and all his friends, to withdraw totally from the organizational side and place everything at Krishnaj's feet,—where it has belonged from the very beginning. And for himself and for us, it is still not too late to explore a quite different field of relationship with each other, and with everything.

Doris received no reply at all to this entreaty.

*   *   *   *

While this correspondence had been taking place, K had driven from Paris to Holland with Mary Zimbalist in her new Mercedes delivered in Paris, and with Alain Naudé following in the Volkswagen. Anneke Korndorffer had rented a beach house for them at Nordwyk on the dreary cold edge of the North Sea. On May 8 K went to Bussum to record for Dutch television the replies to eight questions that were put to him. Mary Zimbalist recalled, 'He did it with the professionalism even the best actor could not equal, looking up and giving a remarkable answer straight to the camera and without hesitation.' While staying at Nordwyk K also gave five talks at the RAI Hall in Amsterdam between May 11 and 23.

On the 25th they left Holland in the two cars. Starting at 8 a.m. they arrived at Gstaad at 10 p.m., 600 miles and twelve hours of actual driving. K stayed with the others at Les Caprices until Vanda Scaravelli arrived on June 30 to open up Tannegg.

At the end of June my husband and I spent a few nights at the Park Hotel, Gstaad, on our way to Siena. On July 2 we went up to lunch at Tannegg and I met our hostess, Signora Scaravelli, for the first time. She was small, quick in speech and movement, aristocratic looking and beautifully dressed. K had told me that she did yoga every day and he had constantly urged me to do the same. I wish I had: the Signora is still as agile as a gazelle. Her small frame hides a great heart. (She now no longer cares about conventional dress, having settled for a uniform-garment, a short Japanese kimono in plain dark materials with trousers underneath, and bare feet and sandals.)

K, not having received a word from Mima Porter since his meeting with her in April, nor from Rajagopal, had sent her a telegram. On June 29 a vague letter had arrived from her saying that when he came to California in the autumn everything would be settled. This had happened too often before. Rajagopal had repeatedly said that when K came to Ojai the situation would be cleared up between them but there had been continual procrastination; so now K had made up his mind that there was no alternative but to break with KWINC completely. While we were at Gstaad there was much talk of the new foundation he intended to set up with its central office in England. This foundation was to be so constituted that no one individual could ever again obtain control of it. K asked me if I would become a trustee of the new foundation but I declined on the plea of age. The school which was to be started in England and which would include a home for K, was discussed at length. A possible house for it had been found, Ayot Place in Hertfordshire, and on July 4, K, Mary and Alain flew to London for the day to see it. They went over it with

Mr and Mrs Simmons, Gérard Blitz and others who met them there.

On the same day K sent a formal letter to Rajagopal and to the latter's lawyer, drawn up by Mr Rubinstein, revoking the document he had signed in Madras in November 1958, by which he had consigned all his copyrights to Rajagopal, and withdrawing permission for Rajagopal to make contracts on his behalf. Mr Rubinstein had taken the view after consulting a firm of lawyers in Madras that the Madras document was not legal. Rajagopal's lawyer was to take the opposite view, and until the final settlement six years later the point was in dispute.

On July 7, the day of K's first talk at the Saanen Gathering, Michael Rubinstein himself arrived at Gstaad. The next day there was a meeting at Tannegg at which K, Mary Zimbalist, Alain Naudé, Michael Rubinstein, Gérard Blitz, Doris Pratt and Mary Cadogan were present, and it was decided to announce next day, before K's second talk, the severance with KWINC. The formation of the new foundation was also discussed.

It was Mr Rubinstein who read out the announcement next morning in the tent:

> Krishnamurti wishes it to be known that he has completely dis-associated himself from Krishnamurti Writings Incorporated of Ojai, California.
>
> He hopes that, as a result of this public announcement, those who wish to be associated with his work and teachings will give support to the new, international, Krishnamurti Foundation of London, England, whose activities will include a school. The Deed which establishes the Foundation ensures that Krishnamurti's intentions will be respected.

The funds available for the school were sufficient to buy Ayot Place, but Mr Blitz did not agree that there was as yet enough money to start a school. He suggested publishing a bulletin to be circulated through the mailing list, appealing for funds. As Mrs Simmons was at Saanen for the Gathering, much excited talk went on about the school.

Vanda Scaravelli, who managed to keep aloof from all the excitement, left for Rome on August 2 when, at her request, Mary Zimbalist moved to Tannegg. K's talks at Saanen lasted until August 6. The domed tent which had been used for the meetings since 1962 was now worn out and had been replaced by a new pavilion made of rigid corrugated plastic sheeting which is still in use. It had the advantage over the old tent of terraced seating and windows of nylon netting to give more air.

In the talks that year K went very deeply into the questions of fear and freedom with which his teaching is largely concerned. 'One of the main features of fear,' he maintained, 'is the non-acceptance of what one is, the inability to face oneself. The more you know about yourself the greater the quality of maturity.' Fear could not be broken up into fear of this and fear of that; there was only total fear and in the understanding of the totality of fear it could be dissolved. And of freedom, he said that it could never be *from* something, for then it was merely reaction. People thought they wanted freedom, but did they really? 'Is not freedom a state of mind,' he asked, 'which is so intensely active, vigorous, that it throws away every dependence, slavery, conformity, acceptance? Does the mind want such freedom? Such freedom implies complete solitude'; and here fear came in again, for people were afraid of solitude although solitude did not mean isolation.

*   *   *   *

Now that K had broken with KWINC he would no longer be sending the tapes of his talks to Ojai; therefore he had asked three people to edit them for him and arrange for their publication. These were George Wingfield Digby and his wife Nelly, and Ian Hammond. The Digbys were close friends and neighbours of Mrs Bindley in London. He was Keeper of the Department of Textiles at the Victorian and Albert Museum and an expert on oriental ceramics; he had published books on textiles and a volume on William Blake.* The Digbys had been interested in K and had attended all his talks in London since 1949 and now came to Saanen every year. Before that they had worked with Ouspensky and his wife at Lyne Place, Virginia Water. K had once visited Ouspensky there who had said of him, according to George Digby, that 'he was not in the position of ordinary mortals who

---

* His *Catalogue Raisonné* of the Tapestries at the V & A was published in 1981.

had to work heroically if ever they were to attain that state. Krishnamurti had, as it were, missed a step.'

Ian Hammond was an architect whose wife, Jane, a first class audio-typist, helped at Saanen to type K's recorded talks. K now wanted his talks published in hardback, and since Gollancz did not wish to handle them, George Digby went to Wassenaar in Holland in November 1968 to arrange for their publication with Mr Verhulst, senior partner in the firm of Servire, who, a devotee of K's and an old friend of Anneke Korndorffer's, had for a long time wanted a chance to publish him. The authentic reports of K's talks were for the next few years beautifully produced by Servire and distributed through the Stanmore Press in London. Six volumes were published in all, the last two under titles—*The Flight of the Eagle* and *You are the World*. Meanwhile a Publications Committee had been formed in London of which I became a member. The other members were the Digbys, the Hammonds and Mary Cadogan. K had also asked Mary Cadogan to be the secretary of the new Foundation.

It was characteristic of K that he had not told the other members of the Committee that he had asked me to write a book for him, which was already finished, any more than he had told me that he had asked them to edit his talks. The others all knew each other well, so I was the interloper; nevertheless, they welcomed me with the utmost kindness. This failure on K's part, for no other reason it seems than vagueness, to inform one person who is working for him of what another is doing at his request in the same field, has occasionally led to hard feelings. He has even been known to appoint a new trustee to one of his foundations without consulting the other trustees. He expects entire co-operation between all those who work for him, expectations which are realised to a remarkable extent, though there are a few who believe that he has laid an exclusive and sacred trust on them which must be jealously guarded.

Although it was afterwards established that Rajagopal had no legal claim on the London office, Mary Cadogan had frozen all the KWINC assets, and until donations started to come in for the new Foundation managed to carry on with a small fund she and Jane Hammond had had the foresight to build up. There was so much work now to be done in England that it could no longer be carried on in Mary's home. A separate office, therefore, was soon opened at Beckenham, Kent, close to where the Cadogans had recently moved.

*   *   *   *

On August 22 K with Alain Naudé and Mary Zimbalist flew to London from Geneva after leaving their cars at Thun for the winter. They stayed in a flat at the White House again. The next morning, a Sunday, my husband and I drove them to Epping Forest where we had a long walk in the woods. My husband asked K during the walk what would happen to his Foundation and all his work after his death. K replied, with a sweeping gesture of pushing everything away, 'It will all disappear,' or words to that effect. His teaching would remain in his books and tapes— everything else could go. I mention this to show how his attitude changed during the course of the next ten years. He discussed making a will but said he had nothing to leave except his watch and perhaps his manuscripts if he ever recovered them from Rajagopal. He spoke of making Mary Zimbalist and me his literary executors.

The next day I went with them to Ayot Place to go over the house again. The Digbys and Simmonses met us there. The general feeling was that it was not suitable after all.

On August 28 a dramatic meeting took place at Michael Rubinstein's office in Raymond Buildings, Gray's Inn. It lasted for several hours—sandwiches were brought in for lunch. The Krishnamurti Foundation was legally constituted, the constitution being so drafted as to make it impossible for the Rajagopal situation ever to occur again. The trustees (officially called governors) were all present. They were K, Mary Zimbalist, Alain Naudé, George Digby, Dorothy Simmons, Count van der Straten and Gérard Blitz who had come over for the day from Paris. Mary Cadogan was present as secretary, and Doris Pratt and I attended as associates, our only function being to help re-elect the trustees, two of whom, apart from K, had to come up for re-election every year.

At the beginning of the meeting K told us that tape-recordings of a few informal conversations which had taken place between him and some Americans at Gstaad that summer about his difficulties with Rajagopal had somehow reached Ojai. As a result, K had just received a cable from Rajagopal threatening legal action. Mr Rubinstein advised K that should Rajagopal take such action against him during his forthcoming visit to California he ought to consult Monsieur Blitz's lawyer there.

After the signing of papers by the trustees, we discussed the school at great length. Gérard Blitz, who was the chief adviser on finance, was adamant that a school could not be started until larger funds had been built up. At the moment every available penny would be needed to buy a property of the size K wanted. Until there was enough money in hand to equip it and run it for a year, the school was not practicable. 'As you know,' I remember Gérard Blitz saying, 'we would do anything for you, Krishnaji—even jump out of this window [a self-deprecating gesture here from K] but to start a school now is *impossible*.' The taxi he had ordered to take him to the airport arrived just then. Hardly had he driven away before K and Mrs Simmons were in a corner discussing the immediate starting of the school as soon as a suitable building could be found. K's policy has always been to do what he feels should be done and let the money find itself some-how. And it invariably has. Moreover, he has always managed to inspire others to do the impossible. Gérard Blitz was the financial adviser he had appointed whose advice he had no intention of following.

14

Brockwood Park

On September 4 Mary Zimbalist flew from London to New York while K and Alain took a flight to Madrid from where they would be flying next day to Puerto Rico and staying as the guests of K's kind old friends, Mr and Mrs Biascoechea, who put a bungalow at their disposal on a hill overlooking San Juan. During the eighteen days they stayed there K gave some public talks at the University of Puerto Rico in San Juan which were attended by large crowds of mostly young people. K and Alain went to see Pablo Casals who lived at San Juan and who, although ninety-five still practised regularly every day. He spoke of the wonder he experienced each morning at being still alive. On the 23rd they arrived in New York where Mary had a rented apartment ready to receive them at 40 East 62nd Street.

In their absence the trustees of the new Foundation in England had been looking for a house for the school. It had to be fairly close to London and with enough land to ensure complete privacy. Ayot Place having been turned down, a second house near Horsham, called Nore, belonging to Dirk Bogarde, was considered sufficiently promising for K to cable, 'Plant 2,000 daffodil bulbs immediately', and for Alain to fly over from New York for the night on September 24 to inspect it. I went with him to see it and we came to the conclusion that it was too small. While K was giving talks in New York at the New School for Social Research, a third property was found which seemed ideal—Brockwood Park, Bramdean, in Hampshire, midway between Petersfield and Winchester about sixty-four miles from London, belonging to Lord Chesham. It was a large, low, white, late-Georgian house, set in thirty-six acres of park and garden, surrounded by farm land in some of the most beautiful country in England, with extensive views to the south of rolling hills and woodlands. It had a small swimming pool, a hard tennis court and a vast derelict walled kitchen garden (ideal for vegetarians when brought under cultivation), and a little way from the house, an enclosed grove full of azaleas and rare trees, including a great 'handkerchief' tree and some of K's favourite sequoias. A beautiful beech avenue led from the Winchester road to the park lodge, and a further avenue of copper beeches curled round to the back entrance.

While we were still looking for houses, Mary Cadogan and I had flown to Paris in the middle of September in response to Gérard Blitz's offer to print for the Foundation the first two issues of a quarterly bulletin which I had agreed to edit with Mary Cadogan's help. We saw Monsieur Blitz at the headquarters of the Club Méditerranée where he showed us his printing works and suggested the cover and format we should use. He regarded the bulletin merely as a vehicle for fund-raising. The first number appeared in the late autumn with a frontispiece of a photograph of K taken at the White House by Mark Edwards, a young photographer who has fulfilled his promise. A message, written and signed by K, occupied the first page:

... the Krishnamurti Foundation is the new organisation without the psychological belonging and dependence which most organisations bring about. This is very important to bear in mind in all the work we are doing together. Co-operation is necessary but the ugly and brutal side of organisation has no part in what we are trying to do. There is a great deal to do which has never been done in the past. We must meet together at least once a year to talk things over as friends, express our problems and resolve them.

The constitution of the new Foundation was then announced with the names of the trustees, and the formation of the Publications Committee. Then came an urgent appeal for funds in which it was stated that 'All those who have so generously given of their time and money to Krishnaji's work, and those prepared to help in the future, can feel assured that their efforts can never be used for any purpose which has not originated with him and does not continue to have his blessing.' This was followed by an account of K's activities in 1968, his schedule of talks for '69, a report on his visit to Puerto Rico, notes on the Saanen Gathering of '68 and a very beautiful unpublished piece by K called *The Lake* in which he wrote of real love: 'When it comes do not hold it, do not treasure it as an experience. Once it touches you, you will never be the same again. Let that operate and not your greed, your anger or your righteous indignation. It is really quite wild, untamed, and its beauty is not respectable at all.' A list of K's available books was given at the end of the bulletin and the names and addresses of associated committees in nineteen different countries.

On October 23, I went with others to look at Brockwood Park. At a trustees' meeting five days later the decision was made to buy it for £42,000 although K had not seen it. Monsieur Blitz immediately resigned. He did not, however, withdraw his interest in fund-raising or his help with the bulletin.

*   *   *   *

K, with Mary and Alain, had flown to Boston from New York on October 17 and been next day to Brandeis University. For the next few days K held meetings there with the students, returning to New York on the 24th and flying next day to Los Angeles and so to Malibu. On November 6 they went to Claremont, a small town about sixty miles east of Los Angeles where there were several small colleges, all with excellent reputations. The Blaisdell Institute had invited K to speak there. He had several meetings and discussions with the students and gave public talks until the 18th. For the rest of the year he remained at Malibu. Quite a few people came to see him there, including Christopher Isherwood and his friend Donn Bachardy, and Deborah Kerr and her husband Peter Viertel.

On December 17 K received a telegram to say that Brockwood Park had been bought. The Simmonses, Doris Pratt, a young architect and one Indian boy moved into the house in the middle of January 1969. Their first task was to scrape the accumulated meat-grease of years off the kitchen stove, a particularly unpleasant task for vegetarians.

In January 1969 I had some research to do for my own work at the Huntington Library, Pasadena, so with my husband I took the opportunity of going to see K at Malibu. We arrived at Los Angeles on January 18 where K, Mary and Alain met us and drove us to the Casa Malibu Motel, not far from Mary's lovely comfortable house. Alain lent us his car and we spent the whole of every day with them for a week, arriving in time for breakfast and not leaving until after dinner. It never stopped raining the whole time we were there; nevertheless, K went into the garden every morning in the rain in his white bathrobe and twisted his body about for the good of his liver. It was a joy to see his bare feet again which I had not seen since we were in India together in 1926. They are as beautiful and young looking as his hands, without a blemish on them. It was the first time I had seen him watching television. He enjoyed using the remote control switch, a gadget new to us, and was thrilled when some favourite old movies came on the screen—a Tom Mix film one evening, and on another I remember his awed whisper, 'By Jove, it's *Lassie!*' By Jove is an habitual expression of his.

One day Mary drove us all to Ojai in the pouring rain. I had spent five months there in 1926–27 and longed for my husband to see it, but the thick misty downpour blotted out its beauty. The young pepper tree under which K had sat during his experience in 1922 which had changed his life had grown so huge that it quite overshadowed his cottage.

We had lunch at Ojai with Erna and Theodor Lilliefelt who had a house quite close to Arya Vihara. Theo was Swedish and Erna American. They had both been Theosophists before they met and had gone independently to Adyar and had become followers of K's when they heard him speak in Madras in 1952. They had then gone to Ojai, again independently, and had worked during 1953 at the Happy Valley School, but realising that it was no longer a true Krishnamurti school they had resigned at the end of the school year. They were married in Santa Barbara in '54 and had then gone overseas while Theo was attached to the United Nations. In 1964, when he retired, they went to live at Ojai, believing that K was still speaking there every year. Having heard of his dis-association with Rajagopal at Saanen, they wrote to him, asking if they could help him, for they had already done some research into KWINC's legal position. While K had been in New York in October, Mrs Lilliefelt had flown there and taken part in discussions attended by Michael Rubinstein who had come to New York at K's request. When K arrived in California he invited both the Lilliefelts to Malibu and asked them if they would be willing to help start a new organisation for him. This became the Krishna-murti Foundation of America which was legally established on February 22, 1969. Mrs Lilliefelt is far the most active of the trustees; in fact she does practically all the administrative work.

We learnt while we were at Malibu that as every attempt to reach a private agreement with Rajagopal since K's return to California had failed (Rajagopal refused to see K except alone and K refused to see Rajagopal except in the presence of the whole Board of KWINC and some of his own friends), a Californ-ian lawyer had been consulted on K's behalf as to what measures to take for the recovery of the KWINC assets—land, property, money and copyrights. Later in January, on the advice of a judge, K, Mary Zimbalist and the Lilliefelts appealed to the Attorney General in California for the intervention of his office. This step was extremely distasteful to K but he was being put in an impos-sible position. Several people who had made donations to KWINC had been pressing for the return of their money which had been contributed for *his* work, to be used only as *he* directed. In a later statement, dated August 29, 1974, K put his dilemma of that time into words: 'I felt forced morally to seek legal advice. I felt the whole of KWINC's affairs were something sacred, thousands of people at great sacrifice had contributed to it in my name and now I had no voice or even information about it.'

*   *   *   *

Alain Naudé had arranged more contacts for K with young people in the early part of '69, so at the end of January he went to San Francisco with Alain and Mary and gave three talks at Berkeley University; on February 10 they drove south again to Palo Alto and stayed in rooms at the Stanford Faculty Club where Buckminster Fuller, the inventor of the geodesic dome that had been used for the Saanen tent, came to see K the next day. K gave four talks at Stanford University, and on the 16th drove to the University of California at Santa Cruz where he gave more talks to students at Cowell College. He returned with Mary and Alain to Malibu on February 21. Alain wrote about K's meeting with American students in the second issue of the Bulletin:

What strikes me most about so many of those we met in America is that they are deeply religious; they want a better world and they understand that that means changing their own minds ... . Quite naturally, yet also a little surprisingly, Krishnamurti is suddenly the hero and friend of these students, for long before they met him the thing he talks about had become for them as important as eating and breathing. They love what he says and feel for him a very familiar affection without awe or fear.

In India, of course, K had been in touch with the young for years through his schools at Rishi Valley and Rajghat.

After K's return to Malibu from Santa Cruz he went on February 27 with Mary Zimbalist, the Lilliefelts and their lawyer to a meeting at the Attorney-General's office in Los Angeles and saw the Deputy Attorney-General, Mr Laurence Tapper, who would be investigating the affairs of KWINC. Alain Naudé, though deploring Rajagopal's behaviour, was strongly opposed to going to law and did not attend any of the meetings with lawyers. Rajagopal's trustees stood solidly behind him and he and Rosalind were united in opposing K. Radha naturally took her father's part. Mr Vigeveno circulated a statement defending Rajagopal and blaming K's change of attitude towards him almost entirely on the influence of Mary Zimbalist and Alain Naudé.[27] This does not hold water since the trouble between K and Rajagopal had started several years before K met either Alain or Mary. Mr Vigeveno was right, however, when he added that K had always admired Rajagopal's work. Rajagopal's efficiency and the excellence of his editing have never been in question.

*   *   *   *

On March 6 K, Mary and Alain flew to England and went to stay at Brockwood Park for the first time. There were then four pupils at the school, all boys. The west wing of the house, which was in future to be K's home whenever he came to England, had been only minimally furnished. This wing consisted of a large hall, drawing-room and sitting-room on the ground floor, and three large bedrooms and bathrooms, a dining-room, kitchen and office on the first floor. During this first visit Mary arranged to have the whole of the wing redecorated and furnished with antiques at her own expense and to her own excellent taste. The Digbys gave some of their beautiful Chinese and Japanese porcelain to go in recessed shelves in the drawing-room.

K was delighted with the place, especially with the grove in the park. In all his walks he always passes through the grove to get to the open fields. During March he gave four talks at the Wimbledon Town Hall, an hour and a half's drive from Brockwood. On April 2 he left with Mary and Alain by car for talks in Paris at the Salle de la Chimie; they stayed again at the same house at Boulogne-Billancourt. At the end of the month they went on to Hilversum where a furnished house had been taken for them. After talks in Amsterdam they were back at Brockwood by the middle of May. During the next seven weeks, which K spent quietly at Brockwood in beautiful weather, with occasional days in London, it was decided that there should be a gathering at Brockwood in September on the lines of the Saanen Gathering.

Freedom from the Known had been published this year and I was now working on two other books for K—*The Only Revolution* and the *Penguin Krishnamurti Reader*, both published in 1970. The first, consisting of pieces written by K in India, California and Europe, was easy to edit as is everything K writes or dictates compared to the talks which the Digbys and Ian Hammond were working on. The second was more difficult. Penguin had asked for three of K's early books—*The First and Last Freedom, Life Ahead* and *This Matter of Culture*—to be turned into one, taking a third from each. Since these were very dissimilar books it was not easy to weld them into a homogeneous volume. However, the *Reader* has brought Krishnamurti to tens of thousands who might never have read a word of his.[28]

I felt it was time for K to say something on the subject of sex which might be troubling many people who believed that sex was incompatible with a religious life. I knew that K did not feel this (although he had felt it in his youth), so I asked him if he would write something on the subject for the third issue of the Bulletin. He agreed, but said he would like to put it in the form of questions and answers. Below is the major part of what he wrote:

LOVE, SEX AND THE RELIGIOUS LIFE

Questioner: Many years ago, when I first became interested in the so-called religious life, I made the strong resolve to cut out sex altogether ... Now I see that that kind of puritanical conformity in which suppression and violence are involved, is stupid, yet I don't want to go back to my old life. How am I to act now in regard to sex?

Krishnamurti: Why is it that you don't know what to do when there is desire? I'll tell you why. Because this rigid decision of yours is still in operation. All religions have told us to deny sex, to suppress it, because they say it is a waste of energy and you must have energy to find God. But this kind of austerity and harsh suppression and conformity does brutal violence to all our finer instincts. This kind of austerity is a greater waste of energy than indulgence in sex.

Why have you made sex a problem? Really it doesn't matter at all whether you go to bed with someone or whether you don't. Get on with it or drop it but don't make a problem of it. The problem comes from this constant preoccupation. The really interesting thing is not whether we do or don't go to bed with someone but why we have all these fragments in our lives. In one restless corner there is sex with all its preoccupations; in another corner there is some other kind of turmoil; in another a striving after this or that, and in each corner there is the continual chattering of the mind. There are so many ways in which energy is wasted.

If one corner of my life is in disorder then the whole of my life is in disorder. So you shouldn't ask how to put one corner in order but why I have broken life into so many different fragments ... I should ask myself whether I am going to stay in some sordid little room of pleasure all my life. Go into the slavery of each pleasure, each fragment, and say to yourself, my God, I am dependent, I am a slave to all these little corners—is that all there is in my life? Stay with it and see what happens.

Questioner: I have fallen in love, but I know there is no future in this relationship. It is a situation I have experienced several times before and I don't want to get involved again in all that misery and chaos. Yet I am desperately unhappy without this person. How can I get myself out of this state?

Krishnamurti: The loneliness, bleakness, wretchedness you feel without this person you love existed before you fell in love. What you call love is merely stimulation, the temporary covering up of your emptiness. You escaped from loneliness through a person, used this person to cover it up. Your problem is not this relationship but rather it is the problem of your own emptiness. Escape is very dangerous because, like some drug, it hides the real problem. It is because you have no love inside you that you continually look for love to fill you from the outside. This lack of love is your loneliness, and when you see the truth of this you will never again try to fill it with things and people from outside.

There is a difference between understanding the futility of this escape and deciding not to get involved in this kind of relationship. A decision is no good because it strengthens the thing you are deciding against . . . Even calling it loneliness is an action of the observer to get rid of it. Such action changes nothing, it merely strengthens the loneliness, but *complete inaction* with regard to this loneliness is change. It is going beyond feeling and thinking, side-stepping them. Whatever is happening inside you—anger, depression, jealousy, or any other conflict at all, drop it instantly.

Questioner: Is it possible for a man and a woman to live together, to have sex and children, without all the turmoil, bitterness and conflict inherent in such a relationship?

Krishnamurti: Can't you fall in love and not have a possessive relationship? I love someone and she loves me and we get married—that is all perfectly straightforward and simple, in that there is no conflict at all. (When I say we get married I might just as well say we decide to live together.) Can't one have that without the other, without the tail, as it were, necessarily following? Can't two people be in love and both be so intelligent and so sensitive that there is freedom, and absence of a centre that makes for conflict? Conflict is not in the feeling of being in love. The feeling of being in love is utterly without conflict. There is no loss of energy in being in love. The loss of energy is in the tail— jealousy, possessiveness, suspicion, doubt, the fear of losing that love, the constant demand for reassurance and security. Surely it must be possible to function in a sexual relationship with someone you love without the nightmare which usually follows. Of course it is.

Earlier K had said more poetically about sex: 'So-called holy men have maintained that you cannot come near to God if you indulge in sex, therefore they push it aside although they are eaten up with it. But by denying sexuality they put out their eyes and cut out their tongues for they deny the whole beauty of the earth. They have starved their hearts and minds; they are dehydrated human beings; they have banished beauty because beauty is associated with woman.'[29]

In the fourth number of the Bulletin a long extract was quoted from a notebook in which K had written for a short time in 1969. There was one passage in it that particularly struck home to me: 'Have no shelter inwardly or outwardly; have a room or a house or a family, but don't let it become a hiding place, an escape from yourself.' I gave up editing the Bulletin after the fourth issue and it was taken over by Miss Sybil Dobinson who joined the Publications Committee and has continued to edit it ever since.

*　　　*　　　*　　　*

K flew to Geneva on July 4 with Desikachar, the young yoga teacher, who had been staying at Brockwood. Alain Naudé had gone on ahead and Mary Zimbalist followed next day. This year she had rented part of another chalet at Gstaad, Les Trois Ours, for herself and Alain, nearer Tannegg where K was staying with Vanda Scaravelli as usual. The Saanen talks and discussions lasted from July 17 until August 9. On July 21, when Vanda returned to Florence for a couple of weeks, Mary moved to Tannegg at her invitation. At 6 a.m. that day they had watched on television the astronauts landing on the moon.

Léon de Vidas resigned this year from the Saanen Gatherings Committee (he died in 1971), and Edgar Graf, who was Swiss, took his place in managing the gatherings. At the end of this summer at Gstaad, Alain ceased to work for K in order to pursue his own spiritual adventure. He now lives in San Francisco, has taken up music again as a teacher and has become keenly interested in homoeopathy. He has recently published an excellent English translation of Hahnemann's *Organon*. He has remained friendly with K, Mary Zimbalist and Vanda Scaravelli and sees them from time to time. I number him among the handful of my really close friends and he stays with us whenever he comes to England. His great value to K was that he brought him in contact with so many young people.

On August 20 K and Mary returned to Brockwood. The first gathering there was from September 6 to 14. K spoke four times at consecutive week-ends in a great tent set up in the field at the end of the lawn south of the house. Count van der Straten and his wife came to stay for the first week-end and Pupul Jayakar paid a short visit after the gathering. The first school term began in the third week in September with twelve pupils of different nationalities, and on the 28th K held the first of many meetings with students and teachers.

K and Mary Zimbalist remained at Brockwood until the end of October. Mary then returned to Malibu when K flew to India, via Rome, after an absence of eighteen months.

15

The Urgency of Change

K went first to Delhi where his audiences were larger than ever before, and they had changed in character. There were now many more young people from the several colleges in the city as well as business men and diplomats and the usual international sprinkling of hippies, contrasting with dignified Buddhist monks in their saffron robes. It is understandable that K should attract new audiences but why do the same people come back year after year to hear him speak, especially as he is not saying anything spectacularly different from what he has been saying for years at countless meetings all over the world? Is it that the possibility he holds out of an almost instantaneous psychological transformation in each one of us which will end sorrow and solve all our problems is so irresistible that when we find we have not changed, we believe we only have to hear him once more to discover a clue we must have missed? Are we not continually on the tail of an understanding that is only just outside our grasp? As someone recently said to me, 'Krishnamurti leads one to the door of truth, opens it and just as one expects to walk in he gently shuts the door in one's face.'

After Delhi, K went as usual to Rajghat, Bombay, Madras and Rishi Valley. In Madras he was not able to stay at Vasanta Vihar because the ownership was in dispute; Rajagopal was claiming it as part of the KWINC assets. K stayed instead with an Indian friend, Mrs Jayalakshmi, who lived close to Vasanta Vihar in Greenways Road. He was still hoping for an amicable settlement with Rajagopal. 'As you know,' he was writing to the trustees of the American Foundation at the beginning of December, 'I am in no way antagonistic to him. I have been trying for over ten years to come to some kind of co-operative settlement with him. All my efforts have been, I am afraid, of no avail.' He went on to outline what he considered would be fair terms for a settlement, and concluded:

I don't know what the financial position of Rajagopal is: I have never known it. I do not know if he personally owns the house, with the grounds or not. If he does not own it, it would be good and proper that he should stay on there until the end of his days. A definite sum of money should be given to him every year for all the days of his life. If he has his own money, he may not need any financial help. There must be an open heart for all the work he has done for all these years.

At the same time he was writing to Mary Zimbalist, '. . . we must settle things gently with him . . . you *must* be gentle; you are in a way acting for me. So please be wisely gentle.'

*   *   *   *

While K was at Rishi Valley in the second half of January 1970 the name of the Foundation for New Education, as the Rishi Valley Trust had become in 1953, was changed to the Krishnamurti Foundation of India. The trustees included Pupul Jayakar, as President (K became President in 1978), Nandini Mehta, Dr S. Balasundarum, Principal of the Rishi Valley School, and Sunanda Patwardhan, a doctor of sociology, whose husband was a partner in Orient Longman. All the Krishnamurti Foundations (there was soon to be a Spanish one and there is now a Canadian one) are charitable organisations exempt from tax, all legally distinct but working in close co-operation. The Indian Foundation, in addition to its educational work, became responsible for arranging K's talks in India, Indian publications in English, translations into the vernacular languages and all other activities connected with K's work in India. It also started its own Bulletin which Sunanda Patwardhan edits.

*   *   *   *

K flew back to California, via Rome and England, at the beginning of February and stayed with Mary Zimbalist at Malibu. The American Foundation was as far away as ever from coming to terms with Rajagopal. On January 21 a six-hour meeting had taken place at Ojai between Rajagopal, the assistant Attorney-General, Mr Tapper, and the lawyers of both parties. Rajagopal had sought this meeting; he was not interested in a settlement and wanted to answer the accusations against him. K telephoned to him on February 13 from Malibu and asked him to come and talk about a settlement but he replied that his lawyer had forbidden him to discuss it.

Apart from this unresolved situation, February was a very peaceful month for K at Malibu. On March 1 he gave the first of four talks at the Civic Auditorium at Santa Monica, fourteen miles from Malibu. The hall, holding 3,000, was so crowded that several hundred people had to be turned away. After the fourth talk on the 8th he told Mary as they drove away that he felt like someone singing to the deaf. At the end of the month he made another attempt to get Rajagopal to come and see him. This time Rajagopal said he could not leave Ojai.

At the beginning of April Mary drove K to San Diego where he gave four talks at the San Diego State College. One day while they were there they visited the naval base at Coronado and went over a heavy cruiser—an expedition that K enjoyed immensely. Before departing with Mary for England on April 18 he had a brief telephone conversation with Rajagopal of quite a friendly nature which gave every hope that an agreement might be reached.

K and Mary were at Brockwood for over nine weeks. K seemed to be very happy there apart from suffering from hay fever. May 11 was his seventy-fifth birthday but he brushed aside any mention of it. On the 16th he gave the first of four evening talks at the Friends Meeting House. He would motor from Brockwood in the morning, picnic in the car and rest at Mrs Bindley's house before going to the hall at seven, then drive back to Brockwood immediately after the talk.

It was during his stay at Brockwood this spring that K asked me to write an account of his early life. Some time before this he had asked his old friend in New Delhi, Shiva Rao, to write it. Shiva Rao had first met him at Adyar in 1909 and had come to England in 1914 to coach him and Nitya in mathematics. For many years he had helped Mrs Besant to edit the daily newspaper she had started in Madras, *New India*, and after Partition he had become a member of Parliament. I had been delighted to hear he was writing this book, for I knew he had access to the Theosophical archives at Adyar. After collecting material and making a draft of the first couple of chapters he fell very ill and did not feel he would ever recover sufficiently to finish it; it was then that K asked me to take it over. Shiva Rao had offered to put all his documentation at my disposal, and K said he would bring it over with him when he next returned from India early in 1971.

Although I was, of course, greatly honoured and flattered to be asked to take over this work which I knew I should enjoy, I felt I had to make two conditions before accepting—that I should not have to submit my manuscript to anyone and that K would give me his assurance that he would not stop it from being published. He agreed to these conditions, and also gave me written permission to quote his letters to my mother as well as his and Nitya's accounts of his Ojai experience.

I did not intend to start the book until I had received Shiva Rao's material; all the same, I went down to Brockwood on June 5 to have my first interview with K about it. I found that he had developed a keen interest in 'the boy', as he referred to himself: why had he been picked out by Leadbeater from the other boys on the beach? What was the quality of 'the boy's' mind then? Was he a freak? What had protected him all these years? Why was it that 'the boy', subjected to all that adulation and Theosophical indoctrination, had not become corrupted or conditioned? K's curiosity, though intense, was quite impersonal. He seemed to hope that the book would reveal something about 'the boy' that would explain the man. He appeared to be equally detached from both. Mary Zimbalist was present at this interview, and we discussed it again when they came to lunch with me in London on June 17. K could not have been more co-operative, but, alas, he really remembered nothing of the past at first hand, and was only able to tell me the things about the early days at Adyar that Shiva Rao had quite recently told him. Perhaps we talked too much, for when he returned to Brockwood that evening he was ill. He 'went off', leaving the body to cry out, 'He shouldn't have gone to town. Who's looking after him?'

*   *   *   *

A book had been published that year purporting to have K's permission to interpret him. This called forth a statement from K which was published in the summer number of the Bulletin:

From the nineteen twenties I have been saying that there should be no interpreters of the teachings for they distort the teachings and it becomes a means of exploitation. No interpreters are necessary, for each person should observe directly his own activities, not according to any theory or authority. Unfortunately interpreters have sprung up, a fact for which we are in no way responsible. In recent years several people have asserted they are my successors and that they have been specially chosen by me to disseminate the teachings. I have said, and I again repeat, that there are no representatives of Krishnamurti personally or of his teachings during or after his lifetime. I am very sorry that this has to be said again.

This statement is important, for after K's death interpreters are bound to proliferate. He cannot ensure against them, but those close to him should reiterate this statement to others and constantly remind themselves of it. K feels as strongly about it today as he has always done.

                    *   *   *   *

On June 30 K and Mary Zimbalist left Brockwood, flew the car from Lydd to Le Touquet and motored slowly to Gstaad, spending four nights on the way. This year Mary was sharing Chalet Tannegg with Vanda Scaravelli who returned to Florence before the gathering, leaving her cook to look after the others. The seven talks and eight discussions at Saanen were between July 16 and August 9. The Lilliefelts arrived from California in time for the third talk and stayed at Tannegg. Driving alone with Mary after this talk, K said that even in India where he had spoken more than anywhere else, there was not one person who had listened to him and 'changed'. 'You all do not make enough use of me,' he added. 'You are not serious enough.' In his next talk he was saying that all fragmentary attempts to deal with a problem led to more problems: 'The urgency of change *is change* not urgency.'

The Urgency of Change became the title of another book I had prepared for K (published in 1971).[30] This was the easiest task I have ever done for him since it consists of deeply probing questions put to him by Alain Naudé. The answers were dictated by K to Alain who partly edited them with K's co-operation before they were sent to me so there was very little left for me to do. One of K's frequently recurring themes and, perhaps, the most difficult of all to grasp, is that of the ending of thought. There is a short section on this in *The Urgency of Change*, partly quoted below:

Questioner: I wonder what you really mean by ending thought. I talked to a friend about it and he said it is some kind of oriental nonsense. To him thought is the highest form of intelligence and action, the very salt of life, indispensable. It has created civilisation and all relationship is based on it. All of us accept this, from the greatest thinker to the humblest labourer. When we don't think we sleep, vegetate or day-dream; we are vacant, dull and unproductive, whereas when we are awake we are thinking, doing, living, quarrelling: these are the only two states we know. You say, be beyond both—beyond thought and vacant inactivity. What do you mean by this?

Krishnamurti: Very simply put, thought is the response of memory, the past. The past is an infinity or a second ago. When thought acts it is this past which is acting as memory, as experience, as knowledge, as opportunity. All will is desire based on this past and directed towards pleasure or the avoidance of pain. When thought is functioning it is the past, therefore there is no new living at all; it is the past living in the present, modifying itself and the present. So there is nothing new in life that way, and when something new is to be found there must be the absence of the past, the mind must not be cluttered up with thought, fear, pleasure, and everything else. Only when the mind is uncluttered can the new come into being, and for this reason we say that thought must be still, operating only when it has to—objectively, efficiently. All continuity is thought; when there is continuity there is nothing new. Do you see how important this is? It's really a question of life itself. Either you live in the past, or you live totally differently: that is the whole point.

K goes so far now as to say, 'Thought contaminates'. He is well aware that when he says this, the statement itself is thought—that all speech, all ideas are thought. It is thought as memory, condi-tioned thought, that contaminates—the past staining the purity of the new, the unknown—although, of course memory is essential for all practical purposes. In his *Notebook* he has written, 'There is a sacredness which is not of thought, nor of a feeling resuscitated by thought. It is not recognizable by thought nor can it be utilized by thought. Thought cannot formulate it. But there's a sacredness, untouched by any symbol or word. It is not com-municable.' This is the whole difficulty of such a concept as the ending of thought—it cannot be communicated except through thought. The nearest K can get to it is surely, 'See what happens when the brain is completely still.'

*   *   *   *

K and Mary Zimbalist flew back from Geneva to Brockwood on August 20. The second Brockwood Gathering, which lasted for ten days, was from September 4. The Lilliefelts were there this year and Pupul Jayakar came again for a few days. Later in the month Sacha de Manziarly spent a week-end there, and on September 27 K was interviewed on film for the BBC by Michael Rabinger. The Brockwood School had now been going for a year and students were invited to send in their impressions to the Bulletin. One fifteen-year-old girl wrote:

At Brockwood Park we are all trying to live together as a family, so that we can learn more about ourselves and live a full and happy life. It is not by any means an easy task, but we hope that in some way we will be able to achieve it. Of course we all have our many problems, but we try to find a new and sensible approach to overcoming them, instead of quarrelling and fighting with each other, as we have done in the past.

It is a school I should love to have gone to. For one thing it is so 'un-schooly'. There is an excellent, ever-increasing library, the strictly vegetarian food is delicious with none of that peculiar smell one associates with vegetarian restaurants and health farms, and not only are the grounds beautiful (that one gets at many schools) but inside it has none of the bleakness and discomfort associated with the usual boarding school. The long, light-oak tables in the dining-room come from the Gordon Russell workshops at Broadway in the Cotswolds, and the other furnishings, though simple, are pleasing to the eye. Ten years after its opening the school was to have its full complement of sixty students— about an equal number of boys and girls, ranging from fourteen to twenty and comprising sixteen different nationalities. All members of the staff, whether teachers, workers in the kitchen or garden or on maintenance are paid the same salary. The fees are a little less than those of the neighbouring co-educational school of Bedales, and 20% of the places are filled by non-paying or part-paying pupils, financed from a special scholarship fund. The students can sit for O and A Level examinations in all subjects. This is an anomaly in a Krishnamurti school, for any form of competition is at variance with K's teaching which maintains that competition is one of the strongest roots of evil ('By comparing A to B you destroy them both,' he has often said), yet without examinations it would be almost impossible to attract pupils, especially in India where jobs depend so much on academic degrees.

Only one case of drug-taking has come to light at Brockwood, resulting in a student being asked to leave, and there are the usual emotional and sexual problems that K seems no more able to avert than anyone else, though my own belief is that if he stayed there throughout the school year such problems would not arise, for although it is a delightful place to be at all times, there *is* a special atmosphere when he is there; one can almost hear, and certainly feel, a dynamic throbbing. That Brockwood so nearly measures up to K's well-nigh impossible demands of what a Krishnamurti school should be is the greatest possible tribute to Dorothy Simmons.

16

Tradition and Revolution

In the winter of 1970 K varied his usual programme by going to Australia before India, but before that he went to Italy when Mary Zimbalist returned to Malibu, and spoke in Rome, Perugia and Florence. He then joined Mary at Malibu from where he had some abortive telephone conversations with Rajagopal. On November 12 he and Mary flew from Los Angeles to Sydney. A flat had been taken for them at Manly, a suburb, on the eleventh floor of a building overlooking the harbour. K loved the view and one day while watching a large aircraft-carrier gliding out of the harbour, he sighed, 'How wonderful it would be to be the Captain of that'. In a television interview with him on November 16 far more time was given to his visit to Sydney in 1925 when it was expected that he would enter the Heads walking on the water than to his current philosophy. From November 21 he gave five talks at the Sydney Town Hall, packed with 1,500 people of a wide variety of backgrounds from all over the Continent. So much enthusiasm was aroused that the audience became rather rowdy. On the 26th he was interviewed again on television for the programme 'This Day Tonight'. The interview started with the reading of the following passage from *The Penguin Krishnamurti Reader*:

Our problem then, as I see it, is that we are bound, weighed down by belief, by knowledge. And is it possible for a mind to be free from yesterday and from the beliefs that have been acquired through the process of yesterday? Is it possible for me, as an individual, and you as an individual to live in this society and yet be free from the beliefs in which we have been brought up? Is it possible for the mind to be free from all that knowledge, all that authority?

The interviewer then asked: 'Krishnamurti, are you saying here that it is wrong to believe in what you have found to be true?' To this K's reply was in part:

Sir, is belief necessary at all? Why do we have beliefs? Probably you believe in something because you don't actually see what is. If you see actually what is—what is, in the sense, what is actually going on, both outwardly in the outward phenomenon and inwardly—then what is the necessity for a belief at all? You don't *believe* the sun is rising. It is there, you have seen it. The whole problem of beliefs seems to be so utterly erroneous . . .

The interviewer then asked: 'This means, doesn't it, a completely different view of education? For, after all, education is implanting beliefs.'

Obviously [K replied]. Education as it now is, is really the cultivation of a corner of a vast field. We are concerned with that little corner, with its technological knowledge, conditioning the mind with information and neglecting the whole field; and therefore there is an imbalance. Technologically we have gone very far, and psychologically we are very primitive. We are still at the stage of tribal conflict with our beliefs, our gods, our separate nationalities . . . All that has to be set aside, which means facing the fear, fear to stand alone, fear to discard all this absurdity, all this, if I may use the word, circus which has become religion. To discard all that implies that a man must be aware, and so be very sensitive and very alert, and therefore intelligent. It is that intelligence that is going to change society.[31]

On December 2 K took a flight to Delhi via Hong Kong while Mary flew back to Los Angeles. K's talks at Rajghat were cancelled that year because of an air strike, so he remained in Delhi until the end of 1970. In January '71 he was in Madras, staying with Mrs Jayalakshmi again and giving talks before going to Rishi Valley; he then went to Bombay in February where he gave more talks. On February 22 he broke his journey back to California at Brockwood and brought with him all Shiva Rao's documentation for the biography. I was immensely grateful for it but saw at once that I would not be able to use any of Shiva Rao's text since mine would be such a very different kind of book from the one he had started. Nevertheless, we exchanged frequent letters and I was constantly consulting him on points of fact. Although I did not start the book for several months, I am glad to say that he lived long enough to see it in print and approve of it.

*   *   *   *

The next weeks at Malibu, until the middle of April, were largely spent by K in trying to reach a settlement with Rajagopal in order to avoid filing a suit against him. K and Mary went to his house at Ojai on March 3 where Mima Porter joined them, but they got nowhere. Another meeting of the four of them a month later was equally fruitless. On April 5 K went a third time to Rajagopal's house. This time they spoke alone while Mary and Mima Porter waited in the car outside and after an hour and a half it was hoped that some basis for a settlement had been agreed upon. Alas, it came to nothing. Meanwhile K had given four talks in March at the Civic Auditorium in Santa Monica, and also held some discussions with students at the University of Southern California. Alain Naudé came to stay at Malibu at the end of the month and three interviews between him and K were recorded. Professor Jacob Needleman, professor of philosophy at San Francisco State College, came at the same time and Alain recorded two interviews between him and K.

On April 12 K and Mary flew to New York where they stayed in the empty apartment of Mary's father in the Ritz Tower on Park Avenue at 57th Street. Two days later they flew to Washington for the night. K spoke there at a meeting of the American Society of Newspaper Editors at the invitation of Newbold Noyes, editor of the *Washington Star*. Back in New York K gave four talks at the Town Hall until April 25. The first talk was video-taped for the first time. There was a queue all round the block to get into the hall and many had to be turned away. On the way back to the Ritz Tower K remarked to Mary, 'That man on the platform must know a great deal.'

K and Mary arrived at Brockwood on April 29 and remained there until May 17. After lunch one day at my flat in London, K filled in for me the background of the situation that had developed with Rajagopal. Like everyone else who had known Rajagopal in the early days and was deeply fond of him, I deplored the possibility of a lawsuit but did understand K's position with regard to people who had given money for his work and were pressing for its return now they knew that Rajagopal had sole control of it.

On May 17 K and Mary went to Holland where a house at Huizen had been lent to them. K gave four talks at the RAI Hall in Amsterdam. By the 27th they were back at Brockwood to stay until the end of June. K talked frequently to the students and staff there, and one day he was invited over to Bedales by the headmaster to give a talk to the students. Another day after being in London he felt very ill. 'I feel if I went through that door,' he said to Mary, 'I could die. The wall between living and dying is very thin; it always has been with me. Suddenly it will be there, but not today.' He told her not to be upset by his illness because that only upset him.

He left Brockwood with Mary on June 29 and drove slowly to Gstaad which they reached on July 3 to find Vanda Scaravelli waiting for them at Tannegg. K's hay fever became very bad as soon as he reached the mountains and developed into slight bronchitis. He heard on July 13 that Rajagopal had been given until the 15th to show cause to the Attorney-General why a suit should not be brought against him and his Board; this date was postponed, however, when Rajagopal changed his lawyer. The Saanen Gathering that year was from July 18 until August 10. K's last talk was about the intelligence that comes when thought sees beyond itself and is still. 'The structure and the nature of the "self" [he said] is measurable by thought; it is measurable in the sense that thought can perceive its own activities, what it has created, what it has accepted, what it has denied. And then one realises the limitations of thought; then perhaps one can go into that which lies beyond thought.'

The third Brockwood Gathering was in the early part of September. Permission for camping in the grounds had now been given by the authorities; there was a crèche for children and the atmosphere during the ten days it lasted was like that of a huge garden fête on a fine warm day. Only inside the packed tent, when K slipped in, did that extraordinary stillness immediately descend on the excited audience. Those moments of complete silence while K sat there regarding his audience before beginning to speak were even more impressive in a tent than in a hall. A great circle of young people sat on the ground at the foot of the raised platform on which his chair was placed; then came rows and rows of chairs filling the tent to capacity, with the overflow standing in the openings. There was a pleasant smell of hot canvas and crushed grass. What struck one most about the audience was the lack of hippies. None of the throng there appeared to be part of the guru-drug culture. Young and old, they were clean, decently dressed people who hung on K's words with serious intentness. After the talk a hot meal, prepared in the Brockwood kitchen, was served at moderate cost in a separate tent where K's books, tapes and cassettes of his talks were on sale.

On September 20, the opening day of term, K talked to the assembled school. At this time the building of an extension to Brockwood, to accommodate the many visitors both at the gathering and at other times, was planned. It was decided to build what were to be called The Cloisters, a little apart from the main house—a quadrangle containing thirty-two small rooms, hardly more than cells, each with its own shower, basin and W.C.—and with a communal sitting-room and small kitchen attached. The corner rooms were to be double ones with baths instead of showers. Ian Hammond was the architect of this project.

In the middle of October K and Mary left for Paris where K broadcast in French for ORTF French television. (Léon de Vidas had died a fortnight before they arrived.) On the 20th K flew to Rome while Mary returned to California. K heard in Rome that Mr Tapper had made a final effort to call together the trustees of KWINC and get them to agree to the terms of a settlement he had drawn up. If unsuccessful the complaint would be filed. A fortnight or so later Rajagopal's lawyer informed Mr Tapper that the KWINC Board refused to see him unless he had a substantially better offer to put forward; thereupon Mr Tapper had authorised the plaintiffs' lawyer to file the complaint against Rajagopal and his Board of seven trustees for the recovery of the KWINC assets and the removal of the trustees. This was done on November 9 in the Superior Court of the State of California for the County of Los Angeles. K was not one of the four plaintiffs. These were three trustees of the Krishnamurti Foundation of America and one man who had contributed money to KWINC for K's work.

Having given one public talk in Rome, K suddenly decided not to go to India that winter, not because there was a threat of war between India and Pakistan at that time, but because he felt in need of a rest from travelling. Consequently, on November 19, he flew to Los Angeles via Brockwood. When he reached Malibu he told Mary that his body was bone-tired but his mind bursting with energy; he needed to slow down to give his body a chance to catch up. He decided to give no more private interviews for the time being. He relaxed for the next few weeks, going to cinemas, walking on the beach and watching television, but as always when resting, his head was bad and he was often awake for hours in the night with the intensity of his meditation. Several times, after sleeping, he woke with a sense of special joy, feeling that the room was full of 'eminent holy beings'. Evidently 'the process' was going on and he felt, as always at such times, that something was happening to his brain, expanding it.

*   *   *   *

In the New Year of 1972, while lunching one day with the Lilliefelts at Ojai, the idea of starting an educational centre there was born in K. In the third week in January Alain Naudé came to stay at Malibu for a week and had four taped discussions with K who spoke of emptying the mind of everything but facts. 'A mind that is not empty can never find truth,' he said, and, 'Memory is the source of the self.' Again he was awake in the night for three hours with 'an extraordinary light burning' in his mind. At the same time he declared that he had not felt so rested since the war, yet his body had become so sensitive that one evening when the television was on and he was 'far away', he had such a shock when Mary spoke to him that he began to shake and felt the shock-effects all night.

In the middle of February K went with Mary to San Diego again where he had interviews with Dr Alan Anderson, Professor of Religious Studies at the San Diego State College, and with Father Eugene Schallert, Professor of Sociology at the Jesuit University in San Francisco, and with another Jesuit from the same University, Father O'Hanlon. (It was Alain Naudé who had arranged these meetings.) After the interviews K's meditation was again so strong that he was unable to sleep.

A month later, just as K was to go on the platform to give the first of four talks at the Santa Monica Civic Auditorium, a summons for deposition was handed to him. This was a cross-complaint by Rajagopal and his Board served not only on those who had brought the complaint against him but on K as well. The others received their summonses by post; it was only K who had his handed to him personally, and, it would appear, at a moment carefully calculated to embarrass him. However, he proceeded to give a splendid talk.

The cross-complainants had made charges against the cross-defendants of (1) Bringing action to unlawfully seize assets (2) Breaking of oral agreement that Krishnamurti would support Rajagopal for life and that Rajagopal could appoint his own trustees (3) Breaking of contract signed by Krishnamurti in Madras in November 1958 (4) Attempting to mislead and defraud publishers (5) Of doing harm to Rajagopal and hurting his reputation. They asked for damages on all counts.

Ten days later K and Mary went to stay with the Lilliefelts at Ojai and meetings were held to discuss with some thirty invited teachers and others the prospect of starting an educational centre there, and on April 8 and 9 K gave two public talks in Libbey Park, the first time he had spoken at Ojai since 1966. While he was there he walked with Mary through the orange groves which were full of the scent of blossom and the hum of bees. Mary, realising how much he loved the place—more than anywhere in the world—offered to sell her house at Malibu and buy a house in the valley. He thanked her but said he would not hear of it.

Rajagopal had now made his deposition for the cross-complaint, and a few days later, on April 12, back at Malibu, K was to make his deposition in the presence of the lawyers of both sides, a Court reporter, Mary Zimbalist and Mrs Lilliefelt. Just as he was about to begin, Rajagopal, Mima Porter and another KWINC trustee turned up unexpectedly. They had a legal right to be there. K testified for two hours in the morning and two hours in the afternoon, and on the following day his deposition continued until the evening with the same people present. When it was over K drew up a statement preventing Rajagopal or KWINC from having anything to do with his work after his death.

K and Mary left Malibu on April 21 for New York where they stayed again at the Ritz Tower. During the early part of May K gave four talks at the Carnegie Hall and also started giving private interviews again. After the third talk on May 6 he stayed on in the hall to meet Leopold Stokowski who had been in the audience and had asked to see him. Stokowski and his wife had stayed a week at Castle Eerde in 1928 during one of K's gatherings. Three days later K and Mary flew to England.

*   *   *   *

1972 saw the appearance of the first important Krishnamurti book from India, *Tradition and Revolution*, edited by Pupul Jayaker and Sunanda Patwardhan and published in Delhi by Orient Longman. It comprised thirty dialogues held during 1970–71 in New Delhi, Madras, Rishi Valley and Bombay with a small group of people from a variety of cultural backgrounds and disciplines—intellectuals, artists, politicians, sanyasis—whom K had been meeting since he went back to India in 1947. In the preface it states: 'These dialogues are not questions and answers. They are an investigation into the structure and nature of consciousness, an exploration of the mind.' Although K does not say anything really new in them, the approach is new and refreshingly different from his other books in being so Indian, even to the necessity of having a glossary of Indian words. There is a tendency in India to portray K as an Indian teacher rather than as a world teacher. The Indians might equally well say that there is a tendency in the West to discount the affinity of his teaching with ancient Hindu scriptures. I do not think that his Indian followers can ever quite forget that he was born in a Brahmin body and therefore belongs to them as he never can to the rest of us, whereas he considers himself raceless and without nationality.

In the first discussion there is a memorable passage by K on sorrow:

> There are various ways of escape but there is only one way of meeting sorrow. The excapes with which we are all familiar are really ways of avoiding the greatness of sorrow. The only way to avoid sorrow is to be without any resistance, to be without any movement away from sorrow, outwardly or inwardly, to remain totally with sorrow without wanting to go beyond it.

*   *   *   *

K and Mary Zimbalist were at Brockwood by the second week in May and apart from a short visit to Paris they remained there for nearly six weeks. During that time K talked regularly to the assembled school as he still does when he is there. I had now begun writing his biography and had many questions to ask him which he answered as far as he was able, but his memory for the twenties, let alone his boyhood, is practically non-existent. He has no recollection, for instance, of the physical agony he had suffered from 'the process'. As I covered his life year by year from childhood until the dissolution of the Order of the Star in 1929 he became more and more of a mystery to me. Who was he? What was he? What *was* 'the process'? Why did he have to suffer it? Shiva Rao had told me that on occasions in New Delhi when he was driving him to the place where he had to speak, he would say, 'What on earth am I going to talk about?' He seemed to have no thoughts in his head at all, yet once on the platform he would talk for an hour or more as if inspired. (I have had this same experience with him recently myself when he gave two talks at the huge RAI Hall in Amsterdam: driving there he asked more than once, 'What am I going to say?' and then spoke magnificently for an hour and a half to a packed hall overflowing into another hall where he could be seen and heard on video—to some five thousand people altogether.) Where did his inspiration come from? Well, if K himself could not enlighten me no one else could; I would just have to tell his story, giving the facts as accurately as possible without offering any explanation. I was, however, to go much deeper into these questions when I came to write the present book.

*　　　*　　　*　　　*

K and Mary left Brockwood on June 22 and crossed to France by the night ferry from Southampton to le Havre and after three nights in Paris drove slowly to Gstaad via Avignon, Arles and Les Baux (where they stayed at the famous Baumanière), and so to Switzerland by the St Julien Pass and a happy reunion with Vanda Scaravelli at Chalet Tannegg. A young American, Alan Kishbaugh, who had become a trustee of the Krishnamurti Foundation of America and a member of the English Publications Committee in order to help with the publication of K's books in America, stayed at Tannegg that summer.

In one talk at the Saanen Gathering K discoursed on the religious life:

I have to find out what it means to live a religious life, because I feel if that can be brought about, or comes into being, then action at any level will always be harmonious, not contradictory.

My mind has rejected the whole structure of belief, which is based on fear and therefore illusion. Therefore I also reject completely any authority, because it is still outside of myself. It is still the act of thought which seeks guidance from another, and that brings about a division, hence a conflict and therefore disharmony.

Then I ask myself will any act of desire, which is will, bring this about? Will, which is the concentration of desire, plays an extraordinary part in our life—I must do this, I must not do that, I will follow this—and this constant decision is part of our existence. The 'I' sees that where there is the act of will there must be division, and therefore conflict. And where there is conflict there can be no harmony. So is there a way of living without the action of will? Will comes into being when there is choice, and choice exists when there is confusion. You do not choose, you do not decide when you see things very clearly; then you act which is not the action of will. . . .

So I have an insight into this question of the action of will. Therefore there is no conflict in the mind, it acts when there is insight. Action is insight—not the action of will, or belief or fear or greed. It is the insight that comes when you observe very closely this pattern of existence established by will. When you have an insight into that, your action is entirely different, non-contradictory, and hence that insight brings harmony.

One has no insight because one lives in the past. Your life is in the past, isn't it? Your remembrances, your imaginings, your contriving is based on the past. Our life is the past which, through the present, modified, becomes the future. So as long as you live in the past there must be contradiction, hence conflict. When you have an insight into all this then harmony comes into being.

At the end of the gathering in the middle of August K told Mary, 'You must take care of yourself and outlive me. I will live at least another ten years till I'm ninety perhaps. You do not belong to yourself any more.' They returned to Brockwood via Paris on August 26 for the Brockwood Gathering early in September. K had heard by this time from Mr Vigeveno that Rajagopal might be willing to agree to a settlement out of court. He had also heard that Rajagopal and all the other members of the Board of K W I N C were still Theosophists. He declared that had he known this he would never have allowed Rajagopal to handle his writings.

On October 13 I took Livia Gollancz down to Brockwood for the day. Although she had been his publisher since 1954 this was the first time they had met. They were both shy sitting next to each other at lunch in the great school dining-room, and they had no private conversation. K usually busies himself at Brockwood lunches with collecting scraps to feed to Mrs Simmons's golden labrador.

Two days after this, K and Mary left for Paris and Rome. In Rome K stayed with Vanda Scaravelli in her flat in via Barnaba Oriani and gave one public talk at the Teatro delle Arte to an overflowing audience and held a discussion with about fifty people at the flat. On November 2 Rajagopal telephoned to him from Ojai to say that he loved him whatever happened. K replied that he could settle the case at once if he wanted to, to which Rajagopal answered that it was now out of his hands. I still believe that love is the basis of much of Rajagopal's behaviour—but an all too human love, not love as K understands the word.

On the 5th K flew to India where he was to remain until February 1973. Mary meanwhile returned to Malibu. In Madras in December K parted company with Mr Madhavachari whose loyalty, it was found, was still with Rajagopal.

K was at Rishi Valley at the beginning of 1973. In talking to the teachers there he said something in answer to the question, 'Does not suffering dull the mind?' which struck me with great force when I read it afterwards: 'I should have thought rather, that the continuation of suffering dulls the mind not the impact of suffering, passion. Unless you resolve suffering immediately it must inevitably dull the mind.'

While K was in India, the Judge of the Ventura County Court, which had jurisdiction over the case against Rajagopal, had granted all the motions of the plaintiffs, including the examination of the KWINC records and accounts.

On February 5 K broke his journey from Bombay to Los Angeles at Brockwood for two nights. I was now deeply absorbed in writing his biography but had formed some doubts as to the advisability of publishing it; it was such a peculiar story, at once so sacred and so crazy. Therefore, on the 6th I went down to

Brockwood for the day to talk the matter over with him. Alone with him after lunch in the large drawing-room in the west wing I put my misgivings to him. I was sitting on a sofa and he on a hard chair facing me (he always sits on a hard chair). 'So ought the book to be published?' I asked after voicing my doubts. To this he replied instantly, 'Can't you feel it in the room?' I am quite devoid of any psychic gift but at that moment I did feel a sudden extraordinary throbbing which seemed to fill the room. 'Well, that is your answer,' he said. I realised at the time that the power I felt might have been produced by him or by auto-suggestion, though he implied that it was coming from somewhere outside himself and was showing its approval. 'What *is* this thing?' I demanded. 'This power? What *is* behind you? I know you have always felt protected, but what or who is it that protects you?'

'It's there, as if it were behind a curtain,' he replied, stretching out a hand behind him as if to feel an imaginary curtain. 'I *could* lift it but I don't feel it is my business to.'

When I left that afternoon K had gone to his room to rest, and my daughter, who had driven me from London and had to get back for an appointment, was impatiently waiting in the car outside. I had been into the main school building to say good-bye but had to return to the west wing to get my coat in the cloakroom at the far end of the hall. As I passed the open door of the drawing-room, with no other thought in my head except the need to hurry, the power that I had felt earlier on rushed out at me. It was menacing, terrifying in its force. Was it hostile to me personally or was it just my weakness frightened by its strength? One thing I do know—that it was not auto-suggestion or imagination this time. I came to the conclusion that it was no more hostile to me personally than the gale from a propeller would have been had I crossed its path too closely. Nevertheless, I can never pass the drawing-room door at Brockwood now without a *frisson* up my spine.

17

The Awakening of Intelligence

Two more Krishnamurti books were published in 1973 by which time his books had well-nigh ceased to be reviewed. The difficulty of reviewing them is easily understood, but John Stewart Collis, who is unknown to K, took up the challenge when he reviewed the first short one, *Beyond Violence*, in the *Sunday Telegraph* in March '73:

To be refreshing it is necessary to be fresh. This is rare enough in the arts. In the field of religious-philosophical-ethical thought it is hardly ever found. J. Krishnamurti is always fresh, he is always surprising. I doubt if a cliché has ever passed his lips.

He is also very difficult. Not because he ever uses a long word but because he doesn't believe in 'beliefs'. This must be appalling for those who rely upon *isms* and *ologies*. He believes in Religion, in the fundamental meaning of the word, but not in religions or in any systems of thought whatever.

The sub-title of *Beyond Violence* is 'Authentic Report of Talks and Discussions in Santa Monica, San Diego, London, Brockwood Park, Rome'. First of all Krishnamurti gives a talk and then answers questions. The questions are ordinary. The answers are never ordinary.

'Is not the belief in the unity of all things just as human as the belief in the division of all things?'

'Why do you want to believe in the unity of all human beings?—we are not united, that is a fact. Why do you want to believe in something that is non-factual? There is this whole question of belief; just think, you have your belief and another has his belief; and we fight and kill each other for a belief.'

Again:

'When should we have psychic experiences?'

'Never! Do you know what it means to have psychic experiences? To have extra-sensory experience, you must be extraordinarily mature, extraordinarily sensitive, and extraordinarily intelligent; and if you are extraordinarily intelligent, you do not want psychic experience.'

The Awakening of Intelligence

This volume is chiefly concerned with changing *ourselves*, so as to go beyond the violence so widespread everywhere:

'To be free from violence implies freedom from everything that man has put to another man, belief, dogma, rituals, my country, your country, your god, my god, my opinion, your opinion.'

How to achieve this freedom? I'm awfully sorry, but I can't give Krishnamurti's message in a neat sentence. He has to be read. The act of reading him alone works a change in the reader. One clue: substitute for thinking, the act of *attention*—the power to *look*.

The second book, *The Awakening of Intelligence*, edited by Cornelia (Nelly) and George Wingfield Digby, is the longest and most comprehensive of all K's works. 530 pages long, with sixteen photographs of K by Mark Edwards, the volume is made up of seven parts, including 'Two Conversations between Krishnamurti and Professor Jacob Needleman'* at Malibu in 1971; 'Two Conversations between Krishnamurti and Alain Naudé,' also at Malibu in '71; 'Two Conversations between Krishnamurti and Swami Venkatesananda' at Saanen in 1969, and a 'Conversation between Krishnamurti and Professor David Bohm' at Brockwood in October '72. Dr Bohm, who had been a friend and colleague of Einstein's at Princeton in the forties, is the eminent Professor of Theoretical Physics at Birkbeck College, London University. He had first become interested in K on coming across *The First and Last Freedom* by chance in a library. He had attended K's talks at Wimbledon in '61 and since then he and his wife had frequently been to Saanen and Brockwood and had held many discussions with K. (He was made a trustee of the Krishnamurti Foundation, England, in 1969.) He is the author of several books on the quantum theory and relativity, and since the publication of his latest book in 1980, *Wholeness and the Implicate Order*, which propounds a revolutionary theory of physics akin to K's teaching of the wholeness of life, he has been widely recognised for his controversial scientific discoveries.

In his first conversation with Professor Needleman, K emphasised the importance of getting rid of all religious conditioning: '. . . one has to discard all the promises, all the experiences, all the

---

* Professor of Philosophy at San Francisco State College, author of *The New Religions* and editor of the Penguin Metaphysical Library.

188

mystical assertions. I think one has to start as if one knew absolutely nothing.' Needleman interposed, 'That is very hard.' 'No, Sir, I don't think that is hard. I think it is hard only for those people who have filled themselves with other people's knowledge.' And further on in the conversation K said, 'I don't read any religious, philosophical, psychological books: one can go into oneself at tremendous depths and find out everything.' This is at the root of K's teaching—that everything can be discovered in oneself and that in understanding oneself one comes to understand others, for fundamentally we are no different from others. As he said in one of his conversations with Alain Naudé: '. . . the world is me and I am the world; my consciousness is the consciousness of the world, and the consciousness of the world is me. So when there is order in the human being then there is order in the world.' To make people feel this was surely 'the function of the religious man'. And later in the conversation with Naudé:

One feels there is absolute goodness, not an emotional concept, but one knows, if one has gone into oneself deeply, that there is such a thing: complete, absolute, irrevocable goodness, or order. And this goodness is not a thing put together by thought; if it is, then it is according to a blueprint . . . the moment your life is planned according to a pattern then you are not living, you are merely conforming to a certain standard and therefore that conformity leads to contradiction in oneself. The 'what is' and the 'what should be' breed contradiction and therefore conflict . . . so order, virtue, goodness is in the moment of the now. And therefore it is free of the past.

The conversations with the Swami are interesting in defining K's attitude to gurus. The Swami opened the conversation by saying that he had come to 'Krishnamurti as a humble speaker to a *guru*—the word *guru* meaning "the remover of darkness—of ignorance"'. The Swami then tried to show how much there was in K's teaching of the *Upanishads*. The gurus in the *Upanishads* told their disciples to 'find out for themselves': 'You cannot describe Brahman [truth] positively,' the Swami said, 'but when you eliminate everything else it is there. As you [K] said the other day, love cannot be described—"this is it"—but only by eliminating what is not love . . . Now what, according to you is the rôle of a *guru*, a preceptor or an awakener?' To this K replied: 'Sir, if you are using the word *guru* in the classical sense, which is the dispeller of darkness, of ignorance, can another, whoever he be, enlightened or stupid, really help to dispel the darkness in oneself?' You might point out the door and say, 'Look, go through the door', but each man has 'to do the work entirely himself', and therefore he, K, did not consider himself to be a guru.

The Swami then asked, 'But would you, Krishnaji, accept that the pointing out was necessary?' to which K answered, 'Yes, of course. I point out, I do that. We all do that. I ask a man on the road, "Will you please tell me which is the road to Saanen", and he tells me; but I do not spend time and expect devotion and say, "My God, you are the greatest of men". That is too childish!'

K's conversation with Professor Bohm was at the other end of the stick so to speak. It was about 'Intelligence'. Both the Swami and the Professor started by defining words—the Swami the word *guru* and Bohm the word *intelligence* which comes from *inter* and *legere*, meaning 'to read between'. Bohm pointed out that it had been amply proved by science that all thought was essentially a physical, chemical process. K agreed that thought was mechanical but said that intelligence was not, so 'thought is measurable, intelligence is not. And how does it happen that this intelligence comes into existence? If thought has no relation to intelligence, then is the cessation of thought the awakening of intelligence? Or is it that intelligence, being independent of thought, being not of time, exists always?' 'Thought is time,' Bohm expounded, 'or, rather, thought has invented time.'[32]

It is as a result of his conversations with David Bohm, which have been going on at intervals for over ten years, that K has come to talk more and more about the ending of thought. He has been excited and stimulated by his discussions with Bohm in which he feels that a bridge has been opened between the scientific and religious minds. It is a new approach to his teaching, what might be called an intellectual rather than an intuitive approach, and as such it appeals to many who have studied K for years as well as to those who come new to him. There is a good deal of semantic play from Bohm in these conversations and of giving dictionary derivations of words. To know that the word 'communicate is based on the Latin "commun" meaning "common" and the suffix "ic" which is similar to "fic", meaning "to make or to do"—

i.e. "to make something common"', though interesting in itself, does not necessarily help us to communicate or receive communication, any more than to know the derivation of the word 'intelligence' awakens intelligence. Since K has been talking to Professor Bohm he has changed his meaning of one important word (though not invariably) and this may lead to confusion. The word is 'reality'. To give an example, in a Saanen talk of 1971 K had said:

If one really wants to find out about God, what God is, whether there is such a thing, something which is not nameable . . . if that is the main interest of your life—that very interest does bring order. This means that to find that *Reality* [my italics] one must live differently, deeply differently. There must be austerity without hardness, there must be tremendous love. And love cannot exist if there is fear, or if the mind is pursuing pleasure. So to find that Reality one must understand oneself.[33]

Now, in talking to David Bohm, 'reality' has become antithetic to, instead of synonymic with, the unknown, with God, with 'something which is not nameable': '. . . anything that thought thinks about [K is now saying], whether unreasonably or reasonably, is a reality . . . reality, I say, has nothing to do with truth.' Reality is the chair we sit on, the pen we hold, the clothes we wear, the pain we feel as well as 'part of the conditioned mind'.[34] Bohm has told K that 'Reality comes from 'res', a thing, a fact. This, of course, is the correct meaning: children ask, 'Is it real?'—meaning 'Can it happen to me?', but for years K has used the word in its other sense, and he still slips into using it sometimes as he did formerly—to mean ultimate truth.*

How far this kind of intellectual semantic discourse helps to bring about the object of K's teaching—a complete transformation of the human psyche—must be a matter of temperament. One has to have the mental equipment to grasp it and be thrilled and enlivened by it. It would certainly attract those who are not inspired by K's poetic mysticism. Others may find their receptiveness more readily quickened by reading as a prelude to his

---

* Other instances of the use of the word in this sense can be found in several earlier quotations in this book. See Index under Krishnamurti.

teaching one of his simple descriptions of nature such as the following:

The evening sun was on the new grass and there was splendour in every blade. The spring leaves were just overhead, so delicate that when you touched them you did not feel them ... It was a beautiful evening, full of that strange glory which is the heart of spring. You stood there without a thought, feeling every tree and every blade of grass, and hearing that bus, loaded with people, passing by.[35]

One of the many remarkable things about K is the equal ease with which he talks to a Swami or a Western scientist, an industrial millionaire or a Prime Minister. He has discoursed on meditation with the Dalai Lama and would have no apprehension in conversing with any of the world's great philosophers, yet he is undoubtedly a shy, diffident man who shuns ordinary conversation, has read very little (and that little forgotten) and who has no intellectual pretensions. The answer to this anomaly is, I think, that he perceives some truth as clearly as he can see his own hand. No counter-argument can disturb such a clear vision. While others discuss and argue about the theory of X, K actually holds X like an apple in his hand.

*　　　*　　　*　　　*

K was staying at Malibu with Mary for the rest of February 1973. On March 7 he drove with her to San Francisco where they stayed at the Huntington Hotel and where he gave four talks at the Masonic Auditorium close by, a hall holding over 3,000 people which was packed each time. On the 20th he and Mary drove back to Malibu and there, a few days later, he held a discussion with a small group of people about starting a school at Ojai. He emphasised how necessary it was to start another school because the world was in 'a dark age' and children should be brought up 'sheltered by an umbrella of goodness'. 'We are already in this goodness,' he declared, 'or we would not be here. I am not speculating. I know this.' He asked those present whether they would be willing to help in running such a school at Ojai; they all assured him that they would. Shortly afterwards he told Mary and the Lilliefelts that they had been sent by 'something' to look after him, that they must be responsible and keep control of the school, that a new tide of energy would be generated and that they must be prepared to handle whatever it would bring.

At the beginning of April K and Mary stayed with the Lilliefelts at Ojai while K gave four talks in Libbey Park again to large audiences; he also gave several private interviews. Towards the end of the month they flew via New York to Paris where they heard that Sacha de Manziarly was dangerously ill in the American Hospital. Marcelle de Manziarly took K to the hospital and he went in alone to see Sacha and came out most moved. Afterwards he said to Mary, 'Never let me die in hospital. I would rather die quietly at home.' Sacha died two days later. He had been almost like a brother to K since they had first met in 1919.

At the end of April K and Mary went to Brockwood and in the third week of June there was a ten-day meeting there of representatives of all the Krishnamurti Foundations. The Cloisters, just completed, the plaster not yet quite dry, were occupied for the first time. Fortunately the weather was fine and warm. Although I was not a trustee I was asked to attend these meetings and met some of the Indian trustees for the first time. Mary Cadogan, as Secretary of the English Foundation, was also there. One morning, in K's presence, we discussed his death. He said that wherever he died he wanted to be cremated and have his ashes scattered. The Indians, I am afraid, were shocked by the almost flippant way we Westerners spoke of this; they wanted his ashes sent to India to be thrown in the Ganges. Naturally, as they felt so strongly in the matter, we at once gave way to them. K was not at all embarrassed. One sensed his total remoteness from his body and his utter lack of sentimentality about death.

The Indian ladies present, Pupul Jayakar and Sunanda Patwardhan, sat cross-legged on the sofa during the meetings. Their grace and their beautiful saris (they wore a fresh one every day to our delight) made the rest of us look clumsy and dowdy. Sunanda Patwardhan, who was taking the minutes of the meeting, was such an expert shorthand-writer that Mary Cadogan could easily read her notes.

At the opening meeting K said in part:

One of the problems is that we all die. Who will take charge of the schools and foundations, and yet be responsible for the spirit of the teaching? If we don't bring in younger people who will get to know all our ways of thinking, of discussing, everything will slip into the hands of strangers and get lost. I would like to ask; how do we continue?— not an apostolic succession—but how do we continue with the same feeling? How do we propose to continue Brockwood? I am taking Brockwood as an example. I include Rishi Valley, Benares [Rajghat], Madras, Bangalore.* How do we give a continuity to this kind of feeling of really working together, creating together, bringing about a different human mind? This is one of the functions of the Foundations.

Trustee: You should choose some young people.

K: I cannot choose. People come to me wearing a mask, and when I say, 'Look, remove that mask', they don't like it. And so I cannot judge. I *can*, but it is like reading a private letter. Most of the young people put a shield between themselves and me. It is the responsibility of the Foundations to find young people. You may find it easier than I, because people fall in love with me, with my face, they are attracted to me personally, or they want to advance spiritually. The Foundations exist at present to arrange talks, publications, tapes. When Krishnamurti dies, no arrangements for travel will have to be made. People won't give money any more—they may but it is most unlikely. What will then be the function of the Foundations? Will it be primarily a business organisation whose only job will be to carry on the practical work of publishing books and looking after the archives?

Trustee: We must establish a community where people work together.

K: The moment you provide a place for a community there will be infinite trouble. Is such a thing our job? But how are you going to see that everything is kept along the lines laid down? I feel personally that if the Foundation becomes merely an entity to publish books and to keep archives, then something is wrong; I feel the perfume is lost. After Krishnamurti dies, will we reduce the Foundations merely to a publishing concern, or will we, as is happening now, be one mind, something real working together, and therefore having a different perfume which will perhaps continue even though we cease to exist? Personally I feel you are losing something marvellous if you reduce everything to producing books and keeping archives. When I am concerned about my intention for the Foundations, my wish is that the other thing, the flowering, should not wither away. Therefore what is the function of the Foundations apart from the schools? Is it merely to form groups or organisations? That is wrong. How is the perfume to be carried on? I don't know—I'll leave it to you! My wish is that the perfume should be carried on, but I can't do anything about it.

* The Valley School at Bangalore did not start functioning until 1978.

194

I don't think we can decide about the continuity of the Foundations, at least, I can't decide. I don't think in terms of continuity at all. For me, it is a continual state of transformation; it will work itself out. But the schools have to go on definitely, because they may produce a different kind of human being. But we must see what happens with the Foundations. If something is operating in us, then something will happen, not the crystalisation of a structure, but much more than that.

This was a far cry from 1968 when K had told my husband in Epping Forest that everything could go after his death. It seemed to me that he was now on rather dangerous ground; he did not want interpreters yet he was in a sense licensing us to interpret him after his death on the grounds that we were preserving 'the perfume' of his teaching. If I came new to him after his death I am sure I should feel closer to him by listening to a cassette of one of his talks or watching him speak on video than in hearing someone talking about him, however close that someone had been to him. 'The perfume' comes across in his voice, his words, his looks. I believe, though, that what he hopes for is that a group of people, who actually '*live*' his teaching, will remain in perpetuity. He has never lost his faith, in spite of so many disappointments, of forming such a group, and the ceaseless love and passionate energy he continues to pour into this effort makes one weep for him at times. He is so certain that if only he can make people *see* the truth of what he says—see it for themselves, not on his authority—a radical change *must* take place in them. The main theme of his talks at the Saanen Gathering that summer was 'how to bring about fundamental, radical, revolutionary psychological change in the mind'.

After this Saanen Gathering he returned with Mary Zimbalist to Brockwood for the gathering there at the beginning of September. When he was in England now he would come up to London with Mary about once a week and we would lunch together. The Aperitif Restaurant in Jermyn Street where we used to go was now closed and we had taken to lunching in the fourth-floor restaurant at Fortnum and Mason at a table by the window where it was quiet and where one vegetarian dish, a cheese flan, is always on the menu. A model-girl, who has been at Fortnum's for a long time, goes round the tables at lunch time. K likes to watch her and has strong opinions about the clothes she models. He has always taken a great interest in clothes, not only his own, and never fails to notice if one is wearing anything new. When he comes to London he carries a beautifully rolled umbrella (I doubt whether it has ever been unfurled) and hogskin gloves. (His humanitarianism has never gone to the lengths of giving up wearing leather.) Although it is difficult not to take the opportunity of talking to him during these meals, it is obvious that he would much rather not talk; he wants to watch all that is going on around him. The people in the restaurant fascinate him, especially the children who occasionally eat there.

After lunch K would often go to see Mrs Bindley who was now over ninety and quite deaf. One day when he came up in September that year I suggested that after lunch we should go to what was said to be a very good thriller at the Odeon, Leicester Square. His face lit up with eagerness; then Mary reminded him that he was going to see Mrs Bindley at three. 'Of course,' he said without the slightest hint in tone or manner that going to see a deaf old lady was anything but a pleasure. I was deeply touched, remembering how he had sat holding my mother's hand after she had lost her memory and the joy it had given her.

Another day when K came up I suggested that he should start writing another journal as he had done in 1961. The idea appealed to him; he bought notebooks and pencils that very afternoon and began to write the next morning, September 14. He continued to write in his notebook every day for the next six weeks. Most of the journal was written at Brockwood but he continued it when he went to Rome in October. These daily writings (published early in 1982 under the title *Krishnamurti's Journal*) reveal more about him personally than any of his other works. He refers to himself throughout in the third person as 'he'. On September 15 he was writing:

He only discovered recently that there was not a single thought during these long walks . . . Ever since he was a boy it had been like that, no thought entered his mind. He was watching and listening and nothing else. Thought with its associations never arose. There was no image-making. One day he was suddenly aware how extraordinary it was; he attempted often to think but no thought would come. On these walks, with people or without them, any movement of thought was absent. This is to be alone.

And on the 17th:

He always had this strange lack of distance between himself and the trees, rivers and mountains. It wasn't cultivated: you can't cultivate a thing like that. There was never a wall between him and another. What they did to him, what they said to him never seemed to wound him, nor flattery to touch him. Somehow he was altogether untouched. He was not withdrawn, aloof, but like the waters of a river. He had so few thoughts; no thoughts at all when he was alone.

And on the 21st:

He has never been hurt though many things happened to him, flattery and insult, threat and security. It was not that he was insensitive, unaware; he had no image of himself, no conclusion, no ideology. Image is resistance and when that is not, there is vulnerability but no hurt.

Two days later he wrote:

He was standing by himself on the low bank of the river . . . He was standing there with no one around, alone, unattached and far away. He was about fourteen or less. They had found his brother and himself quite recently and all the fuss and sudden importance given to him was around him. He was the centre of respect and devotion and in the years to come he would be the head of organizations and great properties. All that and the dissolution of them still lay ahead. Standing there alone, lost and strangely aloof, was his first and lasting remembrance of days and events. He doesn't remember his childhood, the schools and the caning. He was told later by the very teacher who hurt him that he used to cane him practically every day; he would cry and be put out on the verandah until the school closed and the teacher would come out and ask him to go home, otherwise he would still be on the verandah. He was caned, this man said, because he couldn't study or remember anything he had read or been told. Later the teacher couldn't believe that that boy was the man who had given the talk he had heard. He was greatly surprised and unnecessarily respectful. All those years passed without leaving scars, memories, on his mind; his friendships, his affections, even those years with those who had ill-treated him— somehow none of these events, friendly or brutal, have left marks on him. In recent years a writer asked if he could recall all those rather strange events and happenings, and when he replied that he could not remember them and could only repeat what others had told him, the man openly, with a sneer, stated that he was putting it on and pretending. He never consciously blocked any happening, pleasant or unpleasant, entering into his mind. They came, leaving no mark, and passed away.

Apart from this memory of standing by the Adyar River soon after he was 'discovered', K seems to have had only one other recollection of his childhood. This was recorded in his journal on October 4: 'As a young boy, he used to sit by himself under a large tree near a pond in which lotuses grew; they were pink and had a strong smell. From the shade of that spacious tree, he would watch the thin green snakes and the chameleons, the frogs and the watersnakes. His brother, with others, would come and take him home.'

I believe that this is a genuine recollection, that no one ever told him this.

18

Freedom is Not Choice

K and Mary left Brockwood on October 15 and spent a fortnight in Rome. On November 1 K flew to India while Mary returned to America. His usual visit to Rajghat was again cancelled that year because of an air strike so he was in Madras throughout December, staying once more with Mrs Jayalakshmi and giving talks. This winter Dr Trimbeck Parchure, a doctor from the hospital at Rajghat, began to travel everywhere with him in India as his medical adviser, as did also Parameshwaran, the head cook in Rishi Valley, who had looked after him when he was so ill in Kashmir in 1959. A Krishnamurti co-educational day school had just been started in Madras under the auspices of the Krishna-murti Foundation of India. In a shady grove in a peaceful part of Madras, it was called simply 'The School' and accommodated 112 children from the ages of three to twelve. (It has since moved to Damodar Gardens, Adyar.)

After talking in Bombay all through January 1974 K arrived at Malibu again early in February. On the 16th he and Mary went to San Diego where, until the end of the month, he held a series of eighteen dialogues, video-taped in colour, with Dr Allan Anderson with whom he had had one interview two years before.

At this time the terms of a settlement of the case against K W I N C were still being argued by the lawyers but some progress had been made. Indeed one condition had already been agreed: Rajagopal had handed over K's manuscript, written in 1961–62, which he had refused to do when K had asked for it in 1966. This was in exchange for the tapes of K's disclosures to a group of Americans at Saanen in '68 about his reasons for breaking with Rajagopal. Mary, who transcribed the 323 pages of the manuscript and was the first to read it after its return, described it in her diary as 'infinitely beautiful, moving and extraordinary. To me the greatest of his writings, the most sacred'. (This manuscript, as has already been recorded, was published in 1976 under the title *Krishnamurti's Notebook*.)

K was now anxious to buy land for the school at Ojai without waiting for the settlement of the case, so early in March he held some meetings with ten possible teachers and others who might become involved in the school. (It was to be a primary day school.) An architect was consulted about the buildings and in April K appointed Mark Lee, an American who had been a teacher at Rishi Valley, as Principal of the new school. There were great misgivings among the trustees of the Krishnamurti Foundation of America, for there was as yet no money for this project. K, however, applies a force when he really wants something done which no one can resist. 'If it is right it will come right,' he always says, and how often he has proved this. The one thing he will never allow to stand in his way is lack of money. The Foundation made a bid for forty acres of land which was fortunately capped by a higher bid.

K told Mary again at this time that he had to live another ten or fifteen years because there was so much to be done. His body, he said, was slowly deteriorating, but his 'brain was untouched'.

In the middle of March K gave four talks at Santa Monica. At the end of one of them a questioner asked: 'I have been listening to you for some time now but no change has come about. What is wrong?' K answered:

Is it that you are not serious? Is it that you don't care? Is it that you have so many problems that you are caught up in them, no time, no leisure to stop, so that you never look at that flower? . . . Sir, you have not given your life to it. We are talking about life—not about ideas, not about theories, practices, technologies—but looking at the whole of life which is your life. You have a very short time to live, maybe ten, maybe fifty years, but don't waste it, look at it, give your life to understand it.

These talks were followed at the beginning of April by two public discussions in Libbey Park, Ojai, after which K and Mary flew to New York for K to give four talks at the Carnegie Hall. They stayed at the Ritz Tower once more. On their return to California the plaintiffs in the case informed their lawyer that if there was no settlement within a week they would ask for a Court hearing and a trial date. A hearing in the judge's chambers at Ventura on May 28, at which a trial date was set, resulted in the other side agreeing to a settlement, signed on September 30, the main terms of which were, very briefly: (1) that KWINC should be dissolved as soon as possible and that another organisation, K and R Foundation of which Rajagopal had control, should hold the copyrights in Krishnamurti's writings prior to July 1, 1968, but that on Rajagopal's death, resignation or incapacity, Krishnamurti or Krishnamurti's appointed successor trustee should become Rajagopal's successor trustee (2) that some 160 acres of land at the Western end of the valley, including the Oak Grove, and eleven acres at the upper end on which Pine Cottage and Arya Vihara stood, should be conveyed to the Krishnamurti Foundation of America (KFA) with certain restrictions on building at the western end during Rajagopal's lifetime (3) that the cash assets of KWINC should be transferred to the KFA after the deduction of certain sums for pensions and Rajagopal's legal costs (4) that the Krishnamurti archives should remain in the office in Rajagopal's house where they were already stored but that Krishnamurti and the trustees of the KFA should be allowed access to them and the right to obtain copies of all manuscripts, tape recordings and letters contained in them.

So at long last this sad business was at an end, though it was not to be formalised by the Ventura Court until the end of December.[36] In the winter Bulletins of 1974–75 a short statement was published announcing that a settlement had been reached, and ending with the words: 'The parties in the Agreement wish to make it clear to all those who are concerned with the teachings of Krishnamurti that it is the intent of this agreement to settle all differences so that the work of Krishnamurti throughout the world may proceed effectively.'

*   *   *   *

K and Mary arrived at Brockwood on May 30 and stayed throughout June. As usual they came to London about once a week and it was when we were lunching together one day at Fortnum and Mason that K suddenly asked me if I would write the second volume of his biography. I was, of course, honoured and did not want to refuse but I had an immediate sensation of the weight of the world on me. I knew how dreadfully hard it would be, infinitely more difficult than the first volume. Anyway, I had two other books of my own that had to be written first so I could not start it for a long time and by then I might be dead or some other act of fate might have intervened. The first volume was now with the publisher and it was K who suggested the sub-title for it—*The Years of Awakening.* When I showed him the photographs I had collected, including ones of Nitya, he asked me to tell him what Nitya had been like; he remembered, he said, that he had had a brother whom he had loved but he had not been able to recall his face until he saw the photographs, or anything about him. He then spoke of his own clairvoyance as a boy; he said it was a faculty he could still have but did not choose to, and he repeated what he had said in a different context at the meeting of the Foundations the year before—'It would be like reading people's private letters.'

At the beginning of July K and Mary went to the Plaza-Athénée Hotel in Paris for three nights en route to Chalet Tannegg where Vanda Scaravelli awaited them. This year they had gone by train to Lausanne from Paris, K having decided that he wanted no more long drives across Europe; he found them too tiring. A few days after arriving at Gstaad K woke saying that 'something extraordinary' had happened to him, 'something spreading out to take in the universe'. That morning he dictated a letter about the school at Ojai, saying that it must produce people so religiously based that they would carry that quality with them whatever they did, wherever they went, whatever career they took up.

As usual K gave seven talks at the Saanen Gathering but held only five public discussions afterwards. It was very hot now in Gstaad and he felt 'very far away' and his head was bad. He had become physically even more sensitive and could not bear to be touched, yet he was having 'marvellous meditations'. 'The mind,' he said, 'felt as if it had been washed out, clean, healthy, and much more than that—a tremendous sense of joy, of ecstasy.'

At the Brockwood Gathering that year in early September, there was heavy rain and such gales that the tent was almost blown away and two great beech trees in the park were uprooted. At this time a record-player with stereo was installed in K's bedroom from which he derives great joy playing classical music—Bach, Mozart, Beethoven. At the beginning of October, still at Brockwood, he took part in three days' filming for John McGrevey of the Canadian Broadcasting Corporation for a series 'People of Our Time'; and in the middle of the month a six-day conference was held at Brockwood of scientists and psychologists, arranged by Professor Bohm at K's request. As well as Bohm himself, four other physicists attended (including Professor Maurice Wilkins of King's College, University of London, who won the Nobel Prize for Medicine in 1962), three biologists, four psychiatrists and one lady doctor specialising in acupuncture.

The theme of the conference was 'What place has knowledge in the transformation of man and society?'. K had been excited at the prospect of this conference but it was not as fruitful as he had hoped. The participants started by each delivering a long paper on his own ideas, thus engulfing a great deal of the time that might have been spent in general discussion. K spoke only after all the others had had their say. Nevertheless, he was by no means discouraged from holding several such conferences thereafter. It tired him, though, at the time, and he realised that 'the body must be more protected, more alone', and he again repeated to Mary that he had to live another ten years or so because of all there was to do.

On October 25 K went with Mary to Rome. He heard while he was there that his good and generous old friend Enrique Biascoechea had died from cancer of the lungs. The talks K was to have given in Rome had to be cancelled because he had had fever and lost his voice. He was sufficiently recovered, however, to fly to Delhi on November 7 when Mary returned to California. He found himself on the same plane as the Maharishi who came along beamingly to talk to him, carrying a flower. K's aversion to 'gurus' and 'systems' of meditation put a stop to their conversation as soon as it was politely possible.

From Delhi K went to Rajghat where he was asked at the end of one talk to define his own teaching: 'We have listened to you now for 25 years or 30 years. In a sense, many of us could give some substance to this whole field of self-knowing and say what it is, but still I would like to ask you one question: What is the Teaching?' To this K replied: 'Are you asking me? You are asking me what is the Teaching? I don't know myself. I cannot put it in a few words. Can I? I think the idea of the teaching and the taught is basically wrong, at least for me. I think it is a matter of sharing rather than being taught, partaking rather than giving or receiving.'[37]

What is the teaching? Wanting to ask K this same question myself in the course of writing this book, I wrote out a short statement beginning 'The revolutionary core of Krishnamurti's teaching . . .' and sent it to him for his approval. As I had hoped he entirely re-wrote it, retaining only the word 'core':

The core of Krishnamurti's teaching is contained in the statement he made in 1929 when he said 'Truth is a pathless land'. Man cannot come to it through any organisation, through any creed, through any dogma, priest or ritual, not through any philosophical knowledge or psychological technique. He has to find it through the mirror of relationship, through the understanding of the contents of his own mind, through observation and not through intellectual analysis or introspective dissection. Man has built in himself images as a fence of security—religious, political, personal. These manifest as symbols, ideas, beliefs. The burden of these dominate man's thinking, relationships and daily life. These are the causes of our problems for they divide man from man in every relationship. His perception of life is shaped by the concepts already established in his mind. The content of his consciousness *is* this consciousness. This content is common to all humanity. The individuality is the name, the form and superficial culture he acquires from his environment. The uniqueness of the individual does not lie in the superficial but in the total freedom from the content of consciousness.

Freedom is not a reaction; freedom is not choice. It is man's pretence that because he has choice he is free. Freedom is pure observation without direction, without fear of punishment and reward. Freedom is without motive; freedom is not at the end of the evolution of man but lies in the first step of his existence. In observation one begins to discover the lack of freedom. Freedom is found in the choiceless awareness of our daily existence.

Thought is time. Thought is born of experience, of knowledge, which are inseparable from time. Time is the psychological enemy of man. Our action is based on knowledge and therefore time, so man is always a slave to the past.

When man becomes aware of the movement of his own conscious-ness he will see the division between the thinker and the thought, the observer and the observed, the experiencer and the experience. He will discover that this division is an illusion. Then only is there pure observation which is insight without any shadow of the past. This timeless insight brings about a deep radical change in the mind.

Total negation is the essence of the positive. When there is negation of all those things which are not love—desire, pleasure—then love is, with its compassion and intelligence. [October 21, 1980.]

I had wanted a short statement but realised that as K had said himself, his teaching could not be put in a few words.

*   *   *   *

While K was at Rishi Valley early in January 1975 Mary Zimbalist was going over Pine Cottage at Ojai which K had not occupied since 1966, and over Arya Vihara which Rosalind Rajagopal had now vacated and which had been denuded of almost all its furni-ture and was in a bad state of repair. Mary had had the cottage redecorated by the time K arrived at Malibu on February 8. A few days later he went with her to Ojai for the day and walked with her, the Lilliefelts and the architect round the land at the western end of the valley where it had been decided that the buildings for the new school—the Oak Grove School as it was to be called—were to be erected. He also went to see Pine Cottage and Arya Vihara. A fortnight later he and Mary went again to Ojai and lunched at the cottage. K felt that the atmosphere there, which had repelled him at his first visit, had already changed. At the beginning of March they stayed there for three nights. K found it very strange and wanted Mary to stay close by. Shortly afterwards they flew to San Francisco where K gave four talks at the Masonic Hall. On their return to Malibu the architect already had plans to show them for the first school building.

On April 1 K again took up the journal that he had begun at Brockwood in September '73 and continued to write in it every day for the next three weeks—partly at Malibu and partly at Pine Cottage into which they had moved for a fortnight. On the 12th, a beautiful, cloudless day, K gave the first of four talks in the Oak Grove—the first time he had spoken there since October 1966. Mrs Simmons and her husband had come from Brockwood to attend the talks and were put up in the flat above the old office near Arya Vihara where Mary Zimbalist had stayed in '66. (This flat, now enlarged and with its own small kitchen, has been turned into very comfortable guest quarters.) But unfortunately troubles with Rajagopal were not at an end. In spite of the settlement, he was reluctant to allow anyone to see the archives which were in his own house and when he did let K in with Mary and the Lilliefelts, there was only printed material there apart from some letters from Mrs Besant to K. When K asked through Mary to see his own manuscripts of the *Commentaries on Living*, Rajagopal said that they had been destroyed as was the custom after publication— at least he thought so although he could not really remember. He then refused to answer any more questions and asked Mary to leave. (This led to an amended legal agreement between the parties stating with more exactitude at what times access to the archives were to be allowed.) It seemed that Rajagopal would rather be a nuisance value to K than no value at all.

*   *   *   *

April 27 saw K and Mary in New York, staying once more at the Ritz Tower. This time K had gone there for a two-day conference of twenty-five psychotherapists at the Postgraduate Center for Mental Health, arranged by Dr David Shainberg, one of the psychiatrists who had been at the Brockwood conference the previous October. In an account of the proceedings written for the Bulletin (No 16, 1975) Dr Shainberg reported that 'The group represented a variety of theoretical orientations, including those of Freud, Horney, Sullivan and Rogers'. He continued:

Krishnamurti kept pointing out that no process is necessary in order to be aware of the nature of thought and becoming, or of the formation of ideals, and that the interval between what is and the inventor of thought is to be instantaneously finished with . . . Most of the psychotherapists were deeply moved by the discussion. In general they had great difficulty understanding that no process was necessary. This challenged the psychoanalytical assumptions of growth and development. To be nothing and to live directly in the moment intrigued and interested many who appreciated that the endless analysis through thought was not helping their patients . . . It is clear that further dialogue is necessary to comprehend the process of thought.

K and Mary arrived at Brockwood from New York on May 2. Another addition to the house had just been completed—an octagonal assembly hall, designed by Ian Hammond. Attached to the front of the main building, it blends in perfectly with it.

By this time the decision had been taken to publish the extraordinary manuscript of 1961–62 which K had retrieved from Rajagopal the year before. On May 8 I went down to Brockwood to submit to K the short introduction I had been asked to write for it in which I stressed the fact that he had never taken alcohol or any other kind of drug; that he did not even drink coffee or tea, and that he had never suffered from epilepsy or any of the other physical conditions that are said to produce visions; nor were his strange states of consciousness produced by fasting: I hoped thus to forestall facile explanations.

I also took down the advance copy of the first volume of K's biography, published by Murray. K seemed pleased with it, looked first, of course, at the illustrations. He was interested in the account of his parents and of the 'discovery of the boy'. I believe he actually read the whole book by degrees, though he will have forgotten it by now. He kept asking me how it would strike a complete outsider; what would 'an ordinary stockbroker', for instance, think of it? I could only answer that it was highly unlikely that 'an ordinary stockbroker' would read it. When Mary after reading it asked him why, if the Masters existed, they had spoken then but not now, he suggested that 'there is no need now that the Lord is here'.

The book came out in July and received some very understanding reviews as well as a few scathing ones as was to be expected. It was published by Farrar, Straus & Giroux in America and afterwards brought out by Avon in paperback and also issued as a paperback in India. Like K's own books it has been translated into several languages, including Icelandic! (Several of K's books have also been translated into Japanese.) From the innumerable letters I have received I believe that the story of Krishnamurti's early life has helped hundreds of people to a better understanding of him even if some of the revelations in it came as a shock to many who were unaware of his Theosophical upbringing.

Two new books of K's were published that summer, giving his views on education—*The Beginnings of Learning*, informal

Freedom is Not Choice

discussions between him and students and staff at Brockwood School, with four beautiful photographs of Brockwood in colour— and *Krishnamurti on Education* (Orient Longman), discussions with students and teachers at the Rishi Valley and Rajghat schools. This book contains a number of excellent photographs of K taken during these discussions. K insists in both these books that through the right kind of education it is possible to bring about a complete transformation of the human mind: 'The right kind of education cultivates your whole being, the totality of your mind, and gives your heart and mind a depth of understanding and beauty.' (On September 12 *The Times Educational Supplement* was to publish a long article by Professor Bohm on the Brockwood Park School.)

*   *   *   *

On May 11, K's eightieth birthday, Dr Parchure arrived at Brockwood from India to stay for several weeks, and in the middle of the month K held the first of what were to be twelve dialogues with Professor Bohm at Brockwood. At this time Mrs Bindley fell and broke her hip. K drove with Mary to Putney Hospital on May 21 to see her. She was asleep when they went in but when Mary woke her to tell her that K was there, she murmured, 'Oh, lovely, lovely, lovely.' She then woke completely and was, as Mary described it, 'her bright amazing self, interested and wanting to know everything that had happened to Krishnaji'. She died a month later at the age of ninety-six. K had lost one of his oldest and truest friends.

There was another week-end conference of scientists at Brockwood from June 6. Most of the people who had attended the previous conference were there again, including David Bohm, Dr Shainberg and Professor Wilkins and, in addition, Dr Parchure.

Late in June I went to stay at Brockwood for a couple of nights because Pupul Jayakar was there to discuss publication matters. David Bohm had one of his discussions with K while I was there. Bohm had just read the biography and was questioning K as to whether there had been a particular moment of change for him. K said no; physical suffering during 'the process' had made him more sensitive and so had his suffering at his brother's death but 'meeting that fully left no marks'.

K and Mary flew to Paris at the end of June and stayed three nights at the Plaza-Athénée. For once K was glad to be in a town; he had not been out for the last three weeks at Brockwood because his hay fever had been so bad. On July 3 they went on to Gstaad. K devoted one of his talks at the Saanen Gathering that year to what he called 'a very serious matter—Can there be total freedom from psychological fear?' 'If one is to be free of fear one must be free of time,' he pointed out. 'If there were no time one would have no fear. I wonder if you see that? If there were no tomorrow, only the now, fear, as a movement of thought, ends.' Fear arises from the desire for security: 'If there is complete psychological security there is no fear.' But there can never be psychological security 'if one is wanting, desiring, pursuing, becoming'. He went on:

... thought is always trying to find a place where it can abide, abide in the sense of hold. What thought creates, being fragmentary, is total insecurity. Therefore there is complete security in being absolutely nothing—which means not a thing created by thought. To be *absolutely nothing* means a total contradiction of everything you have learnt ... You know what it means to be nothing? No ambition— which does not mean that you vegetate—no aggression, no resistance, no barriers built by hurt? ... The security that thought has created is no security. That is an absolute truth.

K was well aware of what might happen to a marriage or to any close relationship if one partner 'sees the truth that in this nothingness there is complete security' and the other does not. Then what takes place? he asks. If you are the secure one what do you do with your partner? 'What do you do with me [if I am the insecure one]—cajole me, talk to me, comfort me, tell me how stupid I am? What will you do?' K believes that to *be* is enough, for he answers his own question: '... if you are completely, wholly secure—in the sense we are talking about—won't you affect me—I who am insecure, despairing, clinging, attached— won't you affect me? Obviously you will. If you affect a basic transformation in yourself then you will affect not only those close to you but the whole consciousness of the world.'

K had a large photograph of a tiger hanging in his bedroom at Tannegg that summer. 'I talk to the tiger,' he told Mary. 'I say,

"Be careful, avoid humans, kill discreetly." I talk to tiger consciousness.' Many years before this, when being driven through a forest after dark in India, he had come face to face with a tiger, a meeting he afterwards described:

They [K and his host] had given up every hope of seeing the tiger as they drove back. But just as they turned a corner, there it was, sitting on its haunches in the middle of the road, huge, striped, its eyes bright with the headlamps. The car stopped and it came towards them growling and the growls shook the car; it was surprisingly large and its long tail with its black tip was moving slowly from side to side. It was annoyed. The window was open and as it passed growling, he [K himself] put out his hand to stroke this great energy of the forest, but his host hurriedly snatched his arm back, explaining later that it would have torn his arm away.[38]

K has no fear of wild animals; that being so it is possible that the tiger would not have harmed him. In many of his writings there are descriptions of snakes—rattlers and cobras—which evidently have a fascination for him.

*   *   *   *

K had been persuaded not to go to India that winter on account of the state of emergency declared by Mrs Gandhi in June, during which nothing could be published or publicly spoken without submission to the Censorship Committee. To tone down his denunciations of all authority and tyranny was the last thing K was prepared to do; there was no point in his going if he did not talk and a real danger of imprisonment if he did. After the Brockwood Gathering, therefore, he returned with Mary to Malibu in October.

During November and December and the first two months of 1976 K and Mary stayed at Pine Cottage at week-ends and held frequent discussions with teachers and parents of prospective pupils about the Oak Grove School. As well as a school K wanted to create a centre at Ojai where people could come and study his teaching. He also wanted to enlarge Pine Cottage now that he would be spending so much more time at Ojai.

From March 19 there was a six-day conference of scientists at the Lilliefelts' house on the theme 'In a disintegrating society, what is the correct action for survival in freedom?' It started with sixteen participants who swelled to thirty when some of them asked to bring friends. On the first day K startled many of those present who had not heard him speak before by his pronouncement, 'All thought leads to sorrow'. Some of the participants were disappointed at not being given the opportunity to read papers on their own ideas as had been done at Brockwood in October '74. One Canadian, who had brought along friends without asking permission, became over-excited, rude and abusive. He had written a book which he had hoped would be discussed. He left on the third day.

This disappointing conference was followed on April 1 by the Ojai Gathering during which K gave public talks in the Oak Grove (the last talk was attended by over 5,000 people); and then at the end of April another three-day conference of twenty-seven psychotherapists was held at the Postgraduate Center for Mental Health in New York, again arranged by Dr Shainberg.

19

A Dialogue with Death

K came to Brockwood with Mary Zimbalist on May 1, directly after the New York conference. *Krishnamurti's Notebook* was published that month. K must at least have glanced through it for he decided that he would like to review it himself 'for fun'. Part of his review is given below:

... *Krishnamurti's Notebook* appears to me to go beyond the Upanishads and Vedanta. When he talks about knowledge and the ending of it, it is in essence Vedanta, which literally means the ending of knowledge. But the Vedantists and their followers in different parts of the world are really maintaining the structure of knowledge, perhaps thinking knowledge is salvation, as most scientists do.

Tradition has such a strong grip on the mind that few seem to escape its tentacles and I think this is where Krishnamurti begins. He constantly asserts that freedom is the first and last step. The traditionalists maintain that a highly disciplined mind is necessary for freedom: be a slave first and afterwards you will be free. To Krishnamurti what seems the most important thing, and he had repeated this in all his talks and dialogues, is that there must be freedom to observe, not some ideological freedom but freedom from the very knowledge and experience which has been acquired yesterday. This brings about a tremendous problem. If there is no knowledge of many yesterdays, then what is it that is capable of observing? If knowledge is not the root of observation, what have you with which to observe? Can the many yesterdays be totally forgotten, which is the essence of freedom? He maintains that it can. This is possible only when the past ends in the present, meeting it fully, head-on. The past, as he asserts, is the ego, the structure of the 'me' which prevents total observation.

An ordinary person reading this book will inevitably cry out, saying, What are you talking about? To him Krishnamurti explains very carefully in manifold ways the necessary memory and the psychological memory. Knowledge is necessary to function in any field of our daily life but psychological memory of our hurts, anxiety, pain and sorrow is the factor of division and hence there is a conflict between the essential knowledge which is required to drive a car and the experience of knowledge which is the whole movement of the psyche. He points out this fact in relationship, in our fragmented ways of life. I have read this book very carefully. I am familiar with the Upanishads and have delved deeply into the teachings of the Buddha. I am fairly familiar with the psychological studies of modern times. As far as I have come in my studies I have not found the phrase 'the observer is the observed', with its full meaning. Perhaps some ancient thinker may have said it, but one of the most important things that Krishnamurti has found is this great truth which, when it actually takes place, as it has occasionally happened to me personally, literally banishes the movement of time. Let me add here that I am not a follower nor do I accept Krishnamurti as my guru. To him the idea of becoming a guru is an abomination. With critical examination I find this book totally absorbing because he annihilates everything thought has put together. It is a shocking thing when one realises this. It is a real physical shock.

Can a human being live in this state of absolute nothingness except for his daily bread and work—in the total emptiness of consciousness as we know it? As Krishnamurti points out over and over again, consciousness is the movement of all thought. Thought is matter, measurable, and thought is time, which implies that psychologically there is no tomorrow. That means no hope. This is a devastating psychological fact and our everyday mind is not only shocked by this statement but probably will refuse to examine it closely. It is death *now*. From this death arises a totally different quality of energy, of a different dimension, inexhaustible and without an end. He says this is the ultimate benediction.

I can feel through all the pages of this book a sense of extraordinary love which the Tibetans might call the love or the compassion of the Bodhisattva, but when you give it a name and an ideological symbol you will lose the perfume. It has strangely affected my life . . .

It is curious also how he deals with meditation. Meditation, according to him, can never be a conscious thing, and one can see the reason for this. If one meditates purposefully with a deliberate intention, consciousness then continues with all its content. . . .[39]

During May seven discussions took place at Brockwood between K, David Bohm and Dr Shainberg, video-taped in colour by a professional American team.[40] They were so successful that it was decided that the Krishnamurti Foundation must acquire video-recording equipment of its own. At the Saanen Gathering, therefore, in July, one video-recorder and one camera, all that could be afforded, were used. Scott Forbes, a young American teacher at the Brockwood school, sat with the recorder on his lap while using the camera. From that time onwards, with increasingly good equipment, all K's talks in Europe, and some in America and India, have been video-recorded, though to date it has not been possible to afford colour equipment.

After Saanen K returned to Brockwood for the eighth gathering there. In September a new Krishnamurti school was opened on Vancouver Island, called the Wolf Lake School. A large white weather-boarded house with three cottages, set in thirty-five acres of meadows, woodland, gardens and orchards, it is beautifully situated overlooking sea and mountains. A co-educational boarding school for fifteen students, aged twelve to eighteen, it was started by two Indian lady doctors, J. K. and S. K. Siddoo, who run a hospital in India and whose father had emigrated to Canada where he built up a successful business. After the opening of this school K found it necessary to publish a statement in the autumn number of the Bulletin saying that although it was an excellent thing that many people in many parts of the world were anxious to start schools intended to bring about the application of Krishnamurti's teachings, the Krishnamurti Foundations could not be responsible for them. Krishnamurti was in close communication with his existing schools but it would not be possible to be so with every school that might come into being; therefore it was suggested that when new schools were started the Krishnamurti name should not be used. 'It is not that one wants to keep the name exclusive,' the statement concluded, 'but it becomes impossible to be directly responsible for schools beyond one's close observation.'

During their stay at Brockwood that autumn, K and Mary came to London more frequently than usual so I saw more of them. K was undergoing rather extensive dental treatment. He has had wonderful teeth but has worn away some of the enamel by over-cleaning. He asked me at this time whether I had started yet on the second volume of the biography. I was still prevaricating. The more I thought about it the harder it seemed to do justice to the subject. Nevertheless, I wanted to do it. Thereafter, for nearly four years. while I went on stalling, the urge to begin it continually nagged at me.

Mrs Gandhi's state of emergency was still in force that winter; all the same, K decided to go to India after an assurance through Pupul Jayakar, Mrs Gandhi's great friend, that he would be allowed to say anything he liked at his meetings. On October 25 he flew alone to Delhi where he stayed with Mrs Jayakar now that Shiva Rao was dead. Soon after his arrival he had a long interview with Mrs Gandhi. Could there, one wonders, have been any connection between this interview and her surprise decision to hold a general election in 1977?

In India he visited the usual places—Rajghat, Rishi Valley, Madras (where he was able to stay again at Vasanta Vihar since it had now been legally restored to the Indian Foundation) and Bombay. He left India earlier than usual, on January 20, 1977, and spent a week at Brockwood. The reason for this was that he had applied for an immigration visa for the United States. For the past two months Mary Zimbalist had been helping to obtain this for him in Los Angeles while Mrs Simmons was dealing with the American Embassy in London. When Mary heard that he had an appointment with the American Embassy on January 26 she decided to fly to London in order to go with him. The interview went well and he was given his papers. When he and Mary flew to Los Angeles on the 31st he was formally admitted into the U.S. as an immigrant and granted permanent residence. The so-called 'green card' was handed to him which would enable him to apply for American citizenship in five years' time.

*   *   *   *

At K's request, representatives of the Krishnamurti Foundations met at Ojai in March to get to know each other better and understand their separate problems. There were meetings with K every other day from March 3 to 24. He was very insistent that the Foundations should co-operate and act as one body. He not only wanted the schools to continue after his death but for the main ones to become centres where people could go to study his

teachings, and for those in charge of the centres to be able to pass
on the essence of his presence; in fact, he repeated, though more
strongly, what he had said at the meeting of the Foundations at
Brockwood in 1973. He now wanted as many of the Foundation
members as possible to be with him—to go to India when he was
there as well as to Ojai and Brockwood. Especially he wanted the
Americans and Europeans who had never been to India to be with
him there in the coming years. At one meeting he asked in effect,
'If people come here and ask, "What was it like to live with this
man?" would you be able to convey it to them? If any of the
Buddha's disciples were alive would not one travel to the ends of
the earth to see them, to find out from them what it had been like
to live in his presence?'

K's allusion to the Buddha and his disciples could surely mean
only one thing? It was the nearest he had ever come to defining
his own status, yet it is impossible to convey to anyone who does
not know him well how totally without self-importance such a
comparison was made. Where the self is absent there can be no
conceit. 'This man' K spoke of was not his own personality. All
the same, how does one reconcile all this with his constant
reiteration, before and since, that no one has any authority to
represent him after his death and that the guru-disciple relationship is an abomination to him? Is it not perhaps quite simple?
If anyone close to him ever does undergo a complete psychological
transformation will not he or she carry on in the same non-
authoritarian way as K himself? In asking the trustees to be with
him as much as possible surely he is hoping that at least one or
two of them may be granted the depth of perception to bring
about a total revolution in the psyche, thus freeing them from
their need of him as from all other crutches. This is very different
from the guru-worship of disciples. If anyone ever claims after
K's death authority to speak for him, one will know that he or
she has *not* been transformed. But here another question arises
which may never be answered: if a transformation should take
place in anyone close to K would he or she choose to remain under
the Krishnamurti aegis?

These Foundation meetings were followed in April by public
talks in the Oak Grove. It had been decided by this time that
Mary was to sell her house at Malibu in order to build an addition

to Pine Cottage. Since the land belonged to the American Foundation the new building would revert to the Foundation at her death.
At the end of April K was with Mary in New York, staying at the
Ritz Tower once again for another week-end conference of
psychotherapists arranged by Dr Shainberg. Back in California K
had to undergo an operation on May 9 at the Cedars-Sinai
Medical Center in Los Angeles. He had warned Mary beforehand
that she must be watchful and not let him 'slip away', and also
remind him to be watchful himself; otherwise, after 'fifty-two
years [of public speaking] he might feel enough is enough'. He
told her he had 'always lived with a very fine line between living
and dying'. A fortnight or so before the operation he went to the
hospital to give a pint of his own blood in case a transfusion was
necessary. He refused to have a general anaesthetic, convinced
that 'the body' would never be able to stand it. Even a local
anaesthetic, he told Mary, causing a spinal block, might be too
much for the body.

When the day came, Mary went with him to the hospital and
stayed in a room next door. She asked the anaesthetist to talk to
him during the operation, to keep him alert so that he would not
'slip away'. He went to the operating theatre at 7.30 and was
wheeled back to his room at 9.45 looking very cheerful and asking
for a detective story to read, but by the evening he was in great
pain. He was given a child's dose of Demarol which had to be
discontinued for it caused dizziness and nausea. He 'went off' for
about an hour and talked of Nitya, and later had, what he called,
'a dialogue with death'. The next day he dictated to Mary an
account of this latter experience:

It was a short operation and not worth talking about, though there
was considerable pain. While the pain continued I saw or discovered
that the body was almost floating in the air. It may have been an
illusion, some kind of hallucination, but a few minutes later there was
the personification—not a person—but the personification of death.
Watching this peculiar phenomenon between the body and death, there
seemed to be a sort of dialogue between them. Death seemed to be
talking to the body with great insistence and the body reluctantly
was not yielding to what death wanted. Though there were people
in the room this phenomenon went on, death inviting, the body re-
fusing.

A Dialogue with Death

It was not a fear of death making the body deny the demands of death but the body realised that it was not responsible for itself, there was another entity that was dominating, much stronger, more vital than death itself. Death was more and more demanding, insisting and so the other interfered. Then there was a conversation or a dialogue between not only the body, but this other and death. So there were three entities in conversation.

He had warned, before he went to the hospital, that there might be a disassociation with the body and so death might intervene. Though the person [Mary] was sitting there and a nurse came and went, it was not a self-deception or kind of hallucination. Lying in the bed he saw the clouds full of rain and the window lighted up, the town below stretching for miles. There was spattering of rain on the window pane and he saw clearly the saline solution dripping, drop by drop, into the organism. One felt very strongly and clearly that if the other had not interfered death would have won.

This dialogue began in words with thought operating very clearly. There was thunder and lightning and the conversation went on. Since there was no fear at all, neither on the part of the body or the other— absolutely no fear—one could converse freely and profoundly. It is always difficult to put a conversation of that kind into words. Strangely, as there was no fear, death was not enchaining the mind to the things of the past. What came out of the conversation was very clear. The body was in considerable pain and not apprehensive or anxious and the other was discernibly beyond both. It was as though the other was acting as an umpire in a dangerous game of which the body was not fully aware.

Death seemed to be always present but death cannot be invited. That would be suicide which would be utterly foolish.

During this conversation there was no sense of time. Probably the whole dialogue lasted about an hour and time by the watch did not exist. Words ceased to exist but there was an immediate insight into what each one was saying. Of course if one is attached to anything— ideas, beliefs, property or person, death would not come to have a conversation with you. Death in the sense of ending is absolute freedom.

The quality of conversation was urbane. There was nothing whatsoever of sentiment, emotional extravagance, no distortion of the absolute fact of time coming to an end and the vastness without any border when death is part of your daily life. There was a feeling that the body would go on for many years but death and the other would always be together until the organism could no longer be active. There was a great sense of humour amongst the three of them and one could almost

218

hear the laughter. And the beauty of it was with the clouds and the rain.

The sound of this conversation was expanding endlessly and the sound was the same at the beginning and was without end. It was a song without a beginning or an end. Death and life are very close together, like love and death. As love is not a remembrance, so death had no past. Fear never entered this conversation for fear is darkness and death is light.

This dialogue was not illusory or fanciful. It was like a whisper in the wind but the whisper was very clear and if you listened you could hear it; you could then be part of it. Then we would share it together. But you won't listen to it as you are too identified with your own body, your own thoughts and your own direction. One must abandon all this to enter into the light and love of death.

After returning from hospital K remained quietly resting at Malibu so he did not go to England that year until June 21 and stayed only ten days at Brockwood before flying to Geneva. The next three months followed their habitual course—Gstaad in July and August, then back to Brockwood for the gathering there in September. An innovation this autumn was that K and Mary went at the end of September to Bonn for three nights, staying at the Bristol Hotel, to consult Dr Scheef at the Janker Clinic. K underwent some tests the result of which showed, according to the doctor, that he was 'fantastic' for his age. They returned to Brockwood where they remained until November 1 when K flew alone direct to Bombay. When Mary left him the day before to fly to New York, his parting words were, 'An angel goes with you.'

20

Who or What is Krishnamurti?

Late in the year some trustees of the English and American Foundations joined K in Madras where he gave public talks at the end of December and the beginning of January 1978. On January 13 and 14 there were special meetings of the Foundations. Changes had taken place in the Rishi Valley School. In the spring of '77 Dr Balasundaram had resigned as Principal and his place had been taken by G. Narayan, the son of K's eldest brother, who had been teaching for twenty-five years both at Rishi Valley and at a Rudolph Steiner school in England. Narayan's wife had been a teacher at Brockwood almost from the beginning and their daughter, Natasha, their only child, an extremely intelligent and lovely girl, is a pupil at Brockwood. K seems to take little account of his blood relationship with Narayan and to be no more or less fond of Natasha than of any other bright girl in one of his schools. Pupils from Rishi Valley have been encouraged in the past to come to Brockwood but K is beginning to question the wisdom of this. It is so easy to be corrupted by the West. The young in India still show a respect for their elders and an eagerness to learn, regarding education as a privilege.

After giving talks in Bombay in late January, K returned to California. The extension to Pine Cottage was now finished and he moved in there with Mary on March 20. It had been a wrench for Mary to abandon her beautiful home at Malibu, and K also was to miss the house, but Pine Cottage has been transformed into an equally beautiful house.

That year it was too wet in April for K to give his Ojai talks in the Oak Grove, so he gave them in the Nordhoff School Gymnasium or, when the rain held off, in Libbey Park. As soon as the talks were over he and Mary flew to Victoria on Vancouver Island to visit the Wolf Lake School where they had not been before. The two Siddoo sisters met them. K spent four days there talking to the children and the staff. He was immensely impressed by the beauty of the place. Back at Ojai, he made a statement on April 27 that after his and Mary's death Pine Cottage was to become a library and a place of study but that nobody was to sleep there.

At the beginning of May K and Mary arrived back at Brockwood. Shortly afterwards Vanda Scaravelli came to stay for a few days. Although a room in the west wing had always been kept for her, this was the first time she had been there. I went down to Brockwood for the day on May 14 and met her for the second time. She was now wearing one of her becoming dark kimonos over trousers, and sandals on her bare feet. Again I was struck by her wonderful suppleness, and envied her her disregard for conventional dress.

At the end of June K and Mary went to the Janker Clinic again at Bonn on their way to Gstaad. The results of the tests K had there were all satisfactory.

In his second talk at Saanen on July 14 he went with vehemence into that difficult aspect of his teaching, the limitation of thought:

... There is an action, total, complete, holistic action in which thought does not interfere at all. Are you waiting for me to tell you? That's rather cheap! The speaker does all the work and you listen and say, 'Yes, I agree'. What is the point of that? But if you really, desperately want to find out, like a drowning man desperate to find some kind of thing to hang on to, to save himself, then like him you exert all your energy . . .

The long rather confused explanation that followed did nothing more than has already been quoted to clarify the subject. (Interviewed by Bernard Levin on BBC television in May 1981, K began with the bare statement, 'All thought corrupts.' Given no opportunity to develop this theme, those viewers who had never before heard him speak must have been totally mystified. The critics appear to have heard nothing beyond this opening remark which they were able to ridicule.)

During the Brockwood Gathering that year K began to write fortnightly letters to his schools which he continued to do until

Who or What is Krishnamurti?

March 1980—thirty-seven letters altogether of about three pages each.[41] He sometimes wrote them in batches but sent them out fortnightly from September 1. It was a means of keeping in close personal touch with all the schools. In his first letter he stated what his intention was for them: 'They are to be concerned with the cultivation of the whole human being. These centres of education must help the students and educators to flower naturally. Career and profession, as society now exists, is inevitable, but if we lay all our emphasis on that the freedom to flower will gradually wither.' And in a later letter: 'It is the concern of these schools to bring about a new generation of human beings who are free from self-centred action. No other educational centres are concerned with this and it is our responsibility, as educators, to bring about a mind that has no conflict within itself.'

A copy of each letter was given to every teacher and pupil. What he expected the teachers to do seemed impossible—to see that fear in any form did not arise in the student (and for this it was necessary for the teachers to uncover the roots of their own fear), and to help the student 'never to be psychologically wounded, not only while he is part of the school but throughout life'. Comparison was one of the greatest evils in education. As he had said before: 'When in your school you compare B with A you are destroying both of them.'

Over and over again in these letters K stresses that teaching is the highest of callings and that 'the Schools exist primarily to bring about a profound transformation in human beings' for which the educator is wholly responsible. K also goes very deeply into the difference between learning and accumulating knowledge. Learning leads to intelligence, accumulating knowledge to the dulling of the mind: 'To know is not to know and the understanding of this fact that knowledge can never solve our human problems is intelligence.'

In his letter of May 1, 1979, he begins one paragraph: 'God is disorder.' If one goes on reading, his meaning becomes perfectly clear: 'Consider the innumerable gods that man has invented, or the one god, the one saviour, and observe the confusion that this has created in the world, the wars it has brought about, the innumerable divisions, the separating beliefs, symbols and images. Isn't this confusion and disorder?'

The parents of one girl, who had taken this letter home in the holidays, happened to read it, and coming upon this bald statement, 'God is disorder', were so outraged that they considered removing their daughter from the school. With such a lack of understanding of K's teaching it is surprising that they sent the child there in the first place. It is short pronouncements of K's such as this that shock one into full attention. Later on he was to make the point even more strongly, saying at a public talk at Saanen in 1980, 'If man is the creation of God, God must be rather horrible, a monstrous entity . . . He must be total disorder, for we live in disorder. If he created us in his image and we are killing each other, then he *must* be monstrous.'

In a passage in a book published the following year K explained how 'never to be psychologically wounded' could be brought about. He had been enlarging on 'living with sorrow' and continued:

We are seeing the fact, the 'what is', which is suffering. That is an absolute fact. I suffer and the mind is doing everything it can to run away from it. When it does not run away then it observes. Then the observer, if it observes very very closely, is the observed, and that very pain is transformed into passion, which is compassion. The words are not the reality. So, don't escape from suffering, which does not mean you become morbid. Live with it. You live with pleasure, don't you? Why don't you live with suffering completely? Can you live with it in the sense of not escaping from it? What takes place? Watch. The mind is very clear, sharp. It is faced with the fact. The very suffering transformed into passion is enormous. From that arises a mind that can never be hurt. Full stop. That is the secret.[42]

*   *   *   *

In October 1978 Mary Zimbalist went to India with K where he spoke in the usual places. Other members of the English and American Foundations joined him in Madras later in the year and several meetings were held of the combined Foundations. Yet another Krishnamurti school had been opened in the summer of '78 in a lush valley at Haridvanam, ten miles from the centre of Bangalore. The building and purchase of 100 acres of land had been made possible by the gift of one man. Called the Valley School, it is a co-educational day and boarding school for 110 children between the ages of six and thirteen, and receives support and guidance from the Rishi Valley School. K went to visit it in the middle of December.

On January 8, 1979, Mrs Gandhi came to see K at Vasanta Vihar. In December she had been jailed for four days which had caused riots in many parts of India. On February 2 K and Mary left Bombay and broke their journey at Brockwood for a few days before returning to California. The new house at Ojai (it can hardly be called a cottage any more) was in 'exquisite order', according to Mary. She wrote to me in May after the Ojai talks which had followed another conference of scientists:

Krishnaji has been very well, gave some very good talks and has, I think, enjoyed the house. 'We must take care of it, it is a beautiful house,' he says and polishes the counter tops [in the kitchen] carefully each morning after breakfast. He is also a dedicated plant-waterer and is busy with a hose every afternoon on the small plantings round the house. I too find this house a lovely place to live in and have enjoyed it every day. The Oak Grove was more beautiful than ever in memory. There had been a great deal of rain before the talks which had stopped just in time for the ground to dry out.

K and Mary were back at Brockwood later in May. By now the writing of the second volume of K's biography was very much in my mind and I was beginning hesitantly to feel my way towards tackling it. But I needed to make another attempt to discover from K the source of his teaching. I knew that he had gone into this matter at Ojai in 1972 with some members of the American Foundation. On that occasion he had said:

I feel we are delving into something which the conscious mind can never understand, which doesn't mean I am making a mystery of it. There is something. Much too vast to be put into words. There is a tremendous reservoir, as it were, which if the human mind can touch it, reveals something which no intellectual mythology—invention, supposition, dogma—can ever reveal.

I am not making a mystery of it—that would be a stupid childish trick. Creating a mystery out of nothing would be a most blackguardly thing to do because that would be exploiting people and ruthless—that's a dirty trick.

Either one creates a mystery when there isn't one or there is a mystery which you have to approach with extraordinary delicacy and hesitancy, and, you know, tentativeness. And the conscious mind can't do this. It is there but you cannot come to it, you cannot invite it. It's not progressive achievement. There *is* something but the brain can't understand it.

But I was still not satisfied, even after reading these notes. I went down to Brockwood for the day on June 4 and had two conversations with K. Mary Zimbalist was present and made notes of salient points. I took no notes myself and felt that the use of a tape-recorder would inhibit spontaneity. The first conversation took place in K's large bedroom looking out over the lawn and the fields beyond, while he sat up in bed cross-legged, very straight-backed in his pale blue bathrobe. There was a faint scent of sandalwood in the room, a scent I always associate with him. Even his writing paper smells slightly of it.

He was more than co-operative; indeed he seemed as eager as I was to make the discovery. I started by asking him if he could explain what had made him what he was. He countered this by asking me what explanation I thought there could be. The most plausible explanation, I said, was the Besant-Leadbeater theory of the Lord Maitreya taking over a body specially prepared for his occupation, the ego having evolved through a series of incarnations until it was born in a Brahmin body, which was purer than any other, not having touched meat or alcohol for countless generations. This explanation would also account for 'the process' —the body being 'tuned' as it were, rendered more and more sensitive to accommodate its divine occupant, thus ultimately blending the consciousness of the Lord Maitreya with that of Krishnamurti. In other words, everything Mrs Besant and Leadbeater had predicted had come to pass. K agreed that this theory was the most likely but he did not think it was that. Another possible explanation I put forward was that there was a great reservoir of goodness in the world which could be tapped, and had been tapped by many great artists, geniuses and saints. K dismissed this out of hand. The only other theory I could suggest was that Krishnamurti himself had evolved through many lives to become what he was, though this I found hard to accept because the boy Krishna I had known had been quite vacant, childish, almost moronic, interested really in nothing except golf, and mechanical things such as cameras, clocks and motor-bicycles.

I could not see how this being could ever have developed the brain to expound Krishnamurti's teaching.

I now quote from Mary Zimbalist's notes:

ML: The teachings are not simple. How did they come out of that vacant boy?

K: You admit a mystery. The boy was affectionate, vacant, not intellectual, enjoyed athletic games. What is important in this is the vacant mind. How could that vacant mind come to this [the teaching]? Was vacancy necessary for this to manifest? Does this thing that manifests come out of a universal pool as genius comes out of it in other fields? The religious spirit has nothing to do with genius. How is it that the vacant mind was not filled with Theosophy etc.? Was the vacancy intended for the manifestation? The boy must have been strange from the beginning. What made him that way? Was the body prepared through many lives or did this force pick out the vacant body? Why didn't he become an abomination with all that adulation? Why didn't he become cynical, bitter? What kept him from that? This vacancy was guarded. By what?

ML: That is what we are trying to find out.

K: Right through life it has been guarded, protected. When I get into an aeroplane I know nothing will happen. But I don't do anything that will cause danger. I would have loved to go up in a glider [the opportunity had been offered to him at Gstaad] but I felt, 'No, I mustn't.' Always I have felt protected. Or does the impression I am protected come because Amma [Mrs Besant] always saw that I was— always saw that there were two initiates to guard me [for the first few years only after he came to England]. I don't think it is that.

ML: No, because the other thing—'the process'—came for the first time when you were away from them all—alone at Ojai with Nitya.

K: Yes, the vacancy has never gone away. At the dentist for four hours not a single thought came into my head. Only when talking and writing does '*this*' come into play. I am amazed. The vacancy is still there. From that age till now—eighty or so—to keep a mind that is vacant. What does it? You can feel it in the room now. It is happening in this room now because we are touching something very, very serious and it comes pouring in. The mind of this man from childhood till now is constantly vacant. I don't want to make a mystery: why can't it happen to everyone?

ML: When you give talks is your mind vacant?

K: Oh, yes, completely. But I'm not interested in that but in why it stays vacant. Because it is vacant it has no problems.

ML: Is it unique?

K: No. If a thing is unique then others cannot get it. I want to avoid any mystery. I see that the boy's mind is the same now. The other thing is here now. Don't you feel it? It is like throbbing.

ML: The essence of your teaching is that everyone can have it.

K: Yes, if it is unique it is not worth anything. But this isn't like that. Is it kept vacant for this thing to say, 'Though I am vacant, you—X—can also have it?'

ML: You mean it is vacant in order to be able to say that this can happen to everyone?

K: That's right. That's right. But did that thing keep the mind vacant? How did it remain vacant all these years? It is extraordinary. I never thought of it before. It would not be that way if it weren't detached. Why was he not attached? That thing must have said, 'There must be vacancy or I—it—cannot function.' This is admitting all sorts of mystical things. So what is *that* that keeps it vacant in order to say all these things? Did it find a boy that was most likely to remain vacant? This boy apparently didn't have any fear of going against Leadbeater, going against Theosophy, against authority. Amma, Leadbeater—they had great authority. That thing must have been operating. This must be possible for all mankind. If not, what is the point of it?

The conversation broke off here; K had to get up to be in time for lunch in the school dining-room. After lunch we resumed talking in the kitchen of the west wing.

K: We haven't discovered why this boy was kept vacant from then till now. Is the vacancy a lack of selfishness—the self—*my* house, attachment? But how did the vacancy with its non-self come about? It would be simple if we said that the Lord Maitreya prepared this body and kept it vacant. That would be the simplest explanation but the simplest is suspect. Another explanation is that K's ego might have been in touch with the Lord Maitreya and the Buddha and said, 'I withdraw: *that* is more important than my beastly self.' But I suspect this too. It implies a lot of superstition. It doesn't feel clean, right, somehow. The Lord Maitreya saw this body with the least ego, wanted to manifest through it and so it was kept uncontaminated. Amma said the face of K was very important because it represented *that*. It was prepared for *that*. This means everyone cannot have it. K is a biological freak. An easy way out. So what is the truth? I don't know. I really don't know. What is the truth of all this? It is not self-delusion, deception, an induced state, a wish produced—I don't know what to wish for. Another peculiar thing in all this is that K has always been attracted to the Buddha. Was this an influence? I don't think so. Is that reservoir the Buddha?, the Maitreya? What is the truth? Is it something we can never find out?

Mary Zimbalist: Do you ever feel used, feel something coming into you?

K: I wouldn't say that. It comes into the room when we are talking seriously.

ML: How is it related to the pain?

K: Pain comes when I am quiet, not talking. It comes slowly until the body says, 'That is enough'. After reaching a crisis the body faints; the pain peters out or there is some interruption and it goes.

ML: Can we rule out something from outside?

K: I don't. But what is the truth? There is an element in all this which is not man-made, thought-made, not self-induced. I am not like that. Is this something which we cannot discover, mustn't touch, is not penetrable? I am wondering. I have often felt it is not my business, that we will never find out. When we say it comes into being because the mind is vacant, I don't think it is that either. We have come to an impasse. I have talked to you, to her [MZ], to Subba Rao [who had known him since the early days]. He said, 'You have been as you are since the beginning'. I ask myself, 'Is this true?' If it is, there is no hope for others. Is it all something which we cannot touch? We are trying with our minds to touch *that*. Try to find out what *that* is when your mind is completely quiet. To find out the truth of the matter you have to have your mind empty. Not *my* mind which *is* in emptiness. But there is a factor we are missing. We have come to a point where our brains, our instruments of investigation, have no meaning.

ML: Might someone else be able to find out? And would it be right to enquire?

K: *You* might be able to because you are writing about it. I cannot. If you and Maria [MZ] sat down and said, 'Let us enquire', I'm pretty sure you could find out. Or do it alone. I see something: what I said is true—I can never find out. Water can never find out what water is. That is quite right. If you find out I'll corroborate it.

ML: You would know if it were right?

K: Can you feel it in the room? It is getting stronger and stronger. My head is starting. If you asked the question and said, 'I don't know', you might find it. If I was writing it I would state all this. I would begin with the boy completely vacant.

ML: Do you mind it said that you want it explained?

K: I don't care. Say what you like. I'm sure if others put their minds to this they can do it. I am absolutely sure of this. Absolutely, absolutely. Also I am sure *I* can't find it.

ML: What if one could understand it but not be able to put it into words?

K: You could. You would find a way. The moment you discover something you have words for it. Like a poem. If you are open to enquire, put your brain in condition, someone could find out. But the moment you find it, it will be right. No mystery.

ML: Will the mystery mind being found?

K: No, the mystery will be gone.

Mary Zimbalist: But the mystery is something sacred.

K: The sacredness will remain.

Here the conversation ended because K's head had become so bad that he had to go and lie down. It was not only when he was quiet that his head came on but when he was talking about such matters as we had been going into. I returned to London awed by the responsibility he had put on us: he was 'absolutely sure' that we could find out the truth about him if we tried, but I was still reluctant to believe that he himself could not help more towards discovering the truth, so three weeks later, on June 15, I talked to him again at Brockwood before he left for Gstaad. It was after lunch in the kitchen of the west wing again, and again Mary Zimbalist was present and took notes from which I quote:

ML: Your teaching is complicated.

K: Very complicated.

ML: If you read it would you understand it?

K: Oh, yes, yes.

ML: Who made the teachings? You? The mystery?

K: A good question, Who made the teachings?

ML: Knowing you as K, the man, it is hard for me to think of you making the teachings.

K: You mean without study, did you or some other person make them?

ML: Something manifests in you which does not seem to be part of your own brain.

K: Are the teachings extraordinary?

ML: Yes. Different. Original.

K: Let us be clear. If I deliberately sat down to write it, I doubt if I could produce it. I'll tell you something that happens: I said yesterday, 'Thinking about something is different from thinking.' I said, 'I don't quite understand it, let me look at it,' and when I did I saw something clearly. There is a sense of vacuity and then something comes. But if I sat down to do it I might not be able to. Schopenhauer, Lenin, Bertrand Russell etc. had all read tremendously. Here there is the phenomenon of this chap who isn't trained, who has had no discipline. How did he get all this? What is it? If it were only K—he is uneducated, gentle—so where does it come from? This person [K] hasn't thought out the teaching.

ML: He hasn't come to it through thought?

K: It is like—what—what is the biblical term?—revelation. It happens all the time when I'm talking.

ML: Does the audience create something towards the revelation?

K: No. Let's begin again. The deeper question would be: the boy was found, conditioning took no hold—neither the Theosophy, nor the adulation, nor the World Teacher, the property, the enormous sums of money—none of it affected him. Why? Who protected him?

ML: It is difficult for me not to personify a power—protection by *someone*. A *power* to protect is too vast a conception for our limited brains, but perhaps it's like a lightning conductor. The lightning, the electricity, finds a conductor—the most direct way to earth. This power, which I think is really love, finds a conductor in the vacant mind.

K: It must be a special body. How did that body come about and remain uncorrupted? It would have been so easy to corrupt it. It means that the power was guarding it.

ML: And training it—opening it up with 'the process'?

K: That comes later.

ML: It started as soon as the body was strong enough.

K: Yes, but if you admit all this, it is a freak, in the kindly sense. The freak was kept for the teaching, the freak is totally unimportant. Anyone can accept the teaching, see the truth of it. If you make the freak important it rules out everything else.

Mary Zimbalist: The freak is necessary to give out the teachings but non-freaks can receive it?

K: Yes, yes. So we are asking, how was it maintained as a freak? An awful word.

ML: Say a power was waiting . . .

K: Amma and Leadbeater maintained that a Bodhisatva was to manifest and they must find a body—the tradition of the Avatar manifesting. The Buddha went through all that, the suffering etc., then threw it aside and became enlightened. What he taught was original but he went through all that. But here is a freak who didn't go through any of it. Jesus may have been a freak too. The power must have watched over this body from the moment it was born. Why? How did it happen? A boy from a family that was nothing special. How did that boy happen to be there? Was it the power wanting to manifest that created the boy or was it that the power saw a Brahmanical family, an eighth child, and said, 'That is the boy.'?

ML: An Eastern body is usually chosen.

K: That thing is in the room. If you ask it what it is, it wouldn't answer. It would say, 'You are too small'. I think we said the other day that there is a reservoir of good that must manifest. But then we are back where we began. How would you describe this without talking of a biological freak? But all this is sacred and I don't know how you will convey not only the sacredness but everything else we have talked about. It is really quite extraordinary why this boy was not corrupted. They did everything to dominate me. Why was he put through the Ojai experience? Was it because the body wasn't sufficiently tuned?

Mary Zimbalist: You never try to escape pain.

K: Of course not. You see it has begun—the pain. About half an hour ago. Suppose you put all this on paper: what would a sane man, a thinking man, like Joe [my husband], say about it? Would they say this isn't anything? It happens to every genius? If you said, 'Criticise this,' what would be their reaction? Would they say that it is all made up or that it is a mystery? Are we trying to touch a mystery? The moment you understand it, it is no longer a mystery. But the sacredness is not a mystery. So we are trying to remove the mystery leading to the source. What would they say?—that you are making a mystery where there is none? That he was born that way? The sacred is there and because it is sacred it is vast. What happens when I die? What happens here? Is it all depending on one man? Or are there people who will carry on?

ML: There has been a change from what you said about ten years ago in Epping Forest that it could all go after your death.

K: I'm not sure there is a change. There are the books but they are not enough. If they [the people round him] really had it they would be freaks like K. The freak is saying, 'Are there people who have drunk the waters and will carry on?' I would go to someone who had known him and through them get a feeling of what he was like. I would walk many miles to talk to someone who had been with him: 'You have drunk the waters, what is it like?' [He had said much the same thing, referring to the Buddha, at the meeting of the Foundation at Ojai in 1977.]

This was the end of the conversation, for again K had to go and lie down on account of the pain in his head and neck. I was left with the curious feeling, which returns even more strongly when I re-read these notes, that K would love to be on the outside for once, which he has never been. I recalled what he had said on December 28, 1925, after the first manifestation, as we believed, of the Lord Maitreya speaking through him at Adyar: my mother had told him that same evening that his face had altered as well as his words and shone with a glorious radiance as he suddenly changed from the third to the first person singular—'I come for those who want sympathy . . .'. 'I wish I could have seen it,' he had replied wistfully.

I went back to London with a feeling of huge compassion for him, a more protective love than I had ever known. 'Water can never find out what water is,' he had said during our previous conversation. He would never get outside; he would never know what he was; he would never see how transfigured his face became in moments of special inspiration or revelation. *Could* I find out for him? He had told us it was possible, told us to try to find out, whereas in 1972 he had said that no one could ever understand—that it was something 'much too vast to be put into words'. Now he was saying, 'The moment you discover something you have words for it.' Could I find out? The sense of protection he has always felt and his repeated insistence on his vacant mind were the chief clues to go upon. Could I find out? The challenge was thrilling, intoxicating.

21

The Source of All Energy

It had been cold in England in June so K's hay fever had not troubled him, but as soon as he arrived at Gstaad at the beginning of July he had a bad attack of it which went to his chest. He was in bed with fever for a few days and still very hoarse for the first talk at the Saanen Gathering on July 8. There was an uproar in the tent that year when three people were very insulting to K, demanding that he should 'reveal his secret' which they accused him of withholding. K remained perfectly calm during the scene, just waited silently for the clamour to die down.

K returned with Mary to Brockwood on August 25 for the gathering there. It was announced at this gathering that only written questions would be answered at the public discussions which were held between the week-end talks. Over ninety questions were handed in of which K selected five to answer at each meeting. At a Foundation meeting during the gathering K asked the trustees to make it clear that when they spoke about his teachings they were speaking only out of their own understanding and not as his mouthpieces. He reminded them that the Foundations were not spiritual organisations and had no spiritual authority. He found it necessary to repeat in the autumn Bulletin the statement he had made in the Bulletin in the summer of 1970 beginning 'From the nineteen twenties I have been saying there should be no interpreters of the teachings . . .'.

After the gathering, there was a six-day seminar at Brockwood in September attended by about eighty invited people, including the whole of the Brockwood teaching staff. The theme of the seminar was: 'We live in a world of increasing violence and disorder. What can I, as a human being, do to change this?'

K seemed to be particularly contented at Brockwood that autumn. He told Mary in September that he 'felt like a young boy', and remarked during a walk, 'How lucky we are to live in this beautiful place.' On October 19 I went down to Brockwood for the weekend to have further talks about the biography. I wanted to find out if possible whether the 'revelation' he had spoken of came from inside or outside. He began by saying that when he first started speaking he had used the language of Theosophy but that from 1922 (the year of his experience at Ojai) he had found his own language. He then commented again on his vacant mind and said, 'When the mind is empty, it only knows it was empty afterwards.' I now quote once again from Mary Zimbalist's notes:

ML: When does it cease to be empty?
K: When it is necessary to use thought, to communicate. Otherwise it is empty. During the seminar—while I am talking it comes out.
ML: Do you *see* something?
K: No, it comes out. I don't see something and translate. It comes out without my thinking about it. As it comes out, it becomes logical, rational. If I think it out carefully, write it down, repeat it, nothing happens.
ML: Does it come from somewhere outside yourself?
K: After the seminar I said to Maria, 'Something new came out.' With artists and poets it is different because they build up to it. Perception of his [K's] revolutionary teaching must have come slowly, gradually. It was not changing parallel to the language. [He now repeated how he had been invited to go gliding at Gstaad.] I would have gone like a shot—it would have been fun. But I realised I shouldn't do it. I mustn't do anything that is irrelevant for the body. I feel it because of what K has to do in the world. I mustn't get ill because I couldn't talk, so I take as much care as possible. The body is here to talk; it has been brought up that way and its purpose is to talk. Anything else is irrelevant, so the body has to be protected. Another aspect of this is that I feel there is another kind of protection which is not mine. There is a separate form of protection as if the future is more or less laid down. A different kind of protection, not only of the body. The boy was born with that peculiarity—he must have been protected to survive all he did. Somehow the body is protected to survive. Some element is watching over it. Something is protecting it. It would be speculating to say what. The Maitreya is too concrete, is not subtle enough. But I can't look behind the curtain. I can't do it. I tried with Pupul [Jayakar] and various Indian scholars who pressed me. I have said it isn't the Maitreya, the Bodhisatva. That protection is too concrete, too worked-out. But I've always felt the protection.

ML: The truth may never be known.

K: I'm not sure. The very truth protects itself. Truth itself is undamageable, therefore it protects itself. Goodness needs no protection. In itself it has the quality of protection. Truth has inherited in itself the quality of its own protection; but it is much more than that. Much, much more than that. Here there is not only protection of the body but something much more universal. I cannot tell you more but that is not the end of it.

ML: You used to say how you longed to become a sanyasi. You said it was your 'last temptation'. [He had said this to me in 1927.]

K: It is there even now. Here [at Brockwood] it happened. I went out walking by myself. I was going far away. I suddenly realised I must return.

ML: It was an effort to come back?

K: Not an effort. I had to accept it.

ML: By going far away do you mean death?

K: Yes, probably it is death.

ML: You had to come back because your work is to talk?

K: If I didn't it would probably end. I feel when the time comes to stop talking, there is dying. When that time comes the protection ends.

For the rest of the time I was staying there we went over ground we had already covered without coming to any new conclusions and without K revealing anything further. K does not want to make a mystery of who or what he is, or of where his teaching comes from, or of who or what is protecting him, yet, inevitably, a mystery remains, and I must say now, writing this in the autumn of 1981, that I am no nearer to elucidating it; nor, as far as I know, has anyone else come near to doing so. It is part of the mystery of life itself. The answer to the riddle of life may be laughably simple but no one has yet found it.

We are left with the question: is K being used by someone or something from outside? When we felt the throbbing in the room he spoke about it may well have been emanating from K himself, but I cannot forget the great gale of force that rushed at me that afternoon through the open drawing-room door when I was least expecting it and when K himself was upstairs in his bedroom; nor can I forget all that went on during 'the process', as described in *The Years of Awakening*, or Pupul Jayakar's experience in 1948 or Vanda Scaravelli's in 1961 and '62. K does not remember any of this, and how could he since he was away from his body at the time?

I am inclined to believe that K *is* being used and has been used since 1922 by something from outside. I do not mean that he is a medium. A medium is separate from what he or she 'brings through', whereas K and whatever it is that manifests through him are for the most part one. His consciousness is as permeated with this other thing as a sponge with water. There are times, though, when the water seems to drain away, leaving him very much as he used to be when I first remember him—vague, gentle, fallible, shy, simple-minded, compliant, affectionate, delighting to laugh at the silliest jokes, yet unique in his complete absence of vanity and self-assertiveness.

There is little doubt that K *was* born different in being so amazingly selfless. He had said in the course of our conversations that if he were a biological freak his teaching could not be for everyone, but he had also said that if others had 'got' what he had 'got' they would be freaks like K. And is it not freaks that he is asking us all to become—biological freaks, sports, mutations—that is, asking us to break away from the normal pattern of human behaviour and development, to discard those human characteristics of striving, aggression, ambition, greed, hate, envy, jealousy? To bring about a new mind?

The question posed here is whether it is possible for a mutation to pass on the strain, not through the genes but through the awakening of intelligence? It may be remembered that K had said that it was not necessary to be an Edison to turn on the electric light. K at any rate believes with passion that it is possible to bring about a revolution in the human psyche; if he did not so believe he would not go on talking. Or, if it is a power speaking through him, that power must also believe (though how can a power believe?) that it is possible. But K has also said that 'the freak'— that is, the personality of Krishnamurti—is of no importance, only the teaching has importance; therefore, those questions of who he is, what he is, and where his teaching comes from, may well be detrimental to the teaching itself. This enquiry should perhaps never have been undertaken and should not be pursued further.

But then one turns to *The Notebook*, that extraordinary document, and finds a state of consciousness that seems to be entirely

K's own and the very well-spring of his teaching, so I find myself reversing my assumption that he is being used. At the end of this book I am more mystified by him than I was at the beginning, and in spite of doubts as to whether it is right to continue the enquiry, the enquiry goes on in my head. No doubt I have never been able to empty my mind sufficiently for truth to enter.

*   *   *   *

Before the year was out K was to undergo a further psychic experience while he was in India. On February 21, 1980, he dictated an account of it to Mary at Ojai (she had not been with him to India that winter), referring to himself in the third person:

K went from Brockwood to India on November 1, 1979 [actually October 31]. He went after a few days in Madras straight to Rishi Valley. For a long time he has been awakening in the middle of the night with that peculiar meditation which has been pursuing him for very many years. This has been a normal thing in his life. It is not a conscious, deliberate pursuit of meditation or an unconscious desire to achieve something. It is very clearly uninvited and unsought. He has been adroitly watchful of thought making a memory of these meditations. And so each meditation has a quality of something new and fresh in it. There is a sense of accumulating drive, unsought and uninvited. Sometimes it is so intense that there is pain in the head, sometimes a sense of vast emptiness with fathomless energy. Sometimes he wakes up with laughter and measureless joy. These peculiar meditations, which naturally were unpremeditated, grew with intensity. Only on the days he travelled or arrived late of an evening would they stop; or when he had to wake early and travel.

With the arrival in Rishi Valley in the middle of November 1979 the momentum increased and one night in the strange stillness of that part of the world, with the silence undisturbed by the hoot of owls, he woke up to find something totally different and new. The movement had reached the source of all energy. This must in no way be confused with, or even thought of, as god or the highest principle, the Brahman, which are the projections of the human mind out of fear and longing, the unyielding desire for total security. It is none of those things. Desire cannot possibly reach it, words cannot fathom it nor can the string of thought wind itself around it. One may ask with what assurance do you state that it is the source of all energy? One can only reply with complete humility that it is so.

The Source of All Energy

All the time that K was in India until the end of January 1980 every night he would wake up with this sense of the absolute. It is not a state, a thing that is static, fixed, immovable. The whole universe is in it, measureless to man. When he returned to Ojai in February 1980, after the body had somewhat rested, there was the perception that there was nothing beyond this. This is the ultimate, the beginning and the ending and the absolute. There is only a sense of incredible vastness and immense beauty.

Since there is 'nothing beyond this', surely my book must end here. But for K it was not an ending. His health, at eighty-seven, is probably better than it has ever been; his bodily suppleness, like his eyesight, is unimpaired; his new energy is almost fierce; he feels there is still a great deal more to come out in his teaching for which he will have to live for another five years or so. A third volume may have to be written before the physical ending; the teaching is touched with immortality.

Source Notes

Page Note
12   1   These two letters are in the Krishnamurti Archives, Ojai, California
20   2   *Candles in the Sun*, p. 185 (Hart-Davis 1957)
22   3   These questions are from the *Star Bulletin*, June 1931
23   4   *Krishnamurti: The Years of Awakening*, p. 281
23   5   Ibid
24   6   Ibid
28   7   *Bernard Shaw* by Hesketh Pearson, p. 115 (Collins 1942)
29   8   *Commentaries on Living*, p. 131 (1956)
31   9   A collected edition of Krishnamurti's poems under the title *From Darkness to Light* was published by Harper & Row in 1980, and by Gollancz in 1981 under the title *Poems and Parables*
47   10   *My Guru and his Disciple* by Christopher Isherwood, p. 50 (Eyre Methuen, 1980)
47   11   Bedford, II, 71 (Chatto & Windus, 1973)
48   12   MS by K, 1976, Krishnamurti Archives, Brockwood Park
52   13   *Commentaries on Living*, p. 17 (1956)
57   14   *The Flight of the Eagle*, p. 46 (1971)
59   15   *Freedom from the Known*, p. 116 (1969)
59   16   Foreword by Krishnamurti to *Meditations* (1980)
59   17   From K's answers to questions put to him by Mrs Zimbalist when trying to discover what he was doing during the war years. His memory of that time was extremely vague. He thinks he *may* have seen Felix Greene, Stravinsky, John Barrymore and Bertrand Russell. (Mrs Zimbalist's notes, August 1979)
62   18   *Life Ahead* (1963)
65   19   Mrs Zimbalist's notes (August 1979)
67   20   *Trial of Mr Gandhi* by Francis Watson (1969)
70   21   From a copy of Mrs Jayakar's notes, quoted with her kind permission
75   22   *My Contemporaries* by G. Venkatachalam (Bangalore 1966)
92   23   *Commentaries on Living* (Second Series 1957)
109   24   In 1968 it was published under the title *Krishnamurti's Notebook*
114   25   Bedford II, 296–97
141   26   This complete chapter, entitled *On Love*, was issued as a separate booklet by the Krishnamurti Foundation in 1981
161   27   Open letter by James Vigeveno of July 1969, addressed to 'Friends of Mine and Those who are Hurt'

Source Notes

162 28 There are now three other Penguin volumes, *The Second Krishna-murti Reader, The Beginnings of Learning* and *The Impossible Question*

164 29 *Freedom from the Known*, p. 80

171 30 *The Second Penguin Krishnamurti Reader*, published in 1972, contains *The Only Revolution* and *The Urgency of Change* in one volume

176 31 This interview is given in full in Bulletin No 11, Autumn 1971

190 32 Two later duologues between K and Professor Bohm were published in *Truth and Actuality*, 1977

191 33 Bulletin No 11, Autumn 1971

191 34 *Truth and Actuality*, p. 17

192 35 Bulletin No 21, Spring 1974

201 36 A resumé of the terms of the settlement was published in the *Ventura County Star-Free Press* on December 27, 1974, and in the *Ojai Valley News* on January 8, 1975

204 37 *Golden Jubilee Souvenir Book* (Krishnamurti Foundation India, 1979)

210 38 *Krishnamurti's Journal*, p. 40

213 39 June 20, 1976

213 40 An edited version of this video-recording was published in *The Wholeness of Life* (1978)

222 41 Krishnamurti's *Letters to the Schools*, privately printed in 1981, are available from the Krishnamurti Foundations

223 42 *Exploration into Insight*, edited by Pupul Jayakar and Sunanda Patwardhan, p. 77 (Gollancz and Harper & Row, 1979)

Available Books by J. Krishnamurti

PUBLISHED BY GOLLANCZ AND HARPER & ROW

The First and Last Freedom (1954)

Education and the Significance of Life (1955)

Commentaries on Living (1956)

Commentaries on Living, Second Series (1959)

Commentaries on Living, Third Series (1960)

This Matter of Culture (1964)

Freedom From the Known (1969)

The Only Revolution (1970)

The Urgency of Change (1971)

The Impossible Question (1972)

Beyond Violence, paperback (1973)

The Awakening of Intelligence, illustrated (1973)

The Beginnings of Learning, illustrated (1975)

Krishnamurti's Notebook (1976)

Truth and Actuality (1977), paperback

The Wholeness of Life (1978)

Exploration into Insight (1979)

Meditations (1979)

Poems and Parables (1981) (American title, *From Darkness to Light*)

Krishnamurti's Journal (1982)

PUBLISHED BY PENGUIN

The Penguin Krishnamurti Reader (1970)

The Second Penguin Krishnamurti Reader (1972)

The Beginnings of Learning (1978)

The Impossible Question (1978)

Books by Krishnamurti

PUBLISHED BY ORIENT LONGMAN

Tradition and Revolution (1972)
Krishnamurti on Education, illustrated (1974)

Index

243

Index

245

Index

Index